KU-379-868

The Institute of Chartered Accountants in England and Wales

# ASSURANCE

Professional Stage Knowledge Level

For exams in 2013

Study Manual

www.icaew.com

Assurance
The Institute of Chartered Accountants in England and Wales Professional Stage

ISBN: 978-0-85760-450-7

Previous ISBN: 978-0-85760-220-6

First edition 2007
Second edition 2008
Third edition 2009
Fourth edition 2010
Fifth edition 2011
Sixth edition 2012

All rights reserved. No part of this publication may be reproduced or transmitted in any form or by any means or stored in any retrieval system, electronic, mechanical, photocopying, recording or otherwise without prior permission of the publisher.

British Library Cataloguing-in-Publication Data
A catalogue record for this book has been applied for from the British Library

Printed in the United Kingdom by Polestar Wheatons

Polestar Wheatons
Hennock Road
Marsh Barton
Exeter
EX2 8RP

Your learning materials are printed on paper sourced from traceable, sustainable forests.

© The Institute of Chartered Accountants in England and Wales

# Welcome to ICAEW

I am delighted that you have chosen to study for our chartered accountancy qualification, the ACA or the Certificate in Finance, Accounting and Business (CFAB).

If you are a CFAB student, you will be gaining essential knowledge of how businesses work. As your understanding develops you may be surprised by the variety of roles that chartered accountants take on. To gain further insight and develop your career, I hope that you choose to continue onto the ACA qualification.

The ACA will open doors to a highly rewarding career as a financial expert or business leader. Once you are an ICAEW member, you will join over 138,000 others around the world who work at the highest levels across all industry sectors, providing valuable financial and business advice. Some of our earlier members formed today's global Big Four firms, and you can find an ICAEW Chartered Accountant on the boards of 80% of the UK FTSE 100 companies.

As part of a worldwide network of over 19,000 students, you will have access to a range of resources including the online student community, where you can interact with fellow students. Our student support team is dedicated to helping you every step of the way. Take a look at the key resources available to you on page viii.

I wish you the very best of luck with your studies and look forward to supporting you throughout your career.

Michael Izza
Chief Executive
ICAEW

# Contents

# 1 Introduction

## 1.1 What is Assurance and how does it fit within the ACA Professional Stage?

### Structure

The ACA syllabus has been designed to develop core technical, commercial, and ethical skills and knowledge in a structured and rigorous manner.

The diagram below shows the twelve modules at the ACA Professional Stage, where the focus is on the acquisition and application of technical skills and knowledge, and the ACA Advanced Stage which comprises two technical integration modules and the Case Study.

If you are studying for CFAB, you will only complete the first six knowledge modules. However, you may decide to progress to the ACA after you have completed the CFAB qualification.

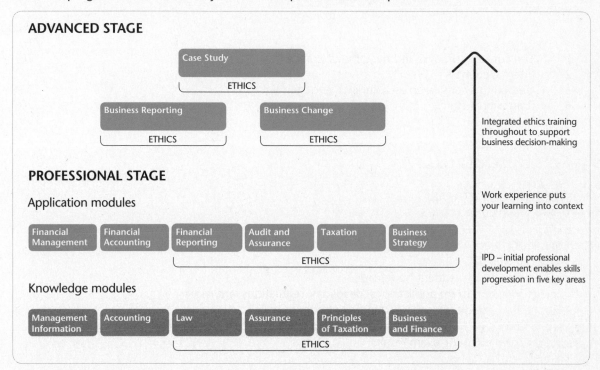

### The knowledge level

The aim of the Assurance module is ensure that students understand the assurance process and fundamental principles of ethics and are able to contribute to the assessment of internal controls and gathering of evidence on an assurance engagement.

### Progression to ACA application level

The knowledge base that is put in place here will be taken further in the Application level Audit and Assurance module where the aim will be to develop the students' understanding of the critical aspects of managing an assurance engagement (including audit engagements): acceptance, planning, managing, concluding and reporting. Students will be expected to have an understanding of the audit of not-for-profit entities as well as non-specialised profit oriented entities.

### Progression to ACA Advanced Stage

The Advanced Stage papers – Business Reporting (BR) and Business Change (BC) – then take things further again. The emphasis in the BR paper is the compliance issues faced by business. Here ethical and audit issues are likely to be important including controls and corporate governance. The BC paper deals with issues arising in business transformations, mergers, acquisitions, alliances and disposals. Students will be expected to deal with a wide range of topics including due diligence, e-commerce and e-business and the raising of finance.

The above illustrates how the knowledge of assurance principles gives a platform from which a progression of skills and assurance expertise is developed.

# 2  Assurance

## 2.1  Module aim

To ensure that students understand the assurance process and fundamental principles of ethics, and are able to contribute to the assessment of internal controls and gathering of evidence on an assurance engagement.

## 2.2  Specification grid

This grid shows the relative weightings of subjects within this module and should guide the relative study time spent on each. Over time the marks available in the assessment will equate to the weightings below, while slight variations may occur in individual assessments to enable suitably rigorous questions to be set.

|   |   | Weighting (%) |
|---|---|---|
| 1 | The concept, process and need for assurance | 20 |
| 2 | Internal controls | 25 |
| 3 | Gathering evidence on an assurance engagement | 35 |
| 4 | Professional ethics | 20 |
|   |   | 100 |

# 3  Key Resources

**STUDENT SUPPORT TEAM**
T +44 (0)1908 248 250
E studentsupport@icaew.com

**STUDENT WEBSITE**
icaew.com/students student homepage
icaew.com/exams exam applications, deadlines, regulations and more
icaew.com/cpl credit for prior learning/exemptions
icaew.com/examresources examiners comments, syllabus, past papers, study guides and more
icaew.com/examresults exam results

**TUITION**
If you are receiving structured tuition, make sure you know how and when you can contact your tutors for extra help. If you aren't receiving structured tuition and are interested in classroom, online or distance learning tuition, take a look at our tuition providers in your area on icaew.com/exams

**ONLINE STUDENT COMMUNITY**
The online student community allows you to ask questions, gain study and exam advice from fellow ACA and CFAB students and access our free webinars. There are also regular Ask an Expert and Ask a Tutor sessions to help you with key technical topics and exam papers. Access the community at icaew.com/studentcommunity

**THE LIBRARY & INFORMATION SERVICE (LIS)**
The Library & Information Service (LIS) is ICAEW's world-leading accountancy and business library. You have access to a range of resources free of charge via the library website, including the catalogue, LibCat. icaew.com/library

# 4 Syllabus and learning outcomes

The following learning outcomes should be read in conjunction with the Assurance and Audit and Ethics Standards tables in section 4.1.

**Covered
in chapter**

## 1 The concept, process and need for assurance

**Candidates will be able to explain the concept of assurance, why assurance is required and the reasons for assurance engagements being carried out by appropriately qualified professionals.**

In the assessment, candidates may be required to:

| | | |
|---|---|---|
| a. | Define the concept of assurance | 1 |
| b. | State why users desire assurance reports and provide examples of the benefits gained from them such as to assure the quality of an entity's published corporate responsibility or sustainability report. | 1 |
| c. | Compare the functions and responsibilities of the different parties involved in an assurance engagement | 1 |
| d. | Compare the purposes and characteristics of, and levels of assurance obtained from, different assurance engagements | 1 |
| e. | Identify the issues which can lead to gaps between the outcomes delivered by the assurance engagement and the expectations of users of the assurance reports, and suggest how these can be overcome | 1 |
| f. | Define the assurance process, including: | 2, 3, 4, 10 |

- Obtaining the engagement
- Continuous risk assessment
- Engagement acceptance
- The scope of the engagement
- Planning the engagement
- Performing the engagement
- Obtaining evidence
- Evaluation of results of assurance work
- Concluding and reporting on the engagement
- Reporting to the engaging party
- Keeping records of the work performed

| | | |
|---|---|---|
| g. | Recognise the need to plan and perform assurance engagements with an attitude of professional scepticism | 3, 4 |
| h. | Define the concept of reasonable assurance. | 1 |

## 2 Internal controls

Candidates will be able to explain the nature of internal controls and why they are important, document an organisation's internal controls and identify weaknesses in internal control systems.

In the assessment, candidates may be required to:

| | | |
|---|---|---|
| a. | State the reasons for organisations having effective systems of control | 5 |
| b. | Identify the fundamental principles of effective control systems | 5 |
| c. | Identify the main areas of a business that need effective control systems | 5 |
| d. | Identify the components of internal control in both manual and IT environments, including: | 5, 9 |

- The overall control environment
- Preventative and detective controls
- Internal audit

| | | |
|---|---|---|
| e. | Define and classify different types of internal control, with particular emphasis upon those which impact upon the quality of financial information | 5 |
| f. | Show how specified internal controls mitigate risk and state their limitations | 5, 6, 7, 8 |
| g. | Identify internal controls for an organisation in a given scenario | 6, 7, 8 |
| h. | Identify internal control weaknesses in a given scenario | 6, 7, 8 |
| i. | Identify, for a specified organisation, the sources of information which will enable a sufficient record to be made of accounting or other systems and internal controls. | 5 |

## 3 Gathering evidence on an assurance engagement

Candidates will be able to select sufficient and appropriate methods of obtaining assurance evidence and recognise when conclusions can be drawn from evidence obtained or where issues need to be referred to a senior colleague.

In the assessment, candidates may be required to:

| | | |
|---|---|---|
| a. | State the reasons for preparing and keeping documentation relating to an assurance engagement | 10 |
| b. | Identify and compare the different methods of obtaining evidence from the use of tests of control and substantive procedures, including analytical procedures | 4, 11 |
| c. | Recognise the strengths and weaknesses of the different methods of obtaining evidence | 11 |
| d. | Identify the situations within which the different methods of obtaining evidence should and should not be used | 11 |
| e. | Compare the reliability of different types of assurance evidence | 11 |
| f. | Select appropriate methods of obtaining evidence from tests of control and from substantive procedures for a given business scenario | 6, 7, 8, 13 |
| g. | Recognise when the quantity and quality of evidence gathered from various tests and procedures is of a sufficient and appropriate level to draw reasonable conclusions on which to base a report | 11 |
| h. | Identify the circumstances in which written confirmation of representations from management should be sought and the reliability of such confirmation as a form of assurance evidence | 12 |
| i. | Recognise issues arising whilst gathering assurance evidence that should be referred to a senior colleague. | 13 |

## 4 Professional ethics

**Candidates will be able to understand the importance of ethical behaviour to a professional and identify issues relating to integrity, objectivity, professional competence and due care, confidentiality, professional behaviour and independence.**

In the assessment, candidates may be required to:

| | | |
|---|---|---|
| a. | State the role of ethical codes and their importance to the profession | 14 |
| b. | Recognise the differences between a rules based ethical code and one based upon a set of principles | 14 |
| c. | Recognise how the principles of professional behaviour protect the public and fellow professionals | 14 |
| d. | Identify the key features of the system of professional ethics adopted by IFAC and ICAEW | 14 |
| e. | Identify the fundamental principles underlying the IFAC and the ICAEW code of ethics | 14 |
| f. | Recognise the importance of integrity and objectivity to professional accountants, identifying situations that may impair or threaten integrity and objectivity | 15 |
| g. | Suggest courses of action to resolve ethical conflicts relating to integrity and objectivity | 15 |
| h. | Respond appropriately to the request of an employer to undertake work outside the confines of an individual's expertise or experience | 15 |
| i. | Recognise the importance of confidentiality and identify the sources of risks of accidental disclosure of information | 16 |
| j. | Identify steps to prevent the accidental disclosure of information | 16 |
| k. | Identify situations in which confidential information may be disclosed | 16 |
| l. | Define independence and recognise why those undertaking an assurance engagement are required to be independent of their clients | 15 |
| m. | Identify the following threats to the fundamental ethical principles and the independence of assurance providers: | 15 |

- Self-interest threat
- Self-review threat
- Management threat
- Advocacy threat
- Familiarity threat
- Intimidation threat

| | | |
|---|---|---|
| n. | Identify safeguards to eliminate or reduce threats to the fundamental ethical principles and the independence of assurance providers | 15 |
| o. | Suggest how a conflict of loyalty between the duty a professional accountant has to their employer and the duty to their profession could be resolved. | 15 |

## 4.1 Technical knowledge

The tables contained in this section show the technical knowledge covered in the ACA syllabus by module.

The level of knowledge required in the relevant Professional stage module and at the Advanced stage is shown.

The knowledge levels are defined as follows:

**Level D**

An awareness of the scope of the standard.

**Level C**

A general knowledge with a basic understanding of the subject matter and training in its application thereof sufficient to identify significant issues and evaluate their potential implications or impact.

**Level B**

A working knowledge with a broad understanding of the subject matter and a level of experience in the application thereof sufficient to apply the subject matter in straightforward circumstances.

**Level A**

A thorough knowledge with a solid understanding of the subject matter and experience in the application thereof sufficient to exercise reasonable professional judgement in the application of the subject matter in those circumstances generally encountered by Chartered Accountants.

Key to other symbols:

→    The knowledge level reached is assumed to be continued

| | Professional Stage | | Advanced Stage |
|---|---|---|---|
| Title | Assurance | Audit & Assurance | |
| The International Auditing and Assurance Standards Board | | D | C |
| The Authority Attaching to Standards Issued by the International Auditing and Assurance Standards Board | | C | A |
| The Authority Attaching to Practice Statements Issued by the International Auditing and Assurance Standards Board | | | A |
| Discussion Papers | | | C |
| Working Procedures | | | C |
| **International Standards on Auditing (UK and Ireland)** | | | |
| 200 Overall Objectives of the Independent Auditor and the Conduct of an Audit in Accordance with International Standards on Auditing | B | A → | |
| 210 Agreeing the Terms of Audit Engagements | | B → | |
| 220 Quality Control for an Audit of Financial Statements | | B → | |
| 230 Audit Documentation | | B | A |
| 240 The Auditor's Responsibilities Relating to Fraud in an Audit of Financial Statements | | B | A |
| 250 A Consideration of Laws and Regulations in an Audit of Financial Statements | | B | A |
| 250 B The Auditor's Right and Duty to Report to Regulators in the Financial Sector | | | C |
| 260 Communication with Those Charged with Governance | | B | A |
| 265 Communicating Deficiencies in Internal Control to Those Charged with Governance and Management | | B | A |
| 300 Planning an Audit of Financial Statements | B | A → | |
| 315 Identifying and Assessing the Risks of Material Misstatement Through Understanding the Entity and its Environment | C | A → | |
| 320 Materiality in Planning and Performing an Audit | C | A | → |

| Title | Professional Stage | | Advanced Stage |
|---|---|---|---|
| | Assurance | Audit & Assurance | |
| **IFAC Statements** | | | |
| ISQC1 Quality Control for Firms that Perform Audits and Reviews of Financial Statements, and Other Assurance and Related Services Engagements | | C | B |
| **APB Bulletins** | | | |
| 2010/2 Compendium of illustrative Auditor's Reports on UK Private Sector Financial Statements | | B | B |

## Ethics Codes and Standards

| Ethics Codes and Standards | Level | Professional Stage modules |
|---|---|---|
| IFAC Code of Ethics for Professional Accountants (parts A, B and C and Definitions) | A | Assurance<br>Business and Finance<br>Law |
| ICAEW Code of Ethics | A | Principles of Taxation<br>Audit and Assurance<br>Business Strategy<br>Financial Reporting<br>Taxation |
| APB Ethical Standards 1-5 (revised)<br>Provisions Available to Small Entities (revised) | A | Assurance<br>Audit and Assurance |

## 5 Faculties and Special Interest Groups

The faculties and special interest groups are specialist bodies within ICAEW which offer members networking opportunities, influence and recognition within clearly defined areas of technical expertise. As well as providing accurate and timely technical analysis, they lead the way in many professional and wider business issues through stimulating debate, shaping policy and encouraging good practice. Their value is endorsed by over 40,000 members of ICAEW who currently belong to one or more of the seven faculties:

- Audit and Assurance
- Corporate Finance
- Finance and Management
- Financial Reporting
- Financial Services
- Information Technology
- Tax

The special interest groups provide practical support, information and representation for chartered accountants working within a range of industry sectors, including:

- Charity and Voluntary sector
- Entertainment and Media
- Farming and Rural Business
- Forensic
- Healthcare
- Interim Management
- Non-Executive Directors
- Public Sector

- Solicitors
- Tourism and Hospitality
- Valuation

Students can register free of charge for provisional membership of one special interest group and receive a monthly complimentary e-newsletter from one faculty of your choice. To find out more and to access a range of free resources, visit icaew.com/facultiesandsigs

# 6 ICAEW publications for further reading

ICAEW produces publications and guidance for its students and members on a variety of technical and business topics. This list of publications has been prepared for students who wish to undertake further reading in a particular subject area and is by no means exhaustive. You are not required to study these publications for your exams. For a full list of publications, or to access any of the publications listed below, visit the Technical Resources section of the ICAEW website at icaew.com

ICAEW no longer prints a Members Handbook. ICAEW regulations, standards and guidance are available at icaew.com/regulations This area includes regulations and guidance relevant to the regulated areas of audit, investment business and insolvency as well as materials that was previously in the handbook.

The TECH and AUDIT series of technical releases are another source of guidance available to members and students. Visit icaew.com/technicalreleases for the most up-to-date releases.

## Audit and Assurance Faculty – icaew.com/aaf

- **Right First Time with the Clarified ISAs,** ICAEW 2010, ISBN 978-0-85760-063-9

  Clarified ISAs provide many opportunities for practitioners in terms of potential efficiencies, better documentation, better reporting to clients, and enhanced audit quality overall.

  This modular guide has been developed by ICAEW's ISA implementation sub-group to help medium-sized and smaller firms implement the clarified ISAs and take advantage of these opportunities. This modular guide is designed to give users the choice of either downloading the publication in its entirety, or downloading specific modules on which they want to focus.

  An international edition is also available.

- **Quality Control in the Audit Environment,** ICAEW 2010, ISBN 0-497-80857-605-5

  The publication identifies seven key areas for firms to consider. Illustrative policies and procedures are provided for selected aspects of each key area, including some examples for sole practitioners. The guide also includes an appendix with answers to a number of frequently asked questions on the standard.

  An international edition is also available.

- **The Audit of Related Parties in Practice,** ICAEW 2010, ISBN 978-1-84125-565-6

  This practical guide to the audit of related party relationships and transactions is set in the context of the significant change in approach that is required under the revised ISA and highlights the importance of planning, the need to involve the entire audit team in this, to assign staff with the appropriate level of experience to audit this area and upfront discussions with the client to identify related parties.

  An international edition is also available.

- **Alternatives to Audit** ICAEW, 2009, ISBN 978-1-84152-819-9

  In August 2006, the ICAEW Audit and Assurance Faculty began a two-year consultation on a new assurance services (the ICAEW Assurance Service), an alternative to audit based on the idea of limited assurance introduced by the International Auditing and Assurance Standards Board (IAASB). This report presents findings from the practical experience of providing the ICAEW Assurance Service over the subsequent two years and views of users of financial information that help in assessing the relevance of the service to their needs.

- **Companies Act 2006 – Auditor related requirements and regulations third edition – March 2012** ICAEW, 2012, ISBN 978-0-85760-442-2

  This third edition of the guide provides a brief summary of the key sections in the Companies Act 2006 (the Act) which relate directly to the rights and duties of auditors. It covers the various types of reports issued by auditors in accordance with the Act. It is designed to be a signposting tool for practitioners and identifies the other pieces of guidance issued by ICAEW, APB, FRC, POB and others to support implementation of the Act.

- **Auditing in a group context: practical considerations for auditors** ICAEW, 2008, ISBN 978-1-84152-628-7

  The guide describes special considerations for auditors at each stage of the group audit's cycle. While no decisions have been taken on UK adoption of the IAASB's clarity ISAs, the publication also covers matters in the IAASB's revised and redrafted 'ISA 600 Special Considerations - Audits of Group Financial Statements (Including the Work of Component Auditors)'. The revised publication contains suggestions for both group auditors and component auditors.

## Corporate Finance Faculty – icaew.com/corpfinfac

- **Private equity demystified –an explanatory guide** Second Edition, Financing Change Initiative, ICAEW, March 2010, John Gilligan and Mike Wright

  This guide summarises the findings of academic work on private equity transactions from around the world. Hard copies of the abstract and full report are free and are also available by download from icaew.com/thoughtleadership

- **Best Practice Guidelines**

  The Corporate Finance Faculty publishes a series of guidelines on best-practice, regulatory trends and technical issues. Authored by leading practitioners in corporate finance, they are succinct and clear overviews of emerging issues in UK corporate finance. icaew.com/corpfinfac

- **Corporate Financier magazine,** ISSN 1367-4544

  The award-winning *Corporate Financier* magazine is published ten times a year for members, stakeholders and key associates of ICAEW's Corporate Finance Faculty.

  Aimed at professionals, investors and company directors involved in corporate finance, it covers a wide range of emerging regulatory, commercial and professional development issues.

  The magazine includes features, news, analysis and research, written by experts, experienced editors and professional journalists.

  In 2011, three major themes were introduced: Innovation & Corporate Finance; Financing Entrepreneurship; and Deal Leadership.

## Corporate governance – icaew.com/corporategovernance

- **The UK Corporate Governance Code 2010**

  The UK Corporate Governance Code (formerly the Combined Code) sets out standards of good practice in relation to board leadership and effectiveness, remuneration, accountability and relations with shareholders. All companies with a Premium Listing of equity shares in the UK are required under the Listing Rules to report on how they have applied the UK Corporate Governance Code in their annual report and accounts.

  The first version of the UK Corporate Governance Code was produced in 1992 by the Cadbury Committee. In May 2010 the Financial Reporting Council issued a new edition of the Code which applies to financial years beginning on or after 29 June 2010.

  The UK Corporate Governance Code contains broad principles and more specific provisions. Listed companies are required to report on how they have applied the main principles of the Code, and either to confirm that they have complied with the Code's provisions or – where they have not – to provide an explanation.

- **Internal Control: Revised Guidance on Internal Control for Directors on the Combined Code (now the UK Corporate Governance Code)**

  Originally published in 1999, the Turnbull guidance was revised and updated in October 2005, following a review by the Financial Reporting Council. The updated guidance applies to listed companies for financial years beginning on or after 1 January 2006.

- **The FRC Guidance on Audit Committees** (formerly known as The Smith Guidance)

  First published by the Financial Reporting Council in January 2003, and most recently updated in 2010. It is intended to assist company boards when implementing the sections of the UK Corporate Governance Code dealing with audit committees and to assist directors serving on audit committees in carrying out their role. Companies are encouraged to use the 2010 edition of the guidance with effect from 30 April 2011.

- **The UK Stewardship Code**

  The UK Stewardship Code was published in July 2010. It aims to enhance the quality of engagement between institutional investors and companies to help improve long-term returns to shareholders and the efficient exercise of governance responsibilities by setting out good practice on engagement with investee companies to which the Financial Reporting Council believes institutional investors should aspire.

  A report summarising the actions being taken by the Financial Reporting Council and explaining how the UK Stewardship Code is intended to operate was also published in July 2010.

## Corporate responsibility – icaew.com/corporateresponsibility

- **Sustainable Business** January 2009

  The new thought leadership prospectus acts as a framework for the work that ICAEW do in sustainability/corporate responsibility. It argues that any system that is sustainable needs accurate and reliable information to help it learn and adapt, which is where the accounting profession plays an important role. A downloadable pdf is available at icaew.com/sustainablebusiness

- **Environmental issues in annual financial statements** ICAEW, May 2009, ISBN 978-1-84152-610-2

  This report is a joint initiative with the Environment Agency. It is aimed at business accountants who prepare, use or audit the financial statements in statutory annual reports and accounts, or who advise or sit on the boards of the UK companies and public sector organisations. It offers practical advice on measuring and disclosing environmental performance. A downloadable pdf is available at icaew.com/sustainablebusiness

- **ESRC seminar series – When worlds collide: contested paradigms of corporate responsibility**

  ICAEW, in conjunction with the British Academy of Management, won an Economic and Social Research Council grant to run a seminar series which aims to bring academics and the business community together to tackle some of the big challenges in corporate responsibility. icaew.com/corporateresponsibility

- **The Business Sustainability Programme (BSP)**

  The Business Sustainability Programme is an e-learning package for accountants and business professionals who want to learn about the business case for sustainability. The course is spread across five modules taking users from definitions of sustainability and corporate responsibility, through case studies and finally towards developing an individually tailored sustainability strategy for their business. The first two modules are free to everyone. For more information and to download a brochure visit icaew.com/bsp

## Ethics – icaew.com/ethics

- **Code of Ethics**

  The Code of Ethics helps ICAEW members meet these obligations by providing them with ethical guidance. The Code applies to all members, students, affiliates, employees of member firms and, where applicable, member firms, in all of their professional and business activities, whether remunerated or voluntary.

- **Instilling integrity in organisations** ICAEW June 2009

  Practical guidance aimed at directors and management to assist them in instilling integrity in their organisations. This document may also be helpful to audit firms discussing this topic with clients and individuals seeking to address issues in this area with their employers.

- **Reporting with Integrity** ICAEW May 2007, ISBN 978-1-84152-455-9

  This publication brings ideas from a variety of disciplines, in order to obtain a more comprehensive understanding of what is meant by integrity, both as a concept and in practice. Moreover, because this report sees reporting with integrity as a joint endeavour of individuals, organisations and professions, including the accounting profession, the concept of integrity is considered in all these contexts.

## Finance and Management Faculty – icaew.com/fmfac

- **Finance's role in the organisation** November 2009, ISBN 978-1-84152-855-7

  This considers the challenges of designing successful organisations, written by Rick Payne, who leads the faculty's finance direction programme.

- **Investment appraisal** SR27: December 2009, ISBN 978-1-84152-854-4

  This special report looks at the key issues and advises managers on how they can contribute effectively to decision making and control during the process of investment appraisal.

- **Starting a business** SR28: March 2010, ISBN 978-1-84152-984-2

  This report provides accountants with a realistic and motivational overview of what to consider when starting a business.

- **Developing a vision for your business** SR30: September 2010, ISBN 978-0-85760-054-7

  This special report looks at what makes a good vision, the benefits of having one, the role of the FD in the process, leadership, storytelling and the use of visions in medium-sized businesses.

- **Finance transformation – the outsourcing perspective** SR31: December 2010, ISBN 978-0-85760-079-0

  The authors of this outsourcing special report share their expertise on topics including service level agreements, people management, and innovation and technology.

- **The Finance Function: A Framework for Analysis September 2011**, ISBN 978-0-85760-285-5

  This report is a source of reference for those analyzing or researching the role of the finance function and provides a foundation for considering the key challenges involved, written by Rick Payne, who leads the faculty's finance direction programme.

## Financial Reporting Faculty – icaew.com/frfac

- **EU Implementation of IFRS and the Fair Value Directive** ICAEW, October 2007, ISBN 978-1-84152-519-8

  The most comprehensive assessment to date of compliance with the requirements of IFRS and the overall quality if IFRS financial reporting.

  The Financial Reporting Faculty makes available to students copies of its highly-regarded factsheets on UK GAAP and IFRS issues, as well as its journal, *By All Accounts*, at icaew.com/frfac

## Financial Services Faculty – icaew.com/fsf

- **Audit of banks: lessons from the crisis,** (Inspiring Confidence in Financial Services initiative) ICAEW, June 2010 ISBN 978-0-85760-051-6

  This research has looked into the role played by bank auditors and examined improvements that can be made in light of lessons learned from the financial crisis. The project has included the publication of stakeholder feedback and development of a final report

- **Measurement in financial services,** (Inspiring Confidence in Financial Services initiative) ICAEW, March 2008, ISBN 978-1-84152-546-4

  This report suggests that more work is required on matching measurement practices in the financial services industry to the needs of different users of financial information, despite the fact that the financial services industry has the greatest concentration of measurement and modelling skills of any industry. A downloadable pdf is available at icaew.com/thoughtleadership

- **Skilled Persons' Guidance – Reporting Under s166 Financial Services and Markets Act 2000 (Interim Technical Release FSF 01/08)**

  This interim guidance was issued by ICAEW in April 2008 as a revision to TECH 20/30 to assist chartered accountants and other professionals who are requested to report under s166 Financial Services and Markets Act 2000. A downloadable pdf is available at icaew.com/technicalreleases

## Information Technology Faculty – icaew.com/itfac

The IT Faculty provides ongoing advice and guidance that will help students in their studies and their work. The online community (ion.icaew.com/itcountshome) provides regular free updates as well as a link to the faculty's Twitter feed which provides helpful updates and links to relevant articles. The following publications should also be of interest to students:

- **Make the move to cloud computing** ICAEW, 2012, ISBN 978-0-85760-617-4

  Cloud computing in its purest form is pay-as-you-go IT, online and on demand. The IT capabilities provided as a service to businesses include: single software applications or software suites; online software development platforms; and virtual computing infrastructure, ranging from data storage to computer grids.

- **Bringing employee personal devices into the business - a guide to IT** consumerisation ICAEW, 2012, ISBN 978-0-85760-443-9

  The gap between business and consumer technology has been growing over the last few years, with the consumer market now leading in terms of ease of use and portability.

- **Making the most of social media - a practical guide for your business** ICAEW, 2011, ISBN 978-0-85760-286-2

  This guide will enable the business manager to develop a philosophy that allies social media's potential with the business's objectives and capabilities, to set objectives and protect against pitfalls, and then to take the first practical steps in a mass communications medium very different from any that British business has encountered before.

## Tax Faculty – icaew.com/taxfac

The Tax Faculty runs a Younger Members Tax Club which provides informal presentations, discussions and socialising. All young professionals interested in tax are welcome to attend. See the website for more details icaew.com/taxfac

- **Tax news service**

  You can keep up with the tax news as it develops on the Tax Faculty's news site icaew.com/taxnews. And you can subscribe to the free newswire which gives you a weekly round up. For more details visit icaew.com/taxfac

- **Demystifying XBRL**

  This booklet, produced jointly by KPMG, the Tax Faculty and the Information Technology Faculty, explains exactly what iXBRL is all about and what must be done in order to e-file corporation tax returns using the new standard.

- **Implementing XBRL**

  This booklet, produced jointly by Thompson Reuters, the Tax Faculty and the Information Technology Faculty, is a practical guide for accountants in business and practice, and follows on from Demystifying XBRL.

- **TAXline Tax Practice series of detailed briefings on current topics:**

  TAXline Tax Practice 27
  Let property - a brief guide by Rebecca Cave (published November 2011)

  TAXline Tax Practice 26
  The new pension rules by Anne Redston (published July 2011)

  TAXline Tax Practice 25
  Tax Credits by Robin Williamson (published April 2011)

  TAXline Tax Practice No 23
  HMRC Powers - an overview of the new powers and penalties regime by Paula Clemett (published October 2010)

# CHAPTER 1

# Concept of and need for assurance

Introduction

Examination context

**Topic List**

    1   What is assurance?

    2   Why is assurance important?

    3   Why can assurance never be absolute?

Summary and Self-test

Answers to Interactive questions

Answers to Self-test

# Introduction

## Learning objectives

Tick off

- Understand the concept of assurance

- Recognise the criteria which constitute an assurance engagement

- Recognise subject matter suitable to be the subject of an assurance engagement

- Understand the different levels of assurance that can be provided in an assurance engagement, including reasonable assurance

- Understand the need for professional accountants to carry out assurance work in the public interest

- Understand the meaning of 'a true and fair view'

- Understand why users desire assurance reports and recognise examples of the benefits gained from them such as to assure the quality of an entity's published corporate responsibility or sustainability report

- Compare the functions and responsibilities of the different parties involved in an assurance engagement

- Understand the issues which can lead to gaps between the outcomes delivered by the assurance engagement and the expectations of users of the assurance reports

- Identify how these 'expectations gaps' can be overcome

Specific syllabus references for this chapter are: 1a, b, c, d, e, h.

## Syllabus links

You have studied the basic books, records and financial statements of a company in the Accounting paper. It is in relation to these records that the auditor will seek evidence to be able to give assurance.

As already mentioned, audit is a key form of assurance and you will be able to apply the basic principles learnt in this paper to that form of assurance service both here and in the Audit and Assurance Paper.

## Examination context

It is crucial to the whole syllabus that you understand the concept of assurance, why it is required and the reason for assurance engagements being carried out by appropriately qualified professionals. You can therefore expect to see questions in the exam testing your understanding of the definition of assurance and the different levels of assurance.

In the sample paper, the first five questions relate to the subject matter you will cover in this chapter.

In the assessment, candidates may be required to:

- Describe the concept of assurance

- State the benefits of an assurance report

- Compare the functions and responsibilities of the different parties involved in an assurance engagement

- Describe the levels of assurance obtained from different types of assurance engagement

- Describe the concept of the 'expectations gap'

# 1 What is assurance?

## Section overview

- An assurance engagement is one in which a practitioner expresses a conclusion, designed to enhance the degree of confidence of the intended users, other than the responsible party, about the outcome of the evaluation or measurement of a subject matter against criteria.

- Key elements are: three party involvement, subject matter, suitable criteria, sufficient appropriate evidence, written report.

- Assurance engagements can give either a reasonable level of assurance or a limited level of assurance.

- There are various examples of assurance services, the key example in the UK is the audit.

## 1.1 Definition (parties, subject matter, criteria)

### Definition

An assurance engagement is one in which a practitioner expresses a conclusion designed to enhance the degree of confidence of the intended users other than the responsible party about the outcome of the evaluation or measurement of a subject matter against criteria.

The key elements of an assurance engagement are as follows:

- Three people or groups of people involved

    - The practitioner (accountant)
    - The intended users
    - The responsible party (the person(s) who prepared the subject matter)

- A subject matter

    As we shall see below, the subject matter of an assurance engagement may vary considerably. However, it is likely to fall into one of three categories:

    - Data (for example, financial statements or business projections)
    - Systems or processes (for example, internal control systems or computer systems)
    - Behaviour (for example, social and environmental performance or corporate governance)

- Suitable criteria

    The person providing the assurance must have something by which to judge whether the information is reliable and can be trusted. So for example, in an assurance engagement relating to financial statements, the criteria might be accounting standards. The practitioner will be able to test whether the financial statements have been put together in accordance with accounting standards, and if they have, then the practitioner can conclude that there is a degree of assurance that they are reliable.

    In the context of company behaviour, suitable criteria to judge whether something is reliable and can be trusted might be the UK Corporate Governance Code, or, if the company has one, its published Code of Practice.

- Sufficient appropriate evidence to support the assurance opinion

    The practitioner must substantiate the opinion that he draws in order that the user can have confidence that it is reliable. The practitioner must obtain evidence as to whether the criteria have been met. We will look at the collection of evidence in detail later in this Study Manual.

- A written report in appropriate form

Lastly, it is required that assurance reports are provided to the intended users in a written form and contain certain specified information. This adds to the assurance that the user is being given, as it ensures that key information is being given and that the assurance given is clear and unequivocal.

## Worked example: Assurance engagement

In order to demonstrate these elements of an assurance engagement, the Worked example is that of a house purchase. Imagine you are buying a house. There are certain issues you would want assurance about, particularly whether the house is structurally sound. In this situation, you would be unlikely just to trust the word of the person who was selling the house but would seek the additional assurance of a qualified professional, such as a surveyor.

You should already be able to see the first key element of an assurance engagement, which is the involvement of three people:

- You (the intended user)
- The house owner (the responsible party)
- The surveyor (the practitioner)

The subject matter of this assurance engagement is the house in question. The surveyor will visit the house to test whether it is sound and will draw a conclusion.

The surveyor will judge whether the house is sound in the context of building regulations, planning rules and best practice in the building industry. These are the criteria by which he will judge whether he can give you assurance that the house is structurally sound.

In order to make a conclusion, the surveyor will obtain evidence from the house (for example, by looking for damp patches and making inspections of key elements of the house).

Lastly, when he has drawn a conclusion, the surveyor will issue a report to you, outlining his opinion as to whether the house is sound or not. This report will contain any limitations to his work, for example, if he was unable to access any of the property or he was unable to lift fitted carpets to inspect the floor underneath them.

Ultimately, when you have read the surveyor's report, you will have more assurance about the state of the property, and correspondingly, more confidence to pay the deposit, take out a mortgage and buy that house.

---

## Interactive question 1: Assurance engagement    [Difficulty level: Easy]

You are an accountant who has been approached by Jamal, who wants to invest in Company X. He has asked you for assurance whether the most recent financial statements of Company X are a reliable basis for him to make his investment decision.

Identify the key elements of an assurance engagement in this scenario, if you accepted the engagement.

See **Answer** at the end of this chapter.

---

## 1.2    Levels of assurance

The definition of an assurance engagement given above is taken from the International Framework for Assurance Engagements, which is issued by the International Federation of Accountants (IFAC), a global organisation for the accountancy profession, which works with its member organisations to protect the public interest by encouraging high quality practices around the world. ICAEW is a member of IFAC.

The Framework identifies two types of assurance engagement:

- Reasonable assurance engagement
- Limited assurance engagement

## Definition

Reasonable assurance: A high level of assurance, that is less than absolute assurance, that engagement risk has been reduced to an acceptably low level, which then allows a conclusion to be expressed positively.

Limited assurance: A meaningful level of assurance, that is more than inconsequential but is less than reasonable assurance, that engagement risk has been reduced to an acceptable level, which then allows a conclusion to be expressed negatively.

The reason that there are two types of assurance engagement is that the level of assurance that can be given depends on the evidence that can be obtained by the practitioner. Using the surveyor example above, a surveyor can only give assurance that a property is structurally sound if he is allowed to enter the property to inspect it. If he is only given access to part of the building, he can only give limited assurance.

The key differences between the two types of assurance engagement are therefore:

- The evidence obtained
- The type of opinion given

We shall look in detail at obtaining evidence later in this Study Manual. The key point about evidence is that in all assurance engagements, sufficient, appropriate evidence must be obtained. We will look at what constitutes sufficient, appropriate evidence as we go through the course. What determines whether evidence is sufficient and appropriate is the level of assurance that the practitioner is trying to give, so it is tied in with the type of opinion being given, which we shall look at here. In summary, a lower level of evidence will be obtained for a limited assurance engagement.

The opinion given in an assurance engagement therefore depends on what type of engagement it is. As noted above, there are two levels of assurance expressed positively and negatively.

Say, for example, that a practitioner is seeking evidence to conclude whether the report issued by the Chairman of a company in the financial statements is reasonable or not. He could seek evidence, conclude that the statement is reasonable and state in a report something like this:

'In my opinion, the statement by the Chairman regarding X is reasonable'.

This is a positive statement of his conclusion that the statement is reasonable. Alternatively, he could state in a report something like this:

'In the course of my seeking evidence about the statement by the Chairman, nothing has come to my attention indicating that the statement is not reasonable.'

This conclusion is less certain, as it implies that matters could exist which cause the statement to be unreasonable, but that the practitioner has not uncovered any such matters. This is therefore called negative assurance. It is the conclusion that a practitioner gives when he carries out a limited assurance engagement and seeks a lower level of evidence.

| SUMMARY OF TYPES OF ENGAGEMENT | | |
| --- | --- | --- |
| Type of engagement | Evidence sought | Conclusion given |
| Reasonable assurance | Sufficient and appropriate | Positive |
| Limited assurance | Sufficient and appropriate (lower level) | Negative |

## 1.3 Examples of assurance engagements

The key example of an assurance engagement in the UK is a statutory audit. We shall look briefly at the nature of this engagement in the next section.

Other examples of assurance engagements include other audits, which may be specialised due to the nature of the business, for example:

- Local authority audits
- Insurance company audits
- Bank audits
- Pension scheme audits
- Charity audits
- Solicitors' audits
- Environmental audits
- Branch audit (where an overseas company trades in the UK through a branch and requires an audit of that branch although an audit is not required by UK law)

There are also many issues users want assurance on, where the terms of the engagement will be agreed between the practitioner and the person commissioning the report, for example:

- Value for money studies
- Circulation reports (for example, for magazines)
- Cost/benefit reports
- Due diligence (where a report is requested on an acquisition target)
- Reviews of specialist business activities
- Internal audit
- Reports on website security, such as WebTrust
- Fraud investigations
- Inventories and receivables reports
- Internal control reports
- Reports on business plans or projections

## 1.4 Audit

An audit is historically the most important type of assurance service in the UK. This is because all large companies have been required by law to have an audit.

### Definition

The objective of an audit of financial statements is to enable the auditor to express an opinion whether the financial statements are prepared, in all material respects, in accordance with an applicable financial reporting framework.

## Worked example: Audit

The key criteria of an assurance engagement can be seen in an audit as follows:

- Three party involvement
    - The shareholders (users)
    - The board of directors (the responsible party)
    - The audit firm (the practitioner)
- Subject matter
    - The financial statements
- Relevant criteria
    - Law and accounting standards
- Evidence
    - As has been said earlier, sufficient and appropriate evidence is required to support an assurance opinion. The specific requirements in relation to evidence on assurance engagements will be looked at in Chapters 4 and 11.
- Written report in a suitable form
    - Again, as has been said, an assurance report is a written report issued in a prescribed form. We will look at the specific requirements for an audit report in Chapter 4.

In the UK, the auditor will normally express his audit opinion by reference to the 'true and fair view', which is an expression of reasonable assurance. Whilst this term is at the heart of the audit, 'true' and 'fair' are not defined in law or audit guidance. However, for practical purposes the following definitions are generally accepted.

## Definitions

**True**: Information is factual and conforms with reality, not false. In addition the information conforms with required standards and law. The accounts have been correctly extracted from the books and records.

**Fair**: Information is free from discrimination and bias in compliance with expected standards and rules. The accounts should reflect the commercial substance of the company's underlying transactions.

Auditors in the UK are subject to both legal and professional requirements. The legal requirements are all contained within the Companies Act. The provisions of the Companies Act 1985 were gradually replaced by the Companies Act 2006, with all changes being in place by the end of 2009.

The Companies Act 2006 requires that auditors are members of a Recognised Supervisory Body (RSB) and are eligible for appointment under the rules of that body. RSBs are required to have rules to ensure that those eligible for appointment as a company auditor are either:

- Individuals holding an appropriate qualification, or
- Firms controlled by qualified persons

The ICAEW is an RSB. Professional qualifications are a prerequisite of membership of an RSB, and these are offered by Registered Qualifying Bodies approved by the Secretary of State.

RSBs must also implement procedures for monitoring their registered auditors on a regular basis.

The Companies Act 2006 also sets out factors which make a person ineligible for being a company auditor, for example, if he or she is:

- An officer or employee of the company
- A partner or employee of such a person
- Any partner in a partnership in which such a person is a partner
- Ineligible by the above for appointment as auditor of any directly connected companies

As you will see later in this course, the professional ethics of the RSBs are usually far stricter in their criteria for ineligibility as an auditor.

In the UK, the Government has delegated the task of independent monitoring of the UK accountancy profession to the Financial Reporting Council (FRC). The FRC is responsible for issuing auditing standards, which it does through its Codes and Standards Committee. The FRC has adopted international standards on auditing, augmented for UK requirements. The FRC is also responsible for issuing the Ethical Standards for Auditors (ESs) in relation to auditors' independence, objectivity and integrity. These standards set professional requirements for auditors. Note that until July 2012, the FRC's work in this area was done by the Auditing Practices Board (APB). Already existing guidance (eg ISAs) were issued by the APB and are still referred to as such.

ISA 200 (UK and Ireland) *Overall Objectives of the Independent Auditor and the Conduct of an Auditor in Accordance with International Standards on Auditing* states that auditors shall comply with relevant ethical requirements relating to audit engagements. These will be outlined later in this Study Manual. An auditor must conduct an audit in accordance with ISAs. Relevant ISAs will be referred to in this Study Manual. Auditors are required to carry out their work with professional scepticism, meaning that they must make a critical assessment.

Auditors must assess the risks associated with the audit and seek to minimise those risks so that the risk of giving the wrong opinion on the financial statements is minimised. This risk is referred to as audit risk and it will be outlined in detail later in this Study Manual.

## 2 Why is assurance important?

### Section overview

- Who the users are will depend on the nature of the subject matter.
- Users benefit from receiving an independent, professional opinion on the subject matter.
- Users may also benefit from additional confidence in the subject matter given to others.
- The existence of an assurance service may prevent errors or frauds occurring in the first place.

### 2.1 Users

In the key assurance service of audit, which we looked at above, the users were the shareholders of a company, to whom the financial statements are addressed. In other cases, the users might be the board of directors of a company or a subsection of them.

### 2.2 Benefits of assurance

The key benefit of assurance is the **independent, professional verification** being given to the users. This can be seen in the example of the house purchase given above. The importance of independence and objectivity in assurance provision will be looked at in Chapters 14 and 15.

In addition, assurance may have subsidiary benefits.

Although an assurance report may only be addressed to one set of people, it may give additional confidence to other parties in a way that benefits the business. For example, audit reports are addressed to shareholders, but the existence of an unqualified audit report might give the bank more confidence to lend money to that business, in other words, it enhances the credibility of the information.

The existence of an independent check might help prevent errors or frauds being made and reduce the risk of management bias. In other words, the fact that an assurance service will be carried out might make people involved in preparing the subject matter more careful in its preparation and reduce the chance of errors arising. Therefore it can be seen that an assurance service may act as a deterrent.

In addition, where problems exist within information, the existence of an assurance report draws attention to the deficiencies in that information, so that users know what those deficiencies are.

Assurance is also important in more general terms. It helps to ensure that high quality, reliable information exists, leading to effective markets that investors have faith in and trust. It adds to the

ICAEW

reputation of organisations and even countries, so that investors are happy to invest in country X because there is a strong culture of assurance provision there.

Businesses are keen to be seen as acting responsibly and are increasingly publishing information such as emissions targets or a pledge not to employ children. There is a growing public perception that this is an important area and stakeholders are unlikely to associate with businesses that could damage their reputation. Corporate responsibility or sustainability reports provide assurance for stakeholders that this published information is reliable and accurate.

# 3 Why can assurance never be absolute?

**Section overview**

- Assurance can never be absolute.
- Assurance provision has limitations which may not be understood by users.
- The expectations gap also adds to the lack of guarantee given by assurance.

Assurance can never be absolute. Assurance providers will never give a certification of absolute correctness due to the limitations set out below.

## 3.1 Limitations of assurance

A key issue for accountants is that there are limitations to assurance services, and therefore there is always a risk involved that the wrong conclusion will be drawn. We shall look in more detail at this issue of assurance engagement risk in Chapter 3.

The limitations of assurance services include:

- The fact that testing is used – the auditors do not oversee the process of building the financial statements from start to finish.

- The fact that the accounting systems on which assurance providers may place a degree of reliance also have inherent limitations (we shall look at control systems and their limitations in Chapter 5).

- The fact that most audit evidence is persuasive rather than conclusive.

- The fact that assurance providers would not test every item in the subject matter (this would be prohibitively expensive for the responsible party, so a sampling approach is used – see Chapter 11).

- The fact that the client's staff members may collude in fraud that can then be deliberately hidden from the auditor or misrepresent matters to them for the same purpose.

- The fact that assurance provision can be subjective and professional judgements have to be made (for example, about what aspects of the subject matter are the most important, how much evidence to obtain, etc).

- The fact that assurance providers rely on the responsible party and its staff to provide correct information, which in some cases may be impossible to verify by other means.

- The fact that some items in the subject matter may be estimates and are therefore uncertain. It is impossible to conclude absolutely that judgemental estimates are correct.

- The fact that the nature of the assurance report might itself be limiting, as every judgement and conclusion the assurance provider has drawn cannot be included in it.

## 3.2 The expectations gap

The problems users may experience in connection with assurance provision also arise from the limitations and restrictions inherent in assurance provision. This is often because users are not aware of the nature of the limitations on assurance provision, or do not understand them and believe that the assurance provider is offering a service (such as a guarantee of correctness) which in fact he is not.

The distinction between reasonable and limited assurance may also be misunderstood by users.

We shall look at the concept of the expectations gap in more detail in Chapter 4, in the context of reporting, but in essence it is this lack of understanding which constitutes the expectations gap – meaning that there is a gap between what the assurance provider understands he is doing and what the user of the information believes he is doing.

Assurance providers need to close this gap as far as possible in order to maintain the value of the assurance provided for the user. This is done in a variety of ways, for example, by issuing an engagement letter spelling out the work that will be carried out and the limitations of that work (which we shall look at in the next chapter) and by regularly reviewing the format and content of reports issued as a result of assurance work.

### Interactive question 2: Benefits of assurance                    [Difficulty level: Exam standard]

Which **three** of the following are benefits of assurance work?

- [ ] An independent, professional opinion
- [ ] Additional confidence given to other related parties
- [ ] Testing as a result of sampling is cheaper for the responsible party
- [ ] Judgements on estimates can be conclusive
- [ ] Assurance may act as a deterrent to error or fraud

See **Answer** at the end of this chapter.

## Summary

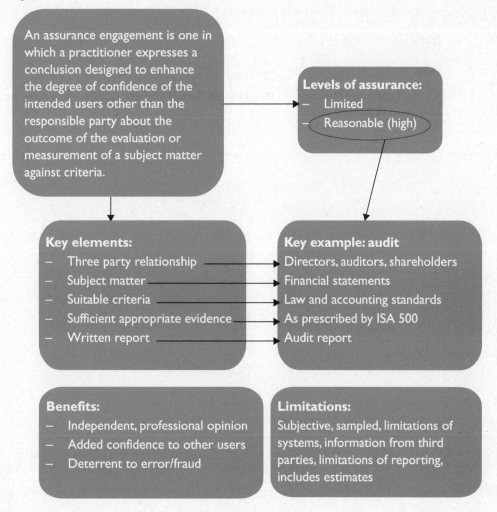

An assurance engagement is one in which a practitioner expresses a conclusion designed to enhance the degree of confidence of the intended users other than the responsible party about the outcome of the evaluation or measurement of a subject matter against criteria.

**Levels of assurance:**
– Limited
– Reasonable (high)

**Key elements:**
– Three party relationship
– Subject matter
– Suitable criteria
– Sufficient appropriate evidence
– Written report

**Key example: audit**
Directors, auditors, shareholders
Financial statements
Law and accounting standards
As prescribed by ISA 500
Audit report

**Benefits:**
– Independent, professional opinion
– Added confidence to other users
– Deterrent to error/fraud

**Limitations:**
Subjective, sampled, limitations of systems, information from third parties, limitations of reporting, includes estimates

## Self-test

Answer the following questions.

1  Assurance services are required by law.

☐  True

☐  False

2  What **five** elements are required for an engagement to be an assurance engagement?

1......................................

2......................................

3......................................

4......................................

5......................................

3    Name **four** limitations of an assurance service.

1.........................................

2.........................................

3.........................................

4.........................................

4    Reasonable assurance is a high level of assurance.

☐    True

☐    False

Now, go back to the Learning Objectives in the Introduction. If you are satisfied you have achieved these objectives, please tick them off.

## Answer to Interactive question 1

1   Three party involvement:

    - Jamal (the intended user)
    - You (the practitioner)
    - The directors of Company X as they produce the financial statements (the responsible party)

2   Subject matter

    The most recent financial statements of Company X are the subject matter

3   Relevant criteria

    It is most likely in this instance that the criteria would be accounting standards, so that Jamal was assured that the financial statements were properly prepared and comparable with other companies' financial statements

4   Evidence

    You would have to agree the extent of procedures in relation to this assignment with Jamal so that he knew the level of evidence you were intending to seek. This would depend on several factors, including the degree of secrecy in the proposed transaction and whether the directors of Company X allowed you to inspect the books and documents

5   Report

    Again, the nature of the report would be agreed between you and Jamal, however, it would be a written report containing your opinion on the financial statements

## Answer to Interactive question 2

An independent, professional opinion
Additional confidence given to other related parties
Assurance may act as a deterrent to error or fraud

1   False (an audit may be required by law if the company does not qualify as a small company)

2   1   Three party relationship
    2   Subject matter
    3   Suitable criteria
    4   Sufficient appropriate evidence
    5   Written report

3   From:

    1   Subjective exercise
    2   Sampling
    3   Limitations in systems
    4   Limitations in report
    5   Information from third parties
    6   Estimations

4   True

# CHAPTER 2

# Process of assurance: obtaining an engagement

### Learning objectives

- Be aware of how assurance firms obtain work

- Understand the key issues practitioners must consider before accepting engagements

- Know what a letter of engagement is and what it does

The specific syllabus reference for this chapter is: 1f.

### Syllabus links

The issues of obtaining engagements will be looked at in much greater detail in the Audit and Assurance paper at the Application level.

### Examination context

This is a fairly minor area for the exam, but you could expect at least one question on the scope of the engagement (there was a question about engagement letters in the sample paper) and possibly another on the considerations of the assurance firm when deciding to accept engagements.

In the assessment, candidates may be required to:

- Identify acceptance procedures
- Identify sources of information about new clients
- Select procedures required by money laundering legislation
- Determine the purpose of a letter of engagement

# 1 Obtaining an engagement

**Section overview**

- Accountants are permitted to advertise for clients, within certain professional guidelines.
- Accountants may sometimes be invited to tender for an audit.

How assurance firms obtain clients is an important practical question, but it is largely outside the scope of this syllabus. In brief, you should be aware that:

- Accountants are permitted to advertise for clients within certain professional guidelines, the details of which you do not need to know.

- Accountants are often invited to tender for particular engagements, which means that they offer a quote for services, outlining the benefits of their firm and personnel, usually in competition with other firms which are tendering at the same time.

In this syllabus, if the topics in this chapter are examined, it will be in the context of an accountant being invited by a potential client to accept an engagement. We will go on now to look at the things which an accountant must consider when he is so invited.

# 2 Accepting an engagement

**Section overview**

- The **present** and **proposed auditors** should normally **communicate** about the client prior to the audit being accepted.

- The client must be asked to give permission for communication to occur. If the client **refuses** to give **permission,** the proposed auditors should normally decline the appointment.

- The auditors must ensure they have sufficient resources (time and staff, for example) to carry out the appointment.

- The audit firm must have client due diligence procedures in place in order to comply with the Money Laundering Regulations 2007.

This section covers the procedures that the **auditors must** undertake to **ensure that their appointment is valid** and that they are clear to act.

## 2.1 Appointment considerations

Section 210 of the ICAEW *Code of Ethics* sets out the rules under which accountants should accept new appointments. Before a new audit client is accepted, the auditors must determine whether there are any **independence** or **other ethical issues** likely to cause significant problems with the ethical code (i.e., significant threats to complying with the fundamental principles of ethical behaviour – see later in this text). Furthermore, new auditors should ensure that they have been appointed in a proper and legal manner.

The nominee auditors must carry out the following procedures.

| Acceptance procedures | |
| --- | --- |
| Ensure **professionally qualified** to act | Consider whether disqualified on legal or ethical grounds, for example if there would be a conflict of interest with another client. We will look in more detail at ethical issues later in this Study Manual. |
| Ensure **existing resources adequate** | Consider available time, staff and technical expertise. |
| **Obtain references** | Make independent enquiries if directors not personally known. |
| **Communicate with present auditors** | Enquire whether there are reasons/circumstances behind the change which the new auditors ought to know, also as a matter of courtesy. |

Some of the basic factors for consideration are given below.

- The integrity of those managing a company will be of great importance, particularly if the company is controlled by one or a few dominant personalities.

- The audit firm will also consider whether the client is likely to be high or low risk to the firm in terms of being able to draw an appropriate assurance conclusion in relation to that client. The following table contrasts low and high risk clients.

| Low risk | High risk |
| --- | --- |
| Good long-term prospects | Poor recent or forecast performance |
| Well-financed | Likely lack of finance |
| Strong internal controls | Significant control weaknesses |
| Conservative, prudent accounting policies | Evidence of questionable integrity, doubtful accounting policies |
| Competent, honest management | Lack of finance director |
| Few unusual transactions | Significant unexplained transactions or transactions with connected companies |

Where the risk level of a company's audit is determined as anything other than low, then the specific risks should be identified and documented. It might be necessary to assign specialists in response to these risks, particularly industry specialists, as independent reviewers. Some audit firms have procedures for closely monitoring audits which have been accepted, but which are considered high risk.

Generally, the expected fees from a new client should reflect the **level of risk** expected. They should also offer the same sort of return expected of clients of this nature and reflect the overall financial strategy of the audit firm. Occasionally, the audit firm will want the work to gain entry into the client's particular industry, or to establish better contacts within that industry. These factors will all contribute to a total expected economic return.

The audit firm will generally want the relationship with a client to be **long term**. This is not only to enjoy receiving fees year after year; it is also to allow the audit work to be enhanced by better knowledge of the client and thereby offer a better service.

Conflict of interest problems can be significant; the firm should establish that no existing clients will cause difficulties as competitors of the new client. Other services to other clients may have an impact here, not just audit.

The audit firm must have the **resources** to perform the work properly, as well as any **specialist knowledge or skills**. The impact on existing engagements must be estimated, in terms of staff time and the timing of the audit.

| Sources of information about new clients | |
|---|---|
| **Enquiries** of other sources | Bankers, solicitors |
| Review of **documents** | Most recent annual accounts, listing particulars, credit rating |
| **Previous accountants/auditors** | Previous auditors should be invited to disclose fully all relevant information |
| Review of **rules and standards** | Consider specific laws/standards that relate to industry |

Prospective auditors should seek the prospective client's permission to contact the previous auditors. If this permission is not given, the prospective auditors should normally decline the appointment. Normally permission will be given, so the prospective auditors can write to the outgoing auditors.

 ## Worked example: Initial communication

This is an example of an initial communication.

> To:        Retiring & Co
>
>            Chartered Accountants
>
> Dear Sirs
>
> Re: New Client Co Ltd
>
> We have been asked to allow our name to go forward for nomination as auditors of the above company, and we should therefore be grateful if you would please let us know whether there are any professional reasons why we should not accept nomination ...... .
>
> Acquiring & Co
>
> Chartered Accountants, Registered Auditors

Having negotiated these steps the auditors will be in a position to accept the nomination, or not, as the case may be.

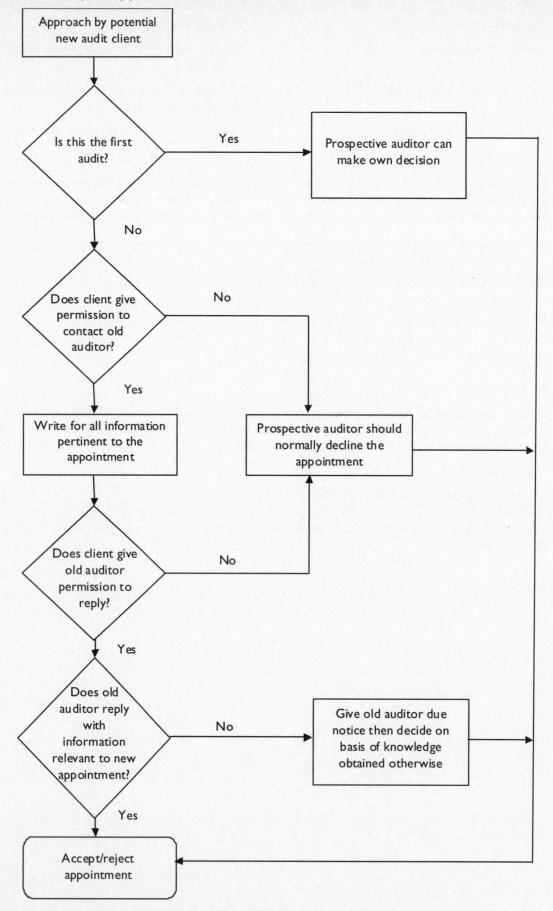

Approach by potential
new audit client

Is this the first
audit?

Yes

Prospective auditor can
make own decision

No

Does client give
permission to
contact old
auditor?

No

Yes

Write for all information
pertinent to the
appointment

Prospective auditor should
normally decline the
appointment

Does client give
old auditor
permission to
reply?

No

Yes

Does old
auditor reply
with
information
relevant to new
appointment?

No

Give old auditor due
notice then decide on
basis of knowledge
obtained otherwise

Yes

Accept/reject
appointment

## Interactive question 1: Accepting appointment [Difficulty level: Easy]

Identify whether the following are true or false. The audit firm should consider the following factors when determining whether to accept an engagement.

|  | True | False |
|---|---|---|
| Whether the firm is ethically barred from acting. |  |  |
| Whether the firm has sufficient resources to carry out the engagement. |  |  |
| Whether the firm can make sufficient profit from the engagement. |  |  |
| Whether the client is new to the firm. |  |  |
| Whether the client gives permission to contact the outgoing auditors. |  |  |

See **Answer** at the end of this chapter.

The following procedures should be carried out after accepting nomination.

- **Ensure** that the **outgoing auditors' removal** or **resignation** has been **properly conducted** in accordance with national legislation.

  The new auditors should see a valid notice of the outgoing auditors' resignation, or confirm that the outgoing auditors were properly removed.

- **Ensure** that the **new auditors' appointment is valid.** The new auditors should obtain a copy of the resolution passed at the general meeting appointing them as the company's auditors.

- Set up and **submit a letter of engagement** to the directors of the company.

Where the outgoing auditors have fees still owing by the client, the new auditors need not decline appointment solely for this reason.

Once a new appointment has taken place, the **new auditors should obtain all books and papers which belong to the client from the outgoing auditors.** The outgoing auditors should ensure that all such documents are transferred promptly, **unless** they have a lien (a legal right to hold on to them) because of unpaid fees. An outgoing auditor cannot have a lien over the accounting records of a registered company as the Companies Act requires these to be available for public inspection. The outgoing auditors should also pass any useful information to the new auditors if it will be of help, without charge, unless a lot of work is involved.

## 2.2 Other assurance engagements

Similar considerations will be required for any assurance engagements. The legal considerations relating to audit will not be relevant to other assurance engagements, but the ethical, risk and practical considerations will be just as valid.

## 2.3 Money laundering regulations

In order to comply with the Money Laundering Regulations 2007, assurance firms must keep certain records about clients and undertake what is known as client due diligence.

It is mandatory to check the identity of all clients before any work is undertaken when an ongoing relationship is envisaged (this would be the case for certain assurance engagements) or where a one-off transaction or a series of transactions greater than €15,000 will take place.

The identity of clients should be checked by:

- **For individuals**: obtaining official documents including a photograph and identifying the client's full name and permanent address, for example, a passport supported by a number of utilities bills or a driving licence.

- **For companies**: obtaining similar legal information from the Registrar of Companies, for example, a certificate of incorporation, the registered address and a list of shareholders and directors.

Client identification documents must be kept for a minimum of five years and until five years have elapsed since the relationship with the client in question has ceased. It is also necessary to keep a full audit trail of all transactions with the client.

**Interactive question 2: Client due diligence** [Difficulty level: Easy]

Drew Brothers, chartered accountants, has recently accepted appointment as the auditor of Abysin Ltd. In terms of client due diligence, they should check which **two** of the following documents?

☐ Certificate of incorporation
☐ Passport
☐ Utilities bills
☐ Annual return

See **Answer** at the end of this chapter.

---

# 3   Agreeing terms of an engagement

**Section overview**

- An engagement letter should be sent to all clients to clarify the terms of the engagement.
- Agreement of audit engagement terms must be in writing.
- It must include an explanation of the scope of the audit, the limitations of an audit and the responsibilities of auditors and those charged with governance.
- It may contain other information concerning practical details of the audit.

The purpose of an engagement letter is to:

- Define clearly the **extent** of the firm's **responsibilities** and so minimise the possibility of any misunderstanding between the client and the firm

- Provide **written confirmation** of the firm's **acceptance** of the appointment, the scope of the engagement and the form of their report

If an engagement letter is not sent to clients, both new and existing, there is scope for argument about the precise extent of the respective obligations of the client and its directors and the auditors. The elements of an engagement letter should be discussed and agreed with management before it is sent.

An engagement letter for any type of assurance engagement will contain the same contents as an audit engagement letter (discussed below). Clearly details will be different (for instance, it will cover the **scope** of the engagement, but the scope of an audit and the scope of a review of forecast information, for example, will be different). An engagement letter for an assurance engagement other than audit is likely to refer to specific fees for the engagement. As you will see below, as an audit engagement is often recurring, specific fees are initially not mentioned.

## 3.1 Audit engagement letters

Auditing standards require that the auditor and the client agree on the terms of the engagement. The agreed terms must be in writing and the usual form would be a **letter of engagement**. Any other form of appropriate contract, however, may be used.

Even in countries where the audit objectives and scope and the auditor's obligations are established by law, an **audit engagement letter** may be informative for clients.

The auditors should send an engagement letter to all new clients soon **after their appointment** as auditors and, in any event, before the commencement of the first audit assignment. They should also consider sending an engagement letter to existing clients to whom no letter has previously been sent as soon as a suitable opportunity presents itself.

The following items shall be included in the engagement letter.

- The **objective** of the **audit** of financial statements.

- The **scope** of the audit, which could include reference to applicable legislation, regulations, or pronouncements of professional bodies to which the auditor adheres.

- The **auditor's responsibility**.

- The **reporting framework** that is applicable for the financial statements being prepared, for example International Financial Reporting Standards.

- **Management's responsibility** to prepare the financial statements and to provide the auditor with **unrestricted access** to whatever records, documentation and other information is requested in connection with the audit.

- The form of any **reports** of results of the engagement.

The form and remaining content of audit engagement letters may vary for each client, but the auditor may wish to include in the letter the following items.

- The form of any **other communication** of the results of the engagement.

- The fact that because of the **test nature** and other **inherent limitations** of an audit, together with the inherent limitations of any accounting and internal control system, there is an unavoidable risk that some material misstatements may remain undiscovered.

- Arrangements regarding the **planning** of the audit.

- Expectation of receiving from management **written confirmation** of **representations** made in connection with the audit.

- Agreement of the client to provide the auditor with information in time to allow the auditor to complete the audit in line with the proposed timetable.

- Basis on which **fees** are computed and any billing arrangements.

- Request for the client to **confirm the terms** of the engagement by acknowledging receipt of the engagement letter.

When relevant, the following points could also be made.

- Arrangements concerning the involvement of **other auditors** and **experts** in some aspects of the audit.

- Arrangements concerning the involvement of **internal auditors** and other client staff.

- Arrangements to be made with the **predecessor auditor**, if any, in the case of an initial audit.

- Any **restriction of the auditor's liability** when such possibility exists.

- A reference to any **further agreements** between the auditor and the client.

- Any obligations to provide audit working papers to **other parties**.

**To the appropriate representative of management or those charged with governance of ABC Company**

**The objective and scope of the audit**

You have requested that we audit the financial statements of ABC Company, which comprise the balance sheet as at December 31, 20X1, and the income statement, statement of changes in equity and cash flow statement for the year then ended, and a summary of significant accounting policies and other explanatory information. We are pleased to confirm our acceptance and our understanding of this audit engagement by means of this letter. Our audit will be conducted with the objective of our expressing an opinion on the financial statements.

**The responsibilities of the auditor**

We will conduct our audit in accordance with International Standards on Auditing (ISAs). Those standards require that we comply with ethical requirements and plan and perform the audit to obtain reasonable assurance about whether the financial statements are free from material misstatement. An audit involves performing procedures to obtain audit evidence about the amounts and disclosures in the financial statements. The procedures selected depend on the auditor's judgment, including the assessment of the risks of material misstatement of the financial statements, whether due to fraud or error. An audit also includes evaluating the appropriateness of accounting policies used and the reasonableness of accounting estimates made by management, as well as evaluating the overall presentation of the financial statements.

Because of the inherent limitations of an audit, together with the inherent limitations of internal control, there is an unavoidable risk that some material misstatements may not be detected, even though the audit is properly planned and performed in accordance with ISAs.

In making our risk assessments, we consider internal control relevant to the entity's preparation of the financial statements in order to design audit procedures that are appropriate in the circumstances, but not for the purpose of expressing an opinion on the effectiveness of the entity's internal control. However, we will communicate to you in writing concerning any significant deficiencies in internal control relevant to the audit of the financial statements that we have identified during the audit.

Our audit will be conducted on the basis that (management and, where appropriate, those charged with governance) acknowledge and understand that they have responsibility:

- For the preparation and fair presentation of the financial statements in accordance with International Financial Reporting Standards;

- For such internal control as (management) determines is necessary to enable the preparation of financial statements that are free from material misstatement, whether due to fraud or error; and

- To provide us with:

  - Access to all information of which (management) is aware that is relevant to the preparation of the financial statements such as records, documentation and other matters;

  - Additional information that we may request from (management) for the purpose of the audit; and

  - Unrestricted access to persons within the entity from whom we determine it necessary to obtain audit evidence.

As part of our audit process, we will request from (management and, where appropriate, those charged with governance), written confirmation concerning representations made to us in connection with the audit.

We look forward to full cooperation from your staff during our audit.

[Other relevant information]

[Insert other information, such as fee arrangements, billings and other specific terms, as appropriate.]

**Reporting**

[Insert appropriate reference to the expected form and content of the auditor's report.]

The form and content of our report may need to be amended in the light of our audit findings.

Please sign and return the attached copy of this letter to indicate your acknowledgement of, and agreement with, the arrangements for our audit of the financial statements including our respective responsibilities.


XYZ & Co.


Acknowledged and agreed on behalf of ABC Company by

(signed)

.....................

Name and Title

---

## Interactive question 3: Engagement letters [Difficulty level: Exam standard]

Which **three** of the following may be contained within a letter of engagement?

☐ Responsibilities of the auditors

☐ Responsibilities of the directors

☐ The names of the staff assigned to the engagement

☐ The scope of the audit

See **Answer** at the end of this chapter.

---

## Summary

> Auditors may advertise their services, within certain boundaries

> Auditors will often be invited to tender for audits

> When an audit firm is invited to accept an engagement (usually as a result of a successful tender), it must:
> – Consider whether it is ethically barred from acting
> – Consider whether it has the resources available to undertake the engagement
> – Obtain permission to contact the outgoing auditors, and so do

> When an audit firm accepts an engagement it must:
> – Check the outgoing auditors' removal was carried out properly
> – Ensure its appointment is valid
> – Carry out customer due diligence in accordance with Money Laundering Regulations 2007
> – Set up Letter of engagement

**Must be sent prior to first audit**

**Clarifies terms of engagement**

## Self-test

Answer the following questions.

1   An audit firm must not accept an engagement if the client is not previously known to them.

☐   True

☐   False

2   If a prospective client declines permission to contact the previous auditors, the audit firm should:

A   Report the client to the Companies Registrar
B   Contact the previous auditors anyway
C   Accept the engagement provisionally and continue to request permission
D   Normally decline the appointment

3    Complete the questions that should be in the diagram.

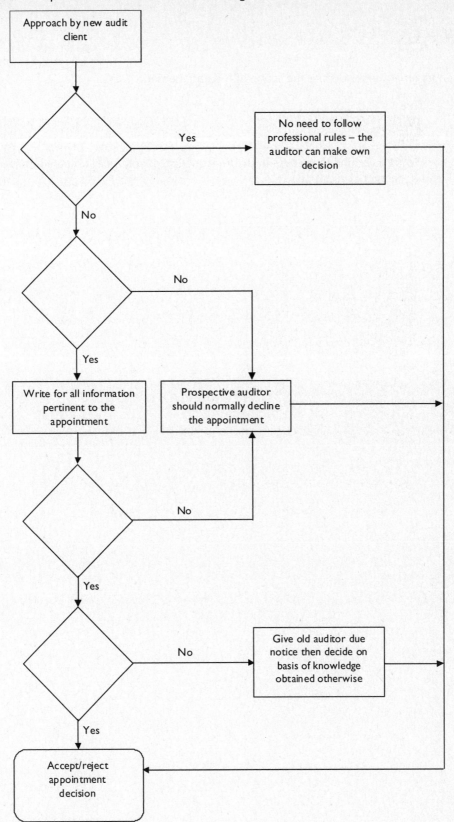

4    In accordance with the money laundering regulations, client identification documents should be kept for:

A    Five years
B    Five years after the cessation of the relationship with the client
C    Seven years
D    Seven years after the cessation of the relationship with the client

5 An engagement letter is only ever sent to a client before the first audit.

☐ True

☐ False

6 An engagement letter defines the scope of the engagement.

☐ True

☐ False

Now, go back to the Learning Objectives in the Introduction. If you are satisfied you have achieved these objectives, please tick them off.

1 Accepting an engagement                                    Section 210, ICAEW Code of Ethics

2 Agreeing terms of an engagement

- Agree the terms in writing                              ISA 210.10 (UK and Ireland)

- Send letter before first audit                         ISA 210.A22 (UK and Ireland)

- Contents of engagement letter                   ISA 210.10, A23 (UK and Ireland)

C
H
A
P
T
E
R

2

### Answer to Interactive question 1

The auditors should consider all these factors except whether the client is new to the firm. This is irrelevant in making the decision, although the firm may have to carry out additional procedures to get to know the client if it is a new client. The auditors must consider if they are ethically qualified to act, whether they have sufficient resources and whether the client gives permission to contact the previous auditors (if this is declined, the auditors must consider carefully the reasons for the refusal). As the audit firm is also a commercial enterprise, it must consider whether taking on the engagement is commercially viable.

### Answer to Interactive question 2

They should check the certificate of incorporation and the annual return (which should give details of the registered office and the shareholders and directors). If they are taking on any work for any individuals connected with Abysin (for example, personal tax for the directors) they should also obtain information for them from passports and utilities bills.

### Answer to Interactive question 3

The specific staff assigned to the engagement will not normally be referred to (as the auditors will reserve the right to change their arrangement and the client should not have influence over assurance staff anyway). The composition of the audit team may be referred to, for example the number of senior and junior staff in the team. The other three items may be included.

1    False. However, if the client is unknown to the audit firm, they should seek references in respect of key personnel associated with the client, and must carry out customer due diligence (as they must with all clients).

2    D. Normally decline the appointment. The auditors must not contact the previous auditors without permission as this would be a breach of confidentiality. The client is legally entitled to refuse this permission so there is no reason to report to the Companies Registrar.

3    •    Is this the first audit?
     •    Does the client give permission to contact the old auditor?
     •    Does the client give old auditor permission to reply?
     •    Does the old auditor reply with information relevant to the new appointment?

4    B

5    False. It should be re-issued if there is a change in circumstances.

6    True

CHAPTER 3

# Process of assurance: planning the assignment

# Introduction

## Learning objectives

Tick off

- Define overall audit strategy and audit plan
- Define professional scepticism
- Understand the need to obtain an understanding of the entity and its environment
- Be aware how such an understanding is obtained
- Understand what analytical procedures are
- Understand the use of analytical procedures at the planning stage
- Define materiality
- Understand the concept of planning materiality and how it is set
- Define audit risk and its individual components
- Understand how auditors use the risk model
- Be able to identify and classify risks

Specific syllabus references for this chapter are: 1f, g.

## Syllabus links

Planning is a large part of the Audit and Assurance syllabus, so when you reach that paper you will build on the knowledge you have gained in this syllabus and learn to apply that knowledge in a more practical way.

## Examination context

Planning and risk are key issues for assurance providers and you should expect this area to come up in your assessment. Ensure that you understand the definitions that are set out in this chapter, since all could be examined. In addition, work through the examples and questions in the chapter identifying risks, as your assessment could include a question in such an area.

In the assessment candidates may be required to:

- Identify the content of an audit strategy and an audit plan
- Select appropriate procedures used by the auditor in obtaining an understanding of the entity
- Describe professional scepticism
- Identify how analytical procedures are applied throughout the course of the audit.
- Describe the concept of materiality
- Describe audit risk and its components
- Identify the type of risks illustrated in a given set of circumstances

# 1 Planning

### Section overview

- The auditors formulate an overall audit strategy which is translated into a detailed audit plan for audit staff to follow.

- A key part of audit planning is obtaining an understanding of the entity – its environment, its internal control, so that risk may be assessed and audit work planned.

- Professional scepticism is an important tool of the auditor when carrying out audit work.

In this chapter, we will look at the major ISAs covering the planning process. Remember that an audit is a high level assurance engagement, and therefore the auditor will carry out more procedures than would be the case on a lower level assurance assignment. However, the general principles discussed in this chapter would be relevant to another assurance assignment such as a review. Remember that in a lower level engagement, less detailed procedures are likely to be carried out.

An effective and efficient audit relies on proper planning procedures. The planning process is covered in general terms by ISA 300 (UK and Ireland) *Planning an Audit of Financial Statements*. ISA 300 states 'The objective of the auditor is to plan the audit so that it will be performed in an effective manner'.

### Definitions

Audit strategy: The formulation of the general strategy for the audit, which sets the scope, timing and direction of the audit and guides the development of the audit plan.

Audit plan: An audit plan is more detailed than the strategy and sets out the nature, timing and extent of audit procedures (including risk assessment procedures) to be performed by engagement team members in order to obtain sufficient appropriate audit evidence.

An **audit plan** shows how the overall audit strategy will be implemented.

Audits are planned to:

- Ensure appropriate attention is devoted to important areas of the audit
- Identify potential problems and resolve them on a timely basis
- Ensure that the audit is properly organised and managed
- Assign work to engagement team members properly
- Facilitate direction and supervision of engagement team members
- Facilitate review of work

Audit procedures may be discussed with the client's management, staff and/or audit committee in order to co-ordinate audit work, including that of internal audit. However, all audit procedures remain the responsibility of the external auditors.

A structured approach to planning will include:

### Step 1
Ensuring that ethical requirements continue to be met.

### Step 2
Ensuring the terms of the engagement are understood.

## Step 3

Establishing the overall audit strategy.

- Identifying the relevant characteristics of the engagement, such as the reporting framework used as this will set the scope for the engagement

- Discovering key dates for reporting and other communications

- Determining materiality, preliminary risk assessment, whether internal controls are to be tested

- Consideration of when work is to be carried out, for example before or after the year end

- Consideration of 'team members' available, their skills and how and when they are to be used, for example particular skills for high risk areas. In addition, appropriate levels of staff are required to facilitate direction, supervision and review of more junior team members' work.

## Step 4

Developing an audit plan including risk assessment procedures, audit tests and any other procedures necessary to comply with ISAs.

The audit plan and any significant changes to it during the audit must be documented.

| Key contents of an overall audit strategy | |
|---|---|
| Understanding the entity's environment | General economic factors and industry conditions. |
| | Important characteristics of the client: (a) business, (b) principal business strategies, (c) financial performance, (d) reporting requirements, including changes since the previous audit. |
| | The general level of competence of management. |
| Understanding the accounting and internal control systems | The accounting policies adopted by the entity and changes in those policies. |
| | The effect of new accounting or auditing pronouncements. |
| | The auditors' cumulative knowledge of the accounting and internal control systems, and the relative emphasis expected to be placed on different types of test (we shall consider this in Chapter 4). |
| Risk and materiality | The expected assessments of risks of fraud or error and identification of significant audit areas. |
| | The setting of materiality for audit planning purposes. |
| | The possibility of material misstatements, including the experience of past periods, or fraud. |
| | The identification of complex accounting areas including those involving estimates. |
| Consequent nature, timing and extent of procedures | Possible change of emphasis on specific audit areas. |
| | The effect of information technology on the audit. |
| Co-ordination, direction, supervision and review | The number of locations. |
| | Staffing requirements. |
| | Need to attend client premises for inventory count or other year-end procedures. |
| Other matters | The possibility that the going concern basis may be subject to question. |
| | Conditions requiring special attention. |
| | The terms of the engagement and any statutory responsibilities. |
| | The nature and timing of reports or other communication with the entity that are expected under the engagement. |

| Area | Typical comment on the audit strategy/explanation |
|---|---|
| The terms of engagement | 'Normal audit report – we write up the nominal ledger and draft statutory accounts from client records.'<br><br>The letter of engagement should be read carefully to see exactly what the contractual commitments are. |
| Understanding the company and its business | 'Old established confectioners, tobacconists and newsagents with main shop in high street and a branch in Kings Road Estate. Revenue £8 million.'<br><br>The auditor will use knowledge of the client to:<br><br>• Assess risks and identify procedures.<br>• Plan and perform the audit effectively and efficiently.<br>• Evaluate the audit evidence. |
| Special audit problems (risks) | 'Review profit margins (profits as a percentage of sales) and directors' salaries to ensure that both appear reasonable in the light of the other evidence, the nature and location of the business and the proprietor's standard of living.'<br><br>Here, it has been identified that in a cash business all earnings might not be reported. The audit team is therefore being alerted that they should see if reported earnings are consistent with other information that is available. |
| Results of analytical procedures | 'No results currently available – we expect gross margins of 26% (newspapers), 10% (tobacco), and 20% (confectionery). Normally sales mix has been approximately 5:3:2.'<br><br>Another influence on how the auditor would perform the audit is the analytical procedures. (We look at this in more detail later in this chapter, but in summary it means looking at ratios and the changes in the accounts to see if anything looks odd.) |
| Materiality | 'Accounting – all posting to be accurate – whenever possible work to be the nearest £ or £10. Audit materiality – £50,000 based on 5% profits.'<br><br>We look at this in more detail later. However, the auditor does not claim to find every misstatement (see the engagement letter), but material misstatements should be discovered.<br><br>This section of the audit strategy gives the audit team some indication as to materiality levels. |
| Risk evaluation and audit approach | 'No reliance can be placed on internal controls or analytical procedures. Generally a substantive approach will be adopted.' (We will see what this means in Chapter 4.)<br><br>'As far as the risk of understatement of sales is concerned, we will check till rolls to cash book, estimate the sales mix and purchase mix and predict gross margins. We will also review cash movements over ten weeks at random and check that they appear reasonable.' |
| Other matters | 'None.'<br><br>This section could contain details of inventory counts and other year-end procedures (which we will look at in Chapter 13). |
| Budget and fee | 'Fee: £15,000.<br><br>Detailed time budget is shown on the current audit file' |

ICAEW

| Area | Typical comment on the audit strategy/explanation |
|---|---|
| Timetable | 'Accounts to be ready for discussion with client by 30 September 20X4.' |
| Staffing | 'Senior – 2 weeks<br>Junior – 1 week.<br><br>There will be one audit visit after year-end commencing 11 August 20X4.<br><br>Manager review: 1 day (23 August 20X4)<br><br>Partner review: 1 day (30 August 20X4).'<br><br>This ties in with the fees section. The auditor will set a time budget for each level of staff involved on the audit. The time budget will be analysed over the different parts of the audit. |

### Interactive question 1: The overall audit strategy     [Difficulty level: Exam standard]

Which **three** of the following would ordinarily be contained in the overall audit strategy?

- ☐ The contract between the audit firm and the client
- ☐ The results of audit risk assessment
- ☐ Calculation of preliminary materiality
- ☐ Detailed plan of audit procedures to be carried out
- ☐ List of staff to be involved with the audit

See **Answer** at the end of this chapter.

## 1.1 Understanding the entity and its environment

ISA 315 (UK and Ireland) *Identifying and Assessing the Risks of Material Misstatement through Understanding the Entity and its Environment* states that 'the objective of the auditor is to **identify and assess the risks of material misstatement,** whether due to fraud or error, at the financial statement and assertion levels, through **understanding the entity and its environment,** including the entity's internal control, thereby providing a basis for designing and implementing responses to the assessed risks of material misstatement'.

In order to be able to identify problem areas which might cause difficulties in collecting evidence or drawing assurance conclusions, auditors must have an understanding of the nature of the business and the context in which it operates.

| Summary | Obtaining an understanding of the entity and its environment |
|---|---|
| Why? | To identify and assess the risks of material misstatement in the financial statements.<br><br>To enable the auditor to design and perform further audit procedures.<br><br>To provide a frame of reference for exercising audit judgement, for example, when setting audit materiality (which we shall look at later in this chapter). |

| | |
|---|---|
| **What?** | Industry, regulatory and other external factors, including the reporting framework. |
| | Nature of the entity, including selection and application of accounting policies. |
| | Objectives and strategies and relating business risks that might cause material misstatement in the financial statements. |
| | Measurement and review of the entity's financial performance. |
| | Internal control (which we shall look at in detail in Chapter 5). |
| **How?** | Inquiries of management and others within the entity. |
| | Analytical procedures (which we shall look at in the next section of this chapter). |
| | Observation and inspection. |
| | Prior period knowledge. |
| | Discussion of the susceptibility of the financial statements to material misstatement among the engagement team. |

As can be seen in the table above, the reasons the auditor is to obtain the understanding of the entity and its environment are very much bound up with assessing risks and exercising audit judgement. We shall look at these aspects further later in this chapter.

## 1.1.1   What?

The ISA sets out a number of requirements about what the auditors must consider in relation to obtaining an understanding of the business. These were summarised in the table above and are covered in more detail in the diagram on page 40.

## 1.1.2   How?

ISA 315 also sets out the methods that the auditor **must** use to obtain the understanding (listed above in the summary). The auditor does not have to use all of these for each area, but a combination of these procedures should be used. These are:

*   Inquiries of management and others within the entity. (The auditors will usually obtain most of the information they require from staff in the accounts department, but may also need to make enquiries of other personnel, for example, internal audit, production staff or directors.)

### Worked example: Inquiries of management and others

Directors may give insight into the environment in which the financial statements are prepared. In-house legal advisers may help with understanding matters such as outstanding litigation, or compliance with laws and regulations. Sales and marketing personnel may give information about marketing strategies and sales trends.

*   Analytical procedures (which we will look at in the next section).

*   Observation and inspection (these techniques are likely to confirm the answers made to inquiries made of management. They will include observing the normal operations of a company, reading documents or manuals relating to the client's operations or visiting premises and meeting staff).

*   If it is a recurring audit, the auditors may have obtained a great deal of knowledge about the entity and the environment in the course of prior year audits. The auditor is entitled to use this information in the current year audit, but he must make sure that he has determined whether any **changes** in the year have affected the relevance of information obtained in previous years.

*   The **audit team** is also required by ISA 315 to **discuss the susceptibility of the financial statements to material misstatement**. Judgement must be exercised in determining which members of the team should be involved in which parts of the discussion, but all team members should be involved in the discussion relevant to the parts of the audit they will be involved in.

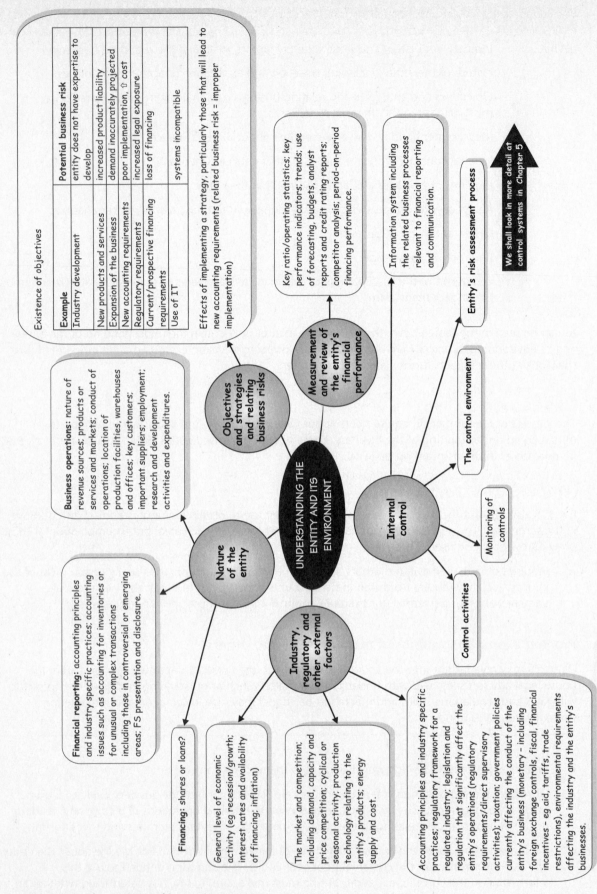

Figure 3.1: The entity and its environment

## Worked example: Understanding the entity

The auditors want to build up a profile of the audit client against the background of the general economic climate. Here is an example for a new audit client, Icket Ltd.

**Icket Ltd**

| | |
|---|---|
| **Shareholders:** | Members of Icket family – (Jane, Chris, Annabel and James) |
| | Other shareholders – (Eddie Stewart, Vikram Sandhu) |
| **Directors:** | Chris Icket, Jane Icket, Eddie Stewart |
| **Operations:** | Manufactures tableware for high street stores and standard lines for a number of wholesalers |
| | Activity tends to be seasonal with new lines being brought into shops in October and April |
| **Customers:** | Three major high street retailers, 50 wholesalers |
| **Suppliers:** | Three key suppliers of fabrics and threads – Fine Fabrics Limited, Sundry Sewing plc and All Sewing Supplies (Manchester) Limited |
| **IT:** | The accounting system is completely computerised |
| **Financial performance:** | Company formed 20 years ago and has always been profitable. Company is financed by equity capital and has a substantial bank loan from National Bank |
| **Future plans:** | No new plans that we are aware of |

This is a very basic company profile. In carrying out risk assessment, more detail would be sought in each area, as you will see when this example is continued in section 4.

## Interactive question 2: Understanding the entity [Difficulty level: Exam standard]

In order to obtain an understanding of the entity, auditors must use a combination of which **four** of the following procedures?

- ☐ Inspection
- ☐ Observation
- ☐ Inquiry
- ☐ Analytical procedures
- ☐ Computation

See **Answer** at the end of this chapter.

## 1.2 Professional scepticism

### Definition

Professional scepticism is an attitude that includes a questioning mind, being alert to conditions which may indicate possible misstatement due to error or fraud, and a critical assessment of audit evidence.

Misstatements which are significant to readers may exist in financial statements and auditors will plan their work on this basis, that is, with **professional scepticism**. The concept of '**significance to readers**' is the concept of materiality, which we will look at in section 3.

Professional scepticism does not mean that auditors should disbelieve everything they are told; however, they must have a questioning attitude.

# 2 Analytical procedures

**Section overview**

- Analytical procedures are used at all stages of the audit, but here we consider only their use in planning the audit.

- Analytical procedures consist of the analysis of significant ratios and trends including the resulting investigations of fluctuations and relationships that are inconsistent with other relevant information or which deviate from predictable amounts.

- During **planning**, analytical procedures are used as a means of **understanding the business** and **identifying audit risk**.

**Definition**

Analytical procedures means evaluations of financial information through analysis of plausible relationships among both financial and non-financial data. Analytical procedures also encompass such investigation as is necessary of identified fluctuations or relationships that are inconsistent with other relevant information or that differ from expected values by a significant amount.

They include consideration of comparisons of the entity's financial information with other information, and the consideration of relationships among elements of financial information that would be expected to conform to a particular pattern or between financial information and relevant non-financial information.

---

ISA 520 (UK and Ireland) *Analytical Procedures* requires auditors to apply analytical procedures in the overall review at the end of the audit and as substantive procedures, to obtain audit evidence directly. ISA 315 (UK and Ireland) *Identifying and Assessing the Risks of Material Misstatement through Understanding the Entity and its Environment* also requires the auditor to use analytical procedures. Here they are used as risk assessment procedures to obtain an understanding of the entity and its environment. We will look at the uses of analytical procedures for purposes other than planning later in the Study Manual.

The ISA states that analytical procedures include:

- The consideration of comparisons with:

    - **Comparable information** for prior periods

    - **Anticipated results** of the entity, from budgets or forecasts or expectations of the auditor

    - Similar **industry information**, such as a comparison of the client's ratio of sales to trade receivables with industry averages, or with the ratios relating to other entities of comparable size in the same industry.

- Consideration of relationships between:

    - Elements of financial information that are expected to conform to a predicted pattern based on the entity's experience, such as the relationship of gross profit to sales.

    - Financial information and relevant non-financial information, such as the relationship of payroll costs to number of employees.

A variety of methods can be used to perform the procedures discussed above, ranging from **simple comparisons** to **complex analysis** using statistics. The choice of procedures is a matter for the auditor's professional judgement.

## 2.1 Analytical procedures in planning the audit

As we have discussed, analytical procedures should be used at the risk assessment stage. Possible sources of information about the client include:

- Interim financial information
- Budgets
- Management accounts
- Non-financial information
- Bank and cash records
- VAT returns
- Board minutes
- Discussions or correspondence with the client at the year-end

Auditors may also use specific industry information or general knowledge of current industry conditions to assess the client's performance.

As well as helping to determine the nature, timing and extent of other audit procedures, such analytical procedures may also indicate aspects of the business of which the auditors were previously unaware. Auditors are looking to see if developments in the client's business have had the expected effects. They will be particularly interested in changes in audit areas where problems have occurred in the past.

Certain accounting ratios may be used as analytical procedures. Here are the key ratios used:

| Heading/Ratio | Formula | Purpose |
|---|---|---|
| **Performance** <br> Return on capital employed | $\dfrac{\text{Profit before interest and tax}}{\text{Equity + net debt}}$ | Effective use of resources |
| Return on shareholders' funds | $\dfrac{\text{Net profit for the period}}{\text{Share capital + reserves}}$ | Effective use of resources |
| Gross profit margin | $\dfrac{\text{Gross profit} \times 100}{\text{Revenue}}$ | Assess profitability before taking overheads into account |
| Cost of sales percentage | $\dfrac{\text{Cost of sales} \times 100}{\text{Revenue}}$ | Assess relationship of costs to revenue |
| Operating cost percentage | $\dfrac{\text{Operating costs} \times 100}{\text{Revenue}}$ | Assess relationship of costs to revenue |
| Net margin = operating margin | $\dfrac{\text{Profit before interest and tax} \times 100}{\text{Revenue}}$ | Assess profitability after taking overheads into account |
| **Short-term liquidity** <br> Current ratio | Current assets : current liabilities | Assess ability to pay current liabilities from reasonably liquid assets |
| Quick ratio | Receivables + current investments + cash : current liabilities | Assess ability to pay current liabilities from reasonably liquid assets |
| **Long-term solvency** <br> Gearing ratio | $\dfrac{\text{Net debt}}{\text{Equity}} \times 100$ | Assess reliance on external finance |
| Interest cover | $\dfrac{\text{Profit before interest payable}}{\text{Interest payable}}$ | Assess ability to pay interest charges |
| **Efficiency** <br> Net asset turnover | $\dfrac{\text{Revenue}}{\text{Capital employed}}$ | Assess revenue generated from asset base |
| Inventory turnover | $\dfrac{\text{Cost of sales}}{\text{Inventories}}$ | Assess level of inventory held |

| Heading/Ratio | Formula | Purpose |
|---|---|---|
| Trade receivables collection period | $\dfrac{\text{Trade receivables} \times 365}{\text{Revenue}}$ | Assess ability to turn receivables into cash |
| Trade payables payment period | $\dfrac{\text{Trade payables} \times 365}{\text{Credit purchases}}$ | Assess ability to pay suppliers |

## Worked example: Analytical procedures

Here are some extracts from an income statement for a company. The areas which analytical procedures suggest may indicate risks are highlighted in grey.

| | 20X6 £'000s | 20X5 £'000s | Comments |
|---|---|---|---|
| Revenue | 1,566,088 | 950,339 | Revenue has risen substantially |
| Cost of sales | 1,237,231 | 757,700 | Cost of sales and gross margin have risen in line with the rise in revenue |
| Gross profit | 328,857 | 192,639 | |
| Salaries and wages | 141,984 | 185,664 | Salaries have fallen despite rise in revenue. If rise is due to increased output, why has related labour cost fallen? |
| Other administrative costs | 10,988 | 9,939 | |
| Audit fee | 5,400 | 5,350 | |
| Bank charges | 64 | 33 | Bank charges have nearly doubled – indicating large loan taken out? Why? Potential problem? |
| Other finance costs | 32 | 35 | |
| Advertising | 276 | 463 | Seems odd that sales appear to have increased when advertising costs have been slashed? |

## Interactive question 3: Analytical procedures    [Difficulty level: Exam standard]

Here is some budget financial information for Fleming plc, contrasted with the management results for the 12 months under review.

| | Budget 20X6 (£) | Actual 20X6 (£) |
|---|---|---|
| Sales | 1,350,000 | 1,339,588 |
| Cost of sales | 850,000 | 994,663 |
| Gross margin | 500,000 | 344,925 |
| Salaries | 245,000 | 243,873 |
| Repairs and renewals | 7,500 | 24,983 |
| Depreciation | 7,500 | 7,551 |
| Motor expenses | 25,750 | 14,678 |
| Other costs | 44,000 | 43,968 |

Which three of the following areas would you be **most likely** to investigate further as a result of carrying out analytical procedures on the above?

- [ ] Sales

- [ ] Cost of sales

- [ ] Sales and cost of sales

- [ ] Depreciation

- [ ] Repairs and renewals

- [ ] Motor expenses

See **Answer** at the end of this chapter.

# 3 Materiality

## Section overview

- Materiality relates to the level of misstatement that affects the decisions of users of the accounts.
- Materiality must be calculated at the planning stages of all audits. The calculation or estimation of materiality is based on experience and judgement.
- Materiality must be reviewed during the audit.

Materiality relates to the level of misstatement that affects the decisions of users of the accounts, where users are taken as a group. The needs of specific individuals are not considered as their needs may vary considerably.

## Definitions

**Materiality**: An expression of the relative significance or importance of a particular matter in the context of financial statements as a whole. The IFRS *Conceptual Framework for Financial Reporting* states that a matter is material if its omission or misstatement could influence the economic decisions of users taken on the basis of the financial statements.

**Performance materiality**: The amount or amounts set by the auditor at less than materiality for the financial statements as a whole to reduce to an appropriately low level the probability that the aggregate of uncorrected and undetected misstatements exceeds materiality for the financial statements as a whole.

ISA 320 (UK and Ireland) *Materiality in Planning and Performing an Audit* states that 'materiality and audit risk are considered throughout the audit, in particular, when:

- Identifying and assessing the risks of material misstatement;
- Determining the nature, timing and extent of further audit procedures; and
- Evaluating the effect of uncorrected misstatements, if any, on the financial statements and in forming the opinion in the auditor's report'.

Figure 3.2 shows how materiality is used in the course of an assurance engagement.

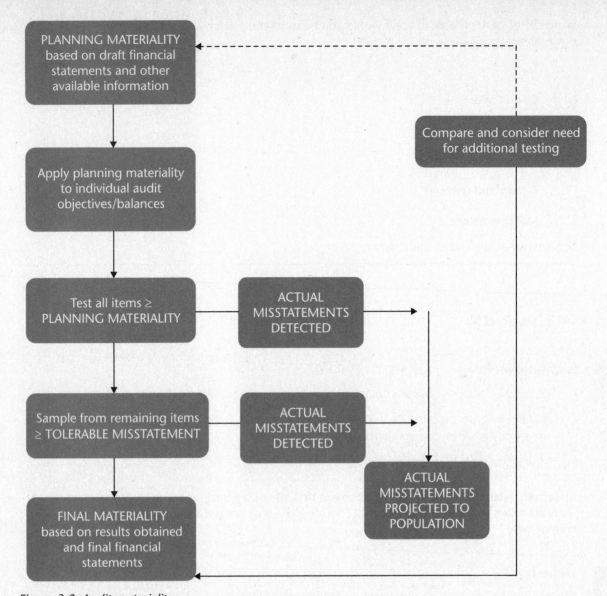

*Figure 3.2: Audit materiality*

Materiality considerations during **audit planning** are extremely important. The assessment of materiality at this stage should be based on the most recent and reliable financial information and will help to determine an effective and efficient audit approach. Materiality assessment will help the auditors to decide:

- How many and what items to examine

- Whether to use sampling techniques

- What level of misstatment is likely to lead to an auditor to say the financial statements do not give a true and fair view.

The resulting combination of audit procedures should help to reduce audit risk to an appropriately low level. This is how risk and materiality are closely connected. The value of discovered misstatements should be aggregated at the end of the audit to ensure the total is still below tolerable misstatement. **Tolerable misstatement** is the maximum misstatement that an auditor is prepared to accept in a class of transactions or balances in the financial statements. It will be considered in more detail in Chapter 11.

To set the materiality level the auditors need to decide the level of misstatement which would distort the view given by the accounts. Because many users of accounts are primarily interested in the profitability of the company, the level is often expressed as a proportion of its profits.

Materiality can be thought of in terms of the size of the business. Hence, if the company remains a fairly constant size, the materiality level should not change; similarly if the business is growing, the level of materiality will increase from year to year.

The size of a company can be measured in terms of revenue and total assets, both of which tend not to be subject to the fluctuations which may affect profit.

Note that the auditors will often calculate a range of values, such as those shown below, and then take an average or weighted average of all the figures produced as the preliminary materiality level. However, **different firms have different methods** and this is **just one of the available approaches.**

| *Value* | *%* |
| --- | --- |
| Profit before tax | 5 – 10 |
| Revenue | ½ – 1 |
| Total assets | 1 – 2 |

However, bear in mind that materiality has qualitative, as well as quantitative, aspects. For example, transactions relating to directors are considered material by nature regardless of their value.

You must not simply think of materiality as being a percentage of items in the financial statements.

## 3.1 Review of materiality

The level of materiality must be reviewed constantly as the audit progresses and **changes** may be required because:

- **Draft financial statements** are **altered** (due to material misstatement and so on) and therefore overall materiality changes.

- **External factors may cause changes** in risk estimates.

  Such changes are caused by **misstatements** found during testing.

# 4 Audit risk

**Section overview**

- The auditor usually adopts a **risk-based approach** to auditing and focuses his testing on the riskiest balances and classes of transactions.

- Audit risk has two elements, the **risk that the financial statements contain a material misstatement** and the **risk that the auditors will fail to detect any material misstatements.**

- Risk of material misstatement in the financial statements has two elements, **inherent** and **control** risk.

- The risk that the auditor will fail to detect material misstatements is known as **detection** risk.

- Auditors set an acceptable level for overall audit risk and carry out sufficient tests to ensure this level is met.

- When the auditor has obtained an understanding of the entity, he must assess the risks of material misstatement in the financial statements, also identifying significant risks.

- **Significant risks** are complex or unusual transactions, ie those that may indicate fraud or other special risks.

Auditors follow a **risk-based approach** to auditing. In the risk-based approach, auditors analyse the risks associated with the client's business, transactions and systems which could lead to misstatements in the financial statements, and direct their testing to risky areas. They are therefore not concerned with individual routine transactions, although they will still be concerned with material, non-routine transactions.

## Definition

Audit risk: The risk that the auditor expresses an inappropriate audit opinion when the financial statements are materially misstated. Audit risk is a function of the risks of material misstatement and detection risk.

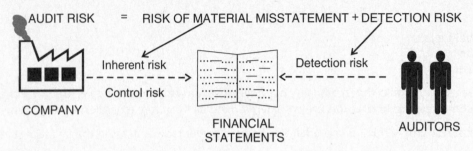

*Figure 3.3: Audit risk*

As you can see from Figure 3.3, audit risk has two major components. One is dependent on the entity, and is the risk of material misstatement arising in the financial statements. The other is dependent on the auditor, and is the risk that the auditor will not detect material misstatements in the financial statements.

## 4.1 Risk of material misstatement in the financial statements

## Definition

Inherent risk: The susceptibility of an assertion about a class of transaction, account balance or disclosure to a misstatement that could be material, either individually or when aggregated with other misstatements, before consideration of any related controls.

Inherent risk is the risk that items will be misstated due to characteristics of those items. Example of issues that might increase inherent risk are:

- Balance is or includes an estimate

- Balance is important in the account

- Financial statements are liable to misstatement because:

  - Company is in trouble

  - Company is seeking to raise finance

  - Other motivation for directors to misstate the figures (such as profit targets or profit related bonuses)

- Financial statements contain balances with complex financial accounting requirements or a choice of treatment.

The auditors must use their professional judgement and all available knowledge to assess inherent risk. If no such information or knowledge is available then the inherent risk is **high**.

Inherent risk is affected by the nature of the entity; for example, the industry it is in and the regulations it falls under, and also the nature of the strategies it adopts. These are the kind of things we looked at in Figure 3.1, when obtaining an understanding of the entity.

### Definition

Control risk: The risk that a misstatement that could occur in an assertion about a class of transaction, account balance or disclosure and that could be material, either individually or when aggregated with other misstatements, will not be prevented, or detected and corrected, on a timely basis by the entity's internal control.

In other words this is the risk that a material misstatement would not be prevented, detected or corrected by the accounting and internal control systems.

We shall look at controls in more detail in Chapter 5, where you will learn about the sort of controls you might expect to see in a company, and therefore be able to identify weaknesses, which indicate control risk.

## 4.2 Risk that the auditor will not detect a material misstatement in the financial statements

### Definition

Detection risk: The risk that the procedures performed by the auditor to reduce audit risk to an acceptably low level will not detect a misstatement that exists and that could be material, either individually or when aggregated with other misstatements.

This is the component of audit risk that the auditors have a degree of control over, because, if risk is too high to be tolerated, the auditors can carry out more work to reduce this aspect of audit risk, and therefore audit risk as a whole.

ISA 200 states that 'the auditor shall obtain sufficient appropriate audit evidence to reduce audit risk to an acceptably low level and thereby enable the auditor to draw reasonable conclusions on which to base the auditor's opinion'.

Auditors will want their overall audit risk to be at an acceptable level, or it will not be worth them carrying out the audit. In other words, if the chance of them giving an inappropriate opinion and being sued is high, it might be better not to do the audit at all.

The auditors will obviously consider how risky a new audit client is during the acceptance process, and may decide not to go ahead with the relationship. However, they will also consider audit risk for each individual audit, and will seek to manage the risk.

As we have seen above, it is not in the auditors' power to affect inherent or control risk. As they are risks integral to the client, the auditor cannot change the level of these risks.

The auditor therefore manages overall audit risk by manipulating detection risk, the only element of audit risk the auditor has control over. This is because, the more audit work the auditors carry out, the lower detection risk becomes, although it can never be entirely eliminated due to the inherent limitations of an audit.

This audit risk management can be shown crudely in a mathematical equation. The auditor will decide what level of overall risk is acceptable, and then determine a level of audit work so that detection risk makes the equation work.

### Worked example 1: Audit risk

| Inherent risk | × Control risk | × Detection risk | = Audit risk |
|---|---|---|---|
| High | × High | × Low | = Acceptable |

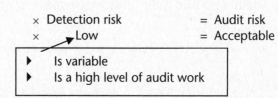

- Is variable
- Is a high level of audit work

In Worked example 1, inherent and control risk were both high. This has the following effects on the audit.

- The auditors are unlikely to rely on tests of controls, but will carry out extended tests of details (we will look at what this means in practice in Chapter 4).

- Detection risk must be rendered low, which will mean carrying out a substantial number of tests of details.

Audits are not all the same, however. A different company could produce the following audit risk calculation.

### Worked example 2: Audit risk

| Inherent risk | | x Control risk | | x Detection risk | | = Audit risk |
|---|---|---|---|---|---|---|
| Medium | | x | Low | x | Medium | = Acceptable |

In Worked example 2, as control risk is low, the auditors are likely to carry out tests of controls and seek to rely on the client's system. As you will see in Chapter 4, this does not mean substantive procedures can be eliminated entirely. Detection risk in this instance would be affected by the amount of tests of controls and tests of details carried out.

It is important to understand that there is not a standard level of audit risk which is considered generally by auditors to be acceptable. This is a matter of audit judgement, and so will vary from firm to firm and audit to audit. Audit firms are likely to charge higher fees for higher risk clients. Regardless of the risk level of the audit, however, it is vital that audit firms always carry out an audit of **sufficient quality**.

### Interactive question 4: Audit risk                                    [Difficulty level: Exam standard]

Audit risk can be split into three components: inherent risk, control risk and detection risk.

For each of the following examples, indicate the type of risk illustrated.

1    The organisation has few employees in the accounts department
2    The organisation is highly connected with the building trade
3    The assurance firm may do insufficient work to detect material misstatements
4    The financial statements contain a number of estimates

See **Answer** at the end of this chapter.

## 4.3    Identifying and assessing the risks

ISA 315 says that 'the objective of the auditor is to **identify** and **assess the risks of material misstatement,** whether due to fraud or error, at the **financial statement and assertion levels**, through understanding the entity and its environment...'. It requires the auditor to take the following steps:

### Step 1
Identify risks throughout the process of obtaining an understanding of the entity and its environment

### Step 2
Assess the identified risks and relate them to what can go wrong at the assertion level (this is the assertions made in the financial statements by the directors, for example, that inventory is £X)

### Step 3
Consider whether the risks are of a magnitude that could result in a material misstatement

### Step 4
Consider the likelihood of the risks causing a material misstatement

## Worked example: Understanding the entity and identifying risks

The audit team at Icket Ltd has been carrying out procedures to obtain an understanding of the entity. In the course of making inquiries about the inventory system, they have discovered that Icket Ltd designs and produces tableware to order for a number of high street stores. It also makes a number of standard lines of tableware, which it sells to a number of wholesalers. By the terms of its contracts with the high street stores, it is not entitled to sell uncalled inventory designed for them to wholesalers. Icket Ltd regularly produces 10% more than the high street stores have ordered, in order to ensure that they meet requirements when the stores do their quality control check. Certain stores have more stringent control requirements than others and regularly reject some of the inventory.

The knowledge above suggests two risks, one that the company may have obsolete inventory, and the other that if their production quality standards are insufficiently high, they could run the risk of losing custom.

We shall look at each of these risks in turn and relate them to the assertion level.

### Inventory

If certain of the inventories are obsolete due to the fact that they have been produced in excess of the customer's requirement and there is no other available market for the inventory, then there is a risk that inventory as a whole in the financial statements will not be carried at the appropriate value. Given that inventory is likely to be a material balance in the balance sheet of a manufacturing company, and the misstatement could be up to 10% of the total value, this has the capacity to be a material misstatement.

The factors that will contribute to the likelihood of these risks causing a misstatement are matters such as:

* Whether management regularly review inventory levels and scrap items that are obsolete
* Whether such items are identified and scrapped at the inventory count
* Whether such items can be put back into production and changed so that they are saleable

### Losing custom

The long-term risk of losing custom is a risk that in the future the company will not be able to operate. It could have an impact on the financial statements, if disputed sales were attributed to customers, sales and trade receivables could be overstated, that is, not carried at the correct value. However, it appears less likely that this would be a material problem in either area, as the problem is likely to be restricted to a few customers, and only a few number of sales to those customers.

Again, review of the company's controls over the recording of sales and the debt collection procedures of the company would indicate how likely these risks to the financial statements are to materialise.

## Interactive question 5: Identifying risks [Difficulty level: Exam standard]

You are involved with the audit of Tantpro Ltd, a small company. You have been carrying out procedures to gain an understanding of the entity. The following matters have come to your attention.

The company offers standard credit terms to its customers of 60 days from the date of invoice. Statements are sent to customers on a monthly basis. However, Tantpro Ltd does not employ a credit controller, and other than sending the statements on a monthly basis, it does not otherwise communicate with its customers on a systematic basis. On occasion, the receivables ledger clerk may telephone a customer if the company has not received a payment for some time. Some customers pay regularly according to the credit terms offered to them, but others pay on a very haphazard basis and do not provide a remittance advice. Receivables ledger receipts are entered onto the receivables ledger but not matched to invoices remitted. The company does not produce an aged list of balances.

Which **one** of the following is the risk most likely to arise out of the above scenario?

| | |
|---|---|
| ☐ Inventory may be overstated | ☐ Inventory may be understated |
| ☐ Purchases may be overstated | ☐ Purchases may be understated |
| ☐ Trade receivables may be overstated | ☐ Trade receivables may be understated |

See **Answer** at the end of this chapter.

## 4.4 Significant risks

Some risks may be **significant risks**, which require **special audit consideration**. ISA 315 sets out the following factors which indicate that a risk might be a significant risk:

- Risk of fraud
- Related to recent significant economic, accounting or other development
- The complexity of the transaction
- It is a significant transaction with a related party
- The degree of subjectivity in the financial information
- It is an unusual transaction

Routine, non-complex transactions are less likely to give rise to significant risk than unusual transactions or matters of director judgement. This is because unusual transactions are likely to have more:

- Management intervention
- Manual intervention
- Complex accounting principles or calculations
- Opportunity for control procedures not to be followed

When the auditor identifies a significant risk, if he hasn't done so already, he must evaluate the design and implementation of the entity's controls in that area.

## Summary

> Planning is necessary to ensure work is carried out efficiently and effectively

Key elements of an overall audit strategy:
- Understanding the entity and its environment
- Risk and materiality
- Practical matters

In order to identify risks.:
- Inquiry
- Analytical procedures
- Inspection and observation

Need professional scepticism

Analysis of significant fluctuations from expected results

The concept of significance to readers. A matter is generally considered to be material if it would affect the decision of a user of financial statements.

Audit risk = inherent risk x control risk x detection risk

→ The risk that a material misstatement exists in the FS

→ The risk that auditors do not uncover material misstatements

## Self-test

Answer the following questions.

1   Complete the definitions:

An ........................................ is the formulation of a general strategy for the audit.

An ........................................ is a set of instructions to the audit team that sets out the further audit procedures to be carried out.

2   Name **four** sources of information which could be used at the planning stage of the audit.

(1)   ........................................

(2)   ........................................

(3)   ........................................

(4)   ........................................

3   Which of the following procedures might an auditor use in gaining an understanding of the entity?

(a)   Inquiry
(b)   Recalculation
(c)   Analytical procedures
(d)   Reperformance of a control
(e)   Observation and inspection

4    The audit team is required to discuss the susceptibility of the financial statements to material misstatements.

☐    True

☐    False

5    Match the percentages to the values for a typical calculation of materiality.

|  | % |
| --- | --- |
| Profit before tax | 5 – 10 |
| Revenue | 1 – 2 |
| Total assets | ½ – 1 |

6    Complete the definitions.

........................................ risk is the risk that........................................ expresses an........................................ opinion when the financial statements are materially misstated.

........................................ risk is the ........................................ of an assertion about a ........................................ ........................................, account balance or disclosure to a ........................................ that could be material, either individually or when aggregated with other misstatements, before consideration of any related controls.

7    If control and inherent risk are assessed as sufficiently low, substantive procedures can be abandoned completely.

☐    True

☐    False

8    Name **four** factors which might indicate a significant risk.

(1)    ........................................

(2)    ........................................

(3)    ........................................

(4)    ........................................

Now, go back to the Learning Objectives in the Introduction. If you are satisfied you have achieved these objectives, please tick them off.

# Technical reference

## 1 Planning

- The role and timing of planning — ISA 300.2 (UK and Ireland)
- Objective — ISA 300.4 (UK and Ireland)
- Requirements — ISA 300.5 – 13 (UK and Ireland)
- Risk assessment procedures — ISA 315.5 – 10 (UK and Ireland)
- Understanding the entity — ISA 315.11 – 24
- Professional scepticism — ISA 200.15 (UK and Ireland)

## 2 Analytical procedures

- Definition — ISA 520.4, A1, A2 (UK and Ireland)
- Analytical procedures in planning — ISA 315.6 (UK and Ireland)

## 3 Materiality

- Definition — ISA 320.9 (UK and Ireland)
- Use in auditing — ISA 320.A1 (UK and Ireland)
- Revision — ISA 320.12 (UK and Ireland)

## 4 Audit risk

- Definitions — ISA 200.13 (UK and Ireland)
- Identifying and assessing the risks — ISA 315.3 (UK and Ireland)
- Significant risks — ISA 315.28 (UK and Ireland)

CHAPTER

3

### Answer to Interactive question 1

The results of audit risk assessment.

Calculation of preliminary materiality.

List of staff to be involved with the audit.

The contract between the firm and client is generally found in the engagement letter which is a separate document. Detailed plan of audit procedures to be carried out would be contained in the audit plan.

### Answer to Interactive question 2

- Inspection
- Observation
- Inquiry
- Analytical procedures

Although the auditor may use computation, particularly when carrying out analytical procedures, it is not a required tool, whereas a combination of the procedures outlined above is required by the ISA.

### Answer to Interactive question 3

Sales and cost of sales

Repairs and renewals

Motor expenses

On the face of it, sales do not appear to have fallen much below what was anticipated for the year, but the fact that the gross margin has changed so much (from 37% to 26%) indicates that there may be a problem somewhere in sales and cost of sales, hence rather than focus on one or the other (you might have selected cost of sales only, due to the fact that the major difference from budget is here) it would be best to look at the whole issue together. Gross margin may look wrong because sales are understated in error – and sales were actually much better for the year than anticipated.

Depreciation, as you might expect, appears to have been predicted accurately and is low risk. Problems with depreciation if they existed would probably be uncovered by an analysis of the balance sheet.

Repairs and renewals and motor expenses vary substantially from budget, so are worth further investigation.

### Answer to Interactive question 4

(1) Control – the fact that there are few employees in the accounts department means that segregation of duties will be limited (see Chapter 5 for more details in this area)

(2) Inherent – this is a naturally risky industry

(3) Detection – this is in essence the definition of detection risk

(4) Inherent – there is a risk that estimates may be inappropriate

## Answer to Interactive question 5

The key risk arising from the above information is that trade receivables will not be carried at the appropriate **value** in the financial statements, as some may be irrecoverable. Where receipts are not matched against invoices in the ledger, the balance on the ledger may include old invoices that the customer has no intention of paying.

It is difficult to assess at this stage whether this is likely to be material. Trade receivables is likely to be a material balance in the financial statements, but the number of irrecoverable balances may not be material. Analytical procedures, for example, to see if the level of accounts receivable has risen year on year, in a manner that is not explained by price rises or levels of production, might help to assess this.

A key factor that affects the likelihood of the material misstatement arising is the poor controls over the receivables ledger. The fact that invoices are not matched against receipts increases the chance of old invoices not having been paid and not noticed by Tantpro Ltd. It appears reasonably likely that the trade receivables balance is overstated in this instance.

# Answers to Self-test

1   Overall audit strategy, audit plan

2   From:

- Interim financial information
- Budgets
- Management accounts
- Non-financial information
- Bank and cash records
- Sales tax returns
- Board minutes
- Discussions or correspondence with the client at the year-end

3   (a), (c), (e)

4   True

5

|  | % |
|---|---|
| Profit before tax | 5 – 10 |
| Revenue | ½ – 1 |
| Total assets | 1 – 2 |

6   Audit, the auditor, inappropriate audit

Inherent, susceptibility, class of transactions, misstatement

7   False

8   Any of:

- Risk of fraud
- Relationship with recent developments
- Degree of subjectivity in the financial information
- The fact that it is an unusual transaction
- Transaction with a related party
- Complexity of the transaction

# CHAPTER 4

# Process of assurance: evidence and reporting

Introduction
Examination context
**Topic List**
    1  Evidence
    2  Reporting
Summary and Self-test
Technical reference
Answers to Interactive questions
Answers to Self-test

# Introduction

## Learning objectives

Tick off

- Define the assurance process, including obtaining evidence

- Identify when tests of controls and substantive procedures will be used

- Understand that assurance may be positive or negative

- Know the contents of the audit report

- Be aware of the other types of report that may be issued after an assurance engagement

This topic will be covered in more detail in subsequent chapters.

Specific syllabus references for this chapter are: 1, f, g, 3b.

## Syllabus links

The issue of drawing conclusions and reporting will be looked at in more detail in Audit and Assurance. Clearly the basic evidence collection that you learn at this level will feed into the drawing of conclusions at the Application level.

## Examination context

Evidence is a very important topic for the exam, and half of this Study Manual is dedicated to the collection of evidence. Gathering evidence on an assurance engagement represents 35% of the syllabus. In contrast, reporting is a minor area of the syllabus, so you should expect no more than one or two questions in this area.

In the assessment, candidates may be required to:

- Identify and compare the different methods of obtaining evidence including tests of control and substantive procedures including analytical procedures

- Evaluate the quality of different types of audit evidence

- Identify the financial statement assertions

- Determine the level of assurance provided by audit reports and other assurance reports

# 1 Evidence

**Section overview**

- Auditors must obtain sufficient, appropriate audit evidence.
- Evidence can be in the form of tests of controls or substantive procedures.
- The reliability of audit evidence is influenced by its source and by its nature.
- Audit tests are designed to obtain evidence about the financial statement assertions.

## 1.1 Evidence

The objective of an assurance engagement is to enable practitioners to express an opinion whether the subject of the assurance engagement is in accordance with the identified criteria. There is an ISA on audit evidence (ISA 500), which we shall look at here.

Remember that audit requires a reasonable level of assurance to be given, and correspondingly detailed audit evidence needs to be obtained. In a lower level assurance engagement, less evidence will be required to support the conclusion. We shall look at the sufficiency of evidence obtained in more detail in a later chapter.

In this section, we shall introduce the **audit evidence** auditors gather, to **enable** them to express an opinion of reasonable assurance on financial statements. We shall look at the process of gathering evidence in more detail later in this study manual, particularly in Chapters 5 – 8 and 11 – 13.

### Definition

Audit evidence: Information used by the auditor in arriving at the conclusions on which the auditor's opinion is based.

---

Audit evidence includes both the information contained within the accounting records underlying the financial statements, and other information gathered by the auditors, such as confirmations from third parties. Auditors are **not expected to look at all the information** that might exist. They will often perform their testing on a sample basis, as we shall see in Chapter 11.

In order to reach a position in which they can express a professional opinion, the auditors need to gather evidence from various sources. There are potentially two types of test which they will carry out: tests of controls and substantive procedures.

### Definitions

Tests of controls: Audit procedures designed to evaluate the operating effectiveness of controls in preventing, or detecting and correcting material misstatements at the assertion level.

Substantive procedures: Audit procedures designed to detect material misstatements at the assertion level. Substantive procedures comprise:

- Tests of detail (of classes of transactions, account balances and disclosures).
- Substantive analytical procedures.

---

We shall look in detail at financial statement assertions later in this chapter.

When the auditors carry out tests of controls, they are seeking to rely on the good operation of the control system that the company has in place to draw a conclusion that the financial statements give a true and fair view. The logic is as follows.

- The directors set up systems of internal controls to ensure they report correctly to the shareholders (we shall look at internal controls in more detail in the next chapter).

- The auditors are required to conclude whether the financial statements give a true and fair view.

- The auditors evaluate the control system put in place to assess whether it is capable of producing financial statements which give a true and fair view.

- The auditors test the control system to assess whether it has operated as it was intended to, therefore giving assurance that the financial statements give a true and fair view.

When the auditors carry out substantive procedures, they are testing whether specific items within balances or transactions in the financial statements are stated correctly.

ISAs require that auditors must always carry out some substantive procedures, because the limitations in internal control systems (which we will look at in the next chapter) mean that the control system can never be fully relied on. However, there may also be instances of cases where it is more appropriate to test controls than to test specific balances or transactions (this will be discussed more later).

## 1.2 Sufficient appropriate audit evidence

ISA 500 (UK and Ireland) *Audit Evidence* requires auditors to 'obtain **sufficient appropriate** audit evidence to be able to draw **reasonable conclusions** on which to base the auditor's opinion'. 'Sufficiency' and 'appropriateness' are interrelated and apply to both tests of controls and substantive procedures.

- **Sufficiency** is the measure of the **quantity** of audit evidence.
- **Appropriateness** is the measure of the **quality** or relevance and **reliability** of the audit evidence.

How much evidence is required will depend on the level of assurance being offered in an engagement.

The **quantity** of audit evidence required is affected by the **level of risk** in the area being audited. It is also affected by the **quality** of evidence obtained. If the evidence is high quality, the auditor may need less than if it were poor quality. However, obtaining a high quantity of poor quality evidence will not cancel out its poor quality. The following generalisations may help in assessing the **reliability** of audit evidence.

| Quality of evidence | |
|---|---|
| **External** | Audit evidence from **external sources** is more reliable than that obtained from the entity's records |
| **Auditor** | Evidence obtained **directly by auditors** is more reliable than that obtained indirectly or by inference |
| **Entity** | Evidence obtained from the entity's records is more reliable when related **control systems operate effectively** |
| **Written** | Evidence in the form of **documents (paper or electronic)** or **written representations** are more reliable than oral representations |
| **Originals** | Original documents are more reliable than photocopies, or facsimiles |

Auditors will often use information produced by the entity when obtaining audit evidence, although this will not always be a strong form of audit evidence. When doing so, the ISA requires that the auditor ensures it is sufficiently reliable, including 'obtaining audit evidence about the **accuracy and completeness** of the information and evaluating whether the information is sufficiently precise and detailed for the auditor's purposes'. This may be achieved by testing controls in the related area.

## 1.3 Financial statement assertions

### Definition

Financial statement assertions: Representations by management, explicit or otherwise, that are embodied in the financial statements, as used by the auditor to consider the different types of potential misstatements that may occur.

By approving the financial statements, the directors are making representations about the information therein. These representations or assertions may be described in general terms in a number of ways.

ISA 315 (UK and Ireland) *Identifying and Assessing the Risks of Material Misstatement through Understanding the Entity and Its Environment* states that 'the auditor shall identify and assess the risks of material misstatement at the financial statement level and the assertion level for **classes of transactions, account balances,** and **disclosures** to provide a basis for designing and performing further audit procedures'. It gives examples of assertions in these areas.

| Assertions used by the auditor | |
| --- | --- |
| Assertions about **classes of transactions** and events for the period under audit | **Occurrence:** transactions and events that have been recorded have occurred and pertain to the entity. |
| | **Completeness:** all transactions and events that should have been recorded have been recorded. |
| | **Accuracy:** amounts and other data relating to recorded transactions and events have been recorded appropriately. |
| | **Cut-off:** transactions and events have been recorded in the correct accounting period. |
| | **Classification:** transactions and events have been recorded in the proper accounts. |
| Assertions about **account balances** at the period end | **Existence:** assets, liabilities and equity interests exist. |
| | **Rights and obligations:** the entity holds or controls the rights to assets, and liabilities are the obligations of the entity. |
| | **Completeness:** all assets, liabilities and equity interests that should have been recorded have been recorded. |
| | **Valuation and allocation:** assets, liabilities, and equity interests are included in the financial statements at appropriate amounts and any resulting valuation or allocation adjustments are appropriately recorded. |
| Assertions about **presentation and disclosure** | **Occurrence and rights and obligations:** disclosed events, transactions and other matters have occurred and pertain to the entity. |
| | **Completeness:** all disclosures that should have been included in the financial statements have been included. |
| | **Classification and understandability:** financial information is appropriately presented and described, and disclosures are clearly expressed. |
| | **Accuracy and valuation:** financial and other information are disclosed fairly and at appropriate amounts. |

## 1.4 Tests of controls or tests of detail?

ISAs require that auditors determine overall responses to assessed risks at the financial statements level and shall design and perform further audit procedures to respond to assessed risks at the assertion level, so that overall audit risk is reduced to an acceptably low level. This is managing detection risk as we saw in Chapter 3.

What that means is that the auditors must carry out tests to reduce the risk of the audit opinion being incorrect. What tests the auditors will carry out is largely a matter of judgement for the auditors and depends on the nature of the risk.

## Worked example: What type of test?

SuperRetail plc is a large retailing operation which has sophisticated point of sale technology and a revenue from sales of £5 billion annually. This represents millions of point of sale transactions.

In order to test the **completeness of revenue** in the financial statements, rather than sample millions of individual transactions and verify them to individual sales receipts, it is going to be significantly more efficient and cost effective for the auditors to test whether the revenue system, with regard to sales recording, operates effectively overall. In this case, the auditors would choose to test controls over revenue recording to establish whether they can rely on the fact that the system worked as it was supposed to and material mistakes in the recording of sales have not occurred.

During the year, SuperRetail plc also invested in new premises for stores. This involved the purchase of three pieces of land. In one case, building work on the new store has started, but in the other two it has not.

In order to test the **valuation** of these **additions to non-current assets** in the financial statements, rather than look in detail at the systems surrounding land purchase and building, it will be more efficient and cost effective for the auditors to verify the cost of the land to purchase documentation and the cost of the building to date to the surveyor's reports. This will be a substantive procedure.

In the first instance, the auditors had to consider a vast number of transactions which were all carried out in a normal, routine fashion through a sophisticated system, in the second, a small number of large transactions, which, although they were probably carried out in line with an established company policy, were easily verified by available, third party evidence. Thus the auditors made a judgement about the best way to collect evidence concerning those different assertions.

---

We will look in more detail at obtaining evidence in the following chapters of this study manual. First we shall look at obtaining evidence by testing controls, then in more detail at obtaining evidence by substantive procedures.

When the auditor believes controls are operating effectively, the auditor shall perform tests of controls to obtain sufficient appropriate audit evidence that the controls were operating effectively at relevant times during the period under audit. So, for example, if controls over revenue and receivables were expected to operate effectively, auditors need to test controls in that area.

It is also necessary to undertake tests of controls when it will not be possible to obtain sufficient appropriate audit evidence simply from substantive procedures. This might be the case if the entity conducts its business using IT systems which do not produce documentation of transactions.

In carrying out tests of control, auditors must use **inquiry**, but must not only use inquiry. Other procedures must also be used. In testing controls, **reperformance** by the auditor will often be a helpful procedure, as will **observation**.

When considering timing in relation to tests of controls, the purpose of the test will be important. For example, if the company carries out a year-end inventory count, controls over the inventory count can only be tested at the year end. Other controls will operate all year, and the auditor will need to test that controls have been effective all year.

Some controls may have been tested in prior audits and the auditor may choose to rely on that evidence of their effectiveness. If this is the case, the auditor must obtain evidence about any changes since the controls were last tested and must test the controls if they have changed. In any case, controls should be tested for effectiveness at least once in every three audits.

If the related risk has been designated a significant risk, the auditor cannot rely on testing carried out in prior years, but shall carry out testing in the current year.

**The auditor must always carry out substantive procedures on material items.**

In addition, the auditor **must** carry out the following substantive procedures:

- Agreeing the financial statements to the underlying accounting records
- Examining material journal entries
- Examining other adjustments made in preparing the financial statements

As you know, substantive procedures fall into two categories: analytical procedures and other procedures. The auditor must determine when it is appropriate to use which type of substantive procedure.

**Analytical procedures** tend to be appropriate for large volumes of predictable transactions (for example, wages and salaries). **Other procedures (tests of detail)** may be appropriate to gain information about account balances (for example, inventories or trade receivables), particularly verifying the assertions of existence and valuation.

Tests of detail rather than analytical procedures are likely to be more appropriate with regard to matters which have been identified as **significant risks**, but the auditor must determine procedures that are specifically responsive to that risk, which may include analytical procedures. Significant risks are likely to be the most difficult to obtain sufficient appropriate evidence about.

## Interactive question 1: Types of procedure                    [Difficulty level: Easy]

For each of the following statements, indicate whether they are true or false.

Tests of controls are tests designed to give evidence whether the controls in a company are operating effectively or not.

| | True |
| | False |

Analytical procedures are a type of substantive procedure.

| | True |
| | False |

See **Answer** at the end of this chapter.

---

# 2 Reporting

### Section overview

- Positive or negative assurance can be given.

- The auditor's report contains a number of elements required by law and by ISAs.

- The auditor's report gives a high level of assurance, but concerns remain about the gap between what users think it means and what it actually means.

- The purpose of gathering evidence is to be able to express an opinion on the subject matter of the assurance engagement.

## 2.1 Types of opinion

We have already mentioned in Chapter 1 the different levels of assurance that can be offered in an assurance engagement and how they may be rendered as positive and negative assurance. The difference between these types of opinion can be seen by comparing the reports produced at the end of an audit and at the end of a review (lower level engagement).

### Worked example: Opinion

**Audit opinion**

In our opinion:

- The financial statements give a true and fair view of the state of the company's affairs as at ... and of its profit (loss) for the year then ended,

- The financial statements have been properly prepared in accordance with United Kingdom Generally Accepted Accounting Practice,

- The financial statements have been prepared in accordance with the requirements of the Companies Act 2006, and

- The information given in the Directors' Report for the financial year for which the financial statements are prepared is consistent with the financial statements.

In this text we refer to the auditor's report as given in Bulletin 2010/2 (Revised) *Compendium of Illustrative Auditor's Reports on UK Private Sector Financial Statements* and ISA 700 (UK and Ireland) *The Auditor's Report on Financial Statements*. This document provides an illustrative example of a standard UK auditor's report which includes references to the Companies Act 2006 and UK GAAP, and to UK auditing standards.

## 2.2 Content of the auditor's report

In this syllabus, you are only concerned with cases where the auditor finds that he **can** conclude that the financial statements give a true and fair view. Such an auditor's report is referred to as an 'unmodified' auditor's report.

The Companies Act 2006 requires the auditors to state **explicitly** whether in their opinion the annual accounts give a **true and fair view,** have been properly prepared in accordance with the Act and have been properly prepared in accordance with the relevant financial reporting framework (eg United Kingdom Generally Accepted Accounting Practice (UK GAAP)). They are also required to state whether in their opinion the directors' report is consistent with the financial statements.

| Explicit opinions |
| --- |
| In respect of the **state of the company's affairs** at the end of the financial year |
| In respect of the **company's profit or loss** for the financial year |
| The **information** given in the **directors' report** is **consistent** with the **financial statements** |

In addition, certain requirements are reported on **by exception**. The auditor only has to report if they have not been met. The following are matters with which the auditors **imply** satisfaction in an unqualified report under the Companies Act 2006.

| Implied opinions |
| --- |
| **Adequate accounting records** have been kept. |
| **Returns adequate for the audit** have been received from branches not visited. |
| The **financial statements** are in **agreement** with the **accounting records** and returns. |
| **All information** and **explanations** have been **received** as the auditors think necessary and they have had access at all times to the company's books, accounts and vouchers. |
| **Details** of **directors' emoluments** and other benefits have been correctly **disclosed** in the financial statements. |
| **Particulars of loans** and other **transactions** in favour of **directors** and others have been correctly disclosed in the financial statements. |

The auditor's report should include the following basic elements, usually in the following layout.

- Title

- Addressee

- **Introductory paragraph** identifying the financial statements audited

- Respective responsibilities of those charged with governance and the auditor

- Scope of the audit paragraph, or a cross reference to the 'Statement of the Scope of an Audit' that is maintained on the website of the Auditing Practices Board

- **Opinion paragraph** containing an expression of opinion on the financial statements

- **Opinion on other matters** such as specific statutory requirements

- Matters on which the auditor is required to report on **by exception**

- **Date** of the report

- **Auditor's address**

- **Auditor's signature**

The Companies Act 2006 prescribes that where the auditor is a firm, the auditor's report must be signed by the **senior statutory auditor** in his own name, for and on behalf of the audit firm. Under ISAs, senior statutory auditor has the same meaning as the term 'engagement partner'.

A measure of uniformity in the form and content of the auditor's report is desirable because it helps to promote the reader's understanding and to identify unusual circumstances when they occur.

An example of a complete UK auditor's report is given below. In the case of a company using IFRS (for example, a listed company) references to United Kingdom Generally Accepted Accounting Practice would be to IFRS.

## Worked example: UK auditor's report

### Independent Auditor's Report to the Members of XYZ Limited/PLC

We have audited the financial statements of (name of company) for the year ended ... which comprise [specify the titles of the primary statements such as the Profit and Loss Account, the Balance Sheet, the Cash Flow Statement, the Statement of Total Recognised Gains and Losses, the Reconciliation of Movements in Shareholders' Funds] and the related notes. The financial reporting framework that has been applied in their preparation is applicable law and United Kingdom Accounting Standards (United Kingdom Generally Accepted Accounting Practice).

### Respective responsibilities of directors and auditors

As explained more fully in the Directors' Responsibilities Statement (set out (on page ...)), the directors are responsible for the preparation of the financial statements and for being satisfied that they give a true and fair view. Our responsibility is to audit the financial statements in accordance with applicable law and International Standards on Auditing (UK and Ireland). Those standards require us to comply with the Auditing Practices Board's (APB's) Ethical Standards for Auditors.

### Scope of the audit of the financial statements

Either:

A description of the scope of an audit of financial statements is ([provided on the APB's website at www.frc.org.uk/apb/scope/private.cfm) / (set out (on page ...) of the Annual Report);

Or

An audit involves obtaining evidence about the amounts and disclosures in the financial statements sufficient to give reasonable assurance that the financial statements are free from material misstatement, whether caused by fraud or error. This includes an assessment of: whether the accounting policies are appropriate to the company's circumstances and have been consistently applied and adequately disclosed; the reasonableness of significant accounting estimates made by the directors; and the overall presentation of the financial statements. In addition, we read all the financial and non-financial information in the [describe the annual report] to identify material inconsistencies with the audited financial statements. If we become aware of any apparent material misstatements or inconsistencies we consider the implications for our report.

### Opinion on financial statements

In our opinion the financial statements:

- give a true and fair view of the state of the company's affairs as at ........ and of its profit (loss) for the year then ended;

- have been properly prepared in accordance with United Kingdom Generally Accepted Accounting Practice; and

- have been prepared in accordance with the requirements of the Companies Act 2006.

ICAEW

**Opinion on other matter prescribed by the Companies Act 2006**

In our opinion the information given in the Directors' Report for the financial year for which the financial statements are prepared is consistent with the financial statements.

**Matters on which we are required to report by exception**

We have nothing to report in respect of the following matters where the Companies Act 2006 requires us to report to you if, in our opinion:

- adequate accounting records have not been kept, or returns adequate for our audit have not been received from branches not visited by us; or

- the financial statements are not in agreement with the accounting records and returns; or

- certain disclosures of directors' remuneration specified by law are not made; or

- we have not received all the information and explanations we require for our audit.

*[Signature]*                                                   *Address*

*John Smith (Senior statutory auditor)*                        *Date*

*for and on behalf of ABC LLP, Statutory Auditor*

## 2.3 Level of assurance and the expectations gap

The above report is designed to give a reasonable (high) level of assurance. However, critics argue that it can fail to do so due to what is known as the 'expectations gap'.

The '**expectations gap**' is defined as the difference between the apparent public perceptions of the responsibilities of auditors on the one hand (and hence the assurance that their involvement provides) and the legal and professional reality on the other. The question remains: how can we make the **meaning** of an unmodified auditor's report clear to the user?

The above definition of the expectations gap is not definitive and it is not a 'static phenomenon'. However, we can highlight some specific issues.

- **Misunderstanding of the nature of audited financial statements,** for example that:

  - The balance sheet provides a fair valuation of the reporting entity.

  - The amounts in the financial statements are stated precisely.

  - The audited financial statements will guarantee that the entity concerned will continue to exist.

- **Misunderstanding as to the type and extent of work undertaken by auditors,** for example that:

  - All items in financial statements are tested
  - Auditors will uncover all errors
  - Auditors should detect all fraud

- **Misunderstanding about the level of assurance provided by auditors,** for example that:

  - The auditors provide absolute assurance that the figures in the financial statements are correct (ignoring the concept of materiality and the problems of estimation).

## 2.4 Other reports

The main assurance report is addressed to users of the assurance material. The international standard on assurance engagements requires that an assurance report must have the following components:

- A title that clearly indicates the report is an independent assurance report

- An addressee

- An identification and description of the subject matter information and, when appropriate, the subject matter

- Identification of the criteria

- Where appropriate, a description of any significant inherent limitations associated with the evaluation or measurement of the subject matter against the criteria

- When the criteria used to evaluate or measure the subject matter are available only to specific intended users, or are relevant only to a specific purpose, a statement restricting the use of the assurance report to those intended users or that purpose

- A statement to identify the responsible party and to describe the responsibilities of the responsible party and the practitioner

- A statement that the engagement was performed in accordance with International Standards on Assurance Engagements (ISAEs)

- A summary of the work performed (usually limited, particularly where a negative conclusion is being given)

- The practitioner's conclusion (positive or negative, depending on the level of assurance being given and the work carried out)

- The assurance report date

- The name of the firm or practitioner, and a specific location, which ordinarily is the city where the practitioner maintains the office that has responsibility for the engagement.

To illustrate some of these points, here is an extract from a sample report on prospective financial information, from the ISAE 3400 *The Examination of Prospective Financial Information*.

## Worked example: Extract from a report on prospective financial information.

We have examined the forecast in accordance with the International Standard on Assurance Engagements applicable to the examination of prospective financial information. Management is responsible for the forecast including the assumptions set out in Note X on which it is based.

Based on our examination of the evidence supporting the assumptions, nothing has come to our attention which causes us to believe that these assumptions do not provide a reasonable basis for the forecast. Further, in our opinion the forecast is properly prepared on the basis of the assumptions and is presented in accordance with.....

Actual results are likely to be different from the forecast since anticipated events frequently do not occur as expected and the variation may be material.

The assurance provider also may sometimes issue reports to the party that has engaged them as well as the main report to users of the assurance material. So for example, in an audit, the auditors will sometimes issue a report to the directors or management as a by-product of the audit. One major issue that such a report might cover is internal control deficiencies, and this is looked at in the next chapter.

## Interactive question 2: Auditor's report
[Difficulty level: Easy]

Which **three** of the following are reported by exception in the auditor's report?

| | All information and explanations required for the audit have been received |

| | Adequate accounting records have been kept |

| | The directors' report is consistent with the financial statements |

| | The financial statements have been prepared in accordance with the Companies Act 2006 |

| | Details of directors' emoluments have been properly disclosed in the financial statements |

See **Answer** at the end of this chapter.

# Summary and Self-test

## Summary

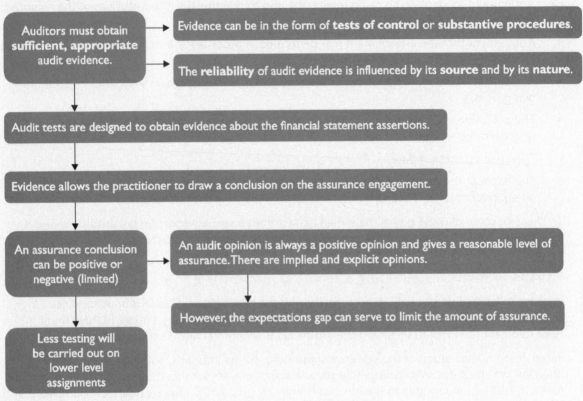

| | |
|---|---|
| Auditors must obtain **sufficient, appropriate** audit evidence. | → Evidence can be in the form of **tests of control** or **substantive procedures**. |
| | → The **reliability** of audit evidence is influenced by its **source** and by its **nature**. |

Audit tests are designed to obtain evidence about the financial statement assertions.

Evidence allows the practitioner to draw a conclusion on the assurance engagement.

| | |
|---|---|
| An assurance conclusion can be positive or negative (limited) | → An audit opinion is always a positive opinion and gives a reasonable level of assurance. There are implied and explicit opinions. |
| | However, the expectations gap can serve to limit the amount of assurance. |

Less testing will be carried out on lower level assignments

## Self-test

Answer the following questions.

1    Name **seven** financial statement assertions.

2    Fill in the **blanks**.

Audit evidence from external sources is .................................... ...................................... than that obtained from the entity's records.

Evidence obtained directly ............................................................................ is more ....................................... than that obtained indirectly or by inference.

3    Complete the standard opinion paragraph.

In our opinion the financial statements:

*   give a .................. ................... ................................... ............................ of the state of the company's affairs as at ... and of its ....................................... for the year then ended,

*   have been .................................... ........................................in accordance with United Kingdom Generally Accepted Accounting Practice,

*   have been ..................................... ....................................... in accordance with the requirements of the Companies Act 2006.

4    Give **three** examples of misunderstandings which contribute to the expectations gap.

1    ..............................................................................

2    ..............................................................................

3    ..............................................................................

Now, go back to the Learning Objectives in the Introduction. If you are satisfied you have achieved these objectives, please tick them off.

# Technical reference

## 1 Evidence

| | |
|---|---|
| • Definition | ISA 500.5 (UK and Ireland) |
| • Types of test | ISA 330.4 (UK and Ireland) |
| • Sufficient appropriate evidence | ISA 500.4 (UK and Ireland) |
| • Quality of evidence | ISA 500.A31 (UK and Ireland) |
| • Use of entity information | ISA 500.9 (UK and Ireland) |
| • Financial statement assertions | ISA 315.25, ISA 315.A124 (UK and Ireland) |
| • Tests of controls or tests of detail | ISA 330.8 – 23 (UK and Ireland) |

## 2 Reporting

| | |
|---|---|
| • Content of the auditor's report | APB Bulletin 2010/2 (Revised) |
| | ISA 700 (UK and Ireland) |

## Answer to Interactive question 1

True

True

## Answer to Interactive question 2

All information and explanations required for the audit have been received

Adequate accounting records have been kept

Details of directors' emoluments have been properly disclosed in the financial statements

1 Any of:

   Existence, rights and obligations, occurrence, completeness, valuation, accuracy, classification, cut-off, allocation

2 More reliable

   By auditors, reliable

3 True and fair view, profit (loss), properly prepared, properly prepared.

4 1 The nature of the financial statements
  2 The type and extent of work undertaken by auditors
  3 The level of assurance given by auditors

# CHAPTER 5

# Introduction to internal control

Introduction
Examination context
**Topic List**
Summary and Self-test
Technical reference
Answers to Interactive questions
Answers to Self-test

## Learning objectives

- Understand the role of internal control within a business

- Understand the limitations of internal control

- Identify the components of internal control

- Understand how the auditor obtains and records information about internal controls

Specific syllabus references for this chapter are: 2a, b, c, d, e, f, i.

## Syllabus links

You will have studied the basic components of an information system when studying for your Accounting paper and should therefore know the basic set up of initial documents, books of prime entry, ledgers, journals, trial balances and financial statements.

You will learn more about a business's risk management and control in your Business and Finance paper.

## Examination context

Internal control is an important practical area in auditing. It is therefore 25% of the syllabus and you should expect that to be reflected in your assessment. In the sample paper there were 15 questions on internal control related issues. This is the first chapter of four in this area.

In the assessment candidates may be required to:

- State the reasons for organisations having effective systems of controls
- Identify factors which contribute to an effective control environment
- Identify the components of internal control in both manual and IT environments
- Identify types of control activity
- Distinguish between general controls and application controls
- Identify inherent limitations of a system of internal controls
- Specify the composition of an audit committee

# 1 What is internal control?

**Section overview**

- Internal control is the process designed to mitigate risks to the business and ensure that the business operates efficiently and effectively.

- Key limitations to internal controls include the fact that they may be expensive, the fact that they generally rely on humans to operate them and the fact that they are generally only designed for routine, normal transactions.

- Small companies in particular may have difficulties implementing effective internal control systems due to employing fewer staff to implement internal controls than larger companies.

## 1.1 Definition

ISA 315 (UK and Ireland) *Identifying and Assessing the Risks of Material Misstatement through Understanding the Entity and Its Environment* contains the following definition of internal control.

**Definition**

Internal control: 'The process designed, implemented and maintained by those charged with governance, management, and other personnel to provide reasonable assurance about the achievement of an entity's objectives with regard to reliability of financial reporting, effectiveness and efficiency of operations and compliance with applicable laws and regulations. The term "controls" refers to any aspects of one or more of the components of internal control.'

'Those charged with governance,' a phrase used in the definition above, are the people who direct the operations of the company. Remember that in the UK, those charged with governance and management are often one and the same thing – the directors of a company, although a distinction may be made between executive directors (who work in the operations of a business) and non-executive directors who are more involved at board level.

**Worked example: Company objectives.**

A company has various objectives:

- To ensure it reports its financial position correctly to shareholders
- To ensure that it operates effectively and efficiently
- To ensure that it complies with relevant laws and regulations

In order to meet these objectives, the directors will take the following steps:

### Step 1
Identify risks to these objectives not being fulfilled, for example, in terms of reporting financial position, the directors might identify that a risk of not being able to report correctly is computer failure and consequent destruction of the financial records.

### Step 2
Implement internal controls to mitigate this risk. The controls to mitigate the above risk could be many and varied, for example, ensuring that all users have passwords to limit unauthorised access to the computer and therefore the risk of it being infected, or, at the other end of the scale, detailed back up and emergency procedures, including a reconstruction plan, to kick into action in the event of computer failure.

## 1.2 Reasons for internal controls

The reasons for internal controls can be seen in the example. They include:

- Minimising the company's business risks
- Ensuring the continuing effective functioning of the company
- Ensuring the company complies with relevant laws and regulations

Most of these reasons funnel back to the ultimate objective that the company continues to operate. For example, if the company failed to comply with relevant laws and regulations, it might be forced to stop operations.

### Worked example: Fairfood Co

Fairfood Co is a food manufacturer. It is subject to a great number of health and safety regulations and therefore must have significant internal controls surrounding the food preparation areas. If these controls were seriously breached, Fairfood Co would be forced to cease operations. The primary objective of each internal control might focus on a particular operation, for example, that all personnel must wear protective clothing when operating machinery however, the ultimate objective is to ensure the operation of the company continues. If the protective clothing wasn't worn and hair or other items, such as jewellery from staff, fell into the food, the company might be forced to stop operating.

## 1.3 Limitations of internal controls

Internal controls have some limitations. In other words, the risk to the business of operating cannot be eliminated entirely.

| Limitation | Explanation |
| --- | --- |
| **Expense** | A key limitation of controls is that they are **expensive**, and therefore may not be worth putting into place, as the continual use of the control is more expensive than the cost of the risk arising. This is a matter of judgement for the directors and often determines the structure and level of controls that are put into place in a business. |
| **Human element** | Another important limitation of controls is the **human element**. Most controls can only function as well as the people that are implementing them. Controls are not necessarily fool-proof. If a human being makes a mistake implementing a control, then that control might be ineffective. Another problem for companies associated with the human element of controls is that of the intention of the people using them. Controls, such as keeping your computer password secret, rely on the integrity of the people being asked to implement them. If people do not understand the importance or relevance of the control they may be less inclined to adhere to it. |
| **Collusion** | Staff members may want to override or avoid controls in order to defraud the company. Controls may be bypassed very effectively and secretly by two or more people working together, that is, colluding in fraud. |
| **Unusual transactions** | Finally, a limitation of internal controls is that they are generally designed to deal with **what normally or routinely happens** in a business. However, it may be the case that an unusual transaction may occur which does not fit into the normal routines, in which case standard controls may not be relevant to the unusual transaction, and hence mistakes may be made in relation to that unusual transaction. |

**Small companies** may have particular problems in implementing effective internal control systems. This is largely because of the **human element** discussed above. Small companies generally have **fewer employees** than larger companies, meaning that there are fewer people to involve in the internal control system.

Involving a large number of people in internal control systems helps to limit the risk of the human element in internal control systems because if a lot of people are involved, there is a greater chance that people's errors or, worse, frauds, will be uncovered by the next person in the control chain. The control of using a number of people in a single system is called **segregation of duties,** and we will look at it in more detail later. In a small company, if its staff capacity is not such to ensure that lots of people are involved in the internal control system, then the control system will be weaker.

### Worked example: Large Co and Small Co

Contrast the following examples.

Large Co is a large company with sophisticated controls systems. In respect of purchase ordering, an order is raised by a member of the purchase team (who all have pre-set limits of the price they are allowed to order up to) on the basis of a requisition note from the relevant department, signed by the department manager. Before the order is despatched to the approved supplier, the purchase manager approves the order. If the order is in excess of £30 million, the purchasing director approves the order.

Small Co is a small company with limited controls systems. When the stores manager needs the stores replacing he rings the approved supplier and orders the goods. The annual cost of purchases is £7 million.

You can see that in the second scenario there are far fewer people, indeed just one, compared with a minimum of four at Large Co, involved in the transaction. If one of the people at Large Co made a mistake with the order, then another member of the team might pick it up. If the stores manager makes a mistake at Small Co, there is not another team member to correct the mistake. Small Co has a control, in that it uses an approved supplier, who might query an unusual order, but the internal control in relation to purchasing is weak due to lack of staff members.

Bear in mind also that although the sums of money discussed in the two scenarios are very different, the materiality of those sums to the businesses themselves might be comparable. A mistake in a £30,000 order may not seem as important as a mistake in a £30 million order, but it might be enough to put Small Co into financial difficulties.

# 2 Components of internal control

### Section overview

- Internal control comprises five components.

- The control environment is the context of the internal control system, influenced by management.

- The entity's risk assessment process is the process by which the company determines what control policies and procedures to implement.

- The information system is the system which captures information about transactions and events for financial reporting purposes.

- Control activities are the heart of the internal control system, comprising policies and procedures which may prevent, or detect and correct errors.

- All control systems should be monitored.

ISA 315 sets out that there are five components of internal control, each of which may impact on the audit process differently. We shall look at each of them in more detail below. An internal control may fall into a particular category.

Each particular internal control may also prevent an error occurring (**preventative control**), or may identify that an error has occurred and correct it (**detective control**). It is an important part of understanding internal controls to be able to identify what it is that each specific control actually does.

Some controls may be relevant to audit while others are not. The auditor will not waste time looking at company controls that are not relevant to whether the financial statements are true and fair, however important those controls might be to the overall operating of the business, for example, control processes over asset utilisation.

The extent of reliance on internal controls in an assurance engagement will depend on the nature of the engagement and the assurance provider's expectation of the effectiveness of controls. In some engagements, very few controls will be relied on and the assurance provider will carry out more tests of detail instead.

## 2.1 The control environment

### Definition

Control environment: The control environment includes the governance and management functions and the attitudes, awareness and actions of those charged with governance and management concerning the entity's internal control and its importance in the entity. The control environment sets the tone of an organisation, influencing the control consciousness of its people.

Where directors feel that internal controls are important, staff members are likely to be better educated about what the controls are and why they are important, so the human element of risk associated with internal controls is reduced. Also, if directors set the tone by taking controls seriously and rigorously applying them, even when they seem silly or unnecessary then other staff members will be encouraged to do the same.

In a strong control environment, management will ensure that individuals have the competence to perform their roles. Authority and responsibility will be assigned to appropriate levels and staff will be made aware of their specific responsibilities and how these affect the organisation as a whole. Policies will be in place to promote best practice in recruitment, training, promotion and compensation so that employees feel valued. Overall, a strong control environment is a foundation for effective internal control.

The control environment is therefore very important to the auditors and they will evaluate it as part of their risk assessment process. If the control environment is strong, then auditors will be more inclined to rely on the controls system in the entity than if it is weak.

However, it is important to understand that the control environment is only one component of the overall internal control system. Equally important are the other aspects of controls, because if other control components are weak, it will not matter as much to the auditors that the directors think that controls are important, because the auditor will not be happy to rely on well-intentioned, but weak, control systems.

### 2.1.1 Audit committees

The audit committee is an important aspect of the control environment of the company. It is a sub-committee of the board of directors responsible for overseeing an entity's internal control structure, financial reporting and compliance with relevant laws and regulations.

The audit committee is comprised of non-executive directors. It is a requirement in UK listed companies under the rules of the UK Corporate Governance Code. The Code requires the committee to have written terms of reference which are likely to include the following:

- To review the integrity of the financial statements of the company and formal announcements relating to the company's performance

- To review the company's internal financial controls and the company's risk management systems (unless there is a separate risk management committee)

- To monitor and review the effectiveness of the company's internal audit function (if relevant)

- To make recommendations to the board in relation to the external auditor

- To monitor the independence of the external auditor

- To implement policy on the provision of non-audit services by the external auditor

The key issue for the audit committee is the financial statements, so the audit committee itself can be seen as a control in relation to the **information system** and the way in which the company produces its financial statements. Note that the committee also has responsibilities with regard to supervising the **identification of risks** and **monitoring controls** (these are all discussed later in this chapter).

## 2.2 Business risk and the entity's risk assessment process

### Definitions

**Entity's risk assessment process:** A component of internal control that is the entity's process for identifying business risks relevant to financial reporting objectives and deciding about actions to address those risks, and the results thereof.

**Business risk:** A risk resulting from significant conditions, events, circumstances, actions or inactions that could adversely affect an entity's ability to achieve its objectives and execute its strategies, or from the setting of inappropriate objectives and strategies.

Internal controls are implemented to minimise business risk.

Assurance providers, particularly auditors focusing on the financial statements, are interested in business risk because issues which pose threats to the business may in some cases also be a risk of the financial statements being misstated. For example, if a particular division of a business was threatened with closure, the valuation of all the assets associated with that division would be affected. In more general terms, if an economic downturn puts pressure on a company to meet the expectations of providers of finance, management might be tempted to manipulate the financial statements.

Not all business risks have a direct impact on the financial statements – for example, the risk that production does not meet quality control requirements of customers does not directly impact upon financial statements – the risk that credit notes are not recorded properly does. However, if an assurance provider is aware of the general business risk that there is a stringent quality control process to be met, he will be aware that there is likely to be a correlation with sales and sales returns if the process is not working adequately.

You can see that if the risk assessment process is weak, then the resulting internal controls may not be effective. The process will involve the following elements:

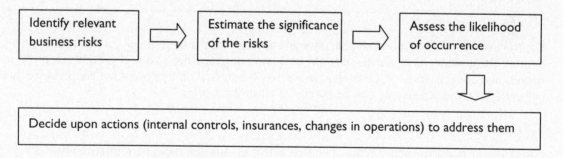

*Figure 5.1: Entity's risk assessment process*

Assessing the risk assessment process will also take place during audit risk assessment, as identifying business risks that management have identified will assist auditors in identifying audit risks as well. In terms of internal control, the auditors will have to evaluate each aspect of this process. If, during the audit, the auditors identify a risk that the entity did not identify, the auditors will evaluate what this means for the effectiveness of the entity's risk assessment process.

ICAEW

## 2.3 The information system relevant to financial reporting

An information system consists of infrastructure (physical and hardware components), software, people, procedures and data.

### Definition

Information system relevant to financial reporting: A component of internal control that includes the financial reporting system, and consists of the procedures and records established to initiate, record, process and report entity transactions (as well as events and conditions) and to maintain accountability for the related assets, liabilities and equity.

The auditors will be interested in:

- The classes of transactions that are significant to the entity's financial statements
- The procedures by which transactions are initiated, recorded, processed, corrected and reported
- The related accounting records and supporting information
- How the information system captures events other than transactions that are significant to the financial statements
- The process of preparing the financial statements

This will typically involve the financial controller and/or director and the use of journals, which the auditors will be interested in.

The auditors will be interested in how this process links in with other internal controls and whether it is at this point that controls are overridden or ignored (by use of journals for example).

## 2.4 Control activities

### Definition

Control activities are the policies and procedures that help ensure that management directives are carried out.

Control activities are the most tangible internal controls that the auditor will concentrate on to a large degree. The auditor will be concerned with understanding whether a control prevents an error or detects and corrects an error. Control activities may be manual or, if relevant, where processes are computerised, then there may also be specific IT control activities.

### 2.4.1 Types of control activity

ISA 315 gives examples of five types of control activities: authorisation, performance reviews, information processing, physical controls and segregation of duties.

| Type of control activity | Examples | Explanation |
|---|---|---|
| Authorisation | Approval of transactions/documents | Transactions/documents should be approved by an appropriate person.<br><br>For example, overtime should be approved by departmental managers, purchase orders by the purchasing manager |
| Performance reviews | Review and analysis of actual performance versus budgets, forecasts and prior period performance | A review highlights and explains any unexpected variances. This reduces the likelihood of errors or deliberate misstatement. |
| | Relating different sets of data (operating or financial) to one another | For example, comparing sales reports by units sold to sales in the profit and loss account. |
| | Comparing internal data with external sources of information | For example, comparison of key performance indicators (KPIs) with industry sector KPIs. |
| | Review of functional or activity performance | For example, a review of sales by branch, region, and product type. |
| Information processing | Controls to check the accuracy, completeness and authorisation of transactions | The two broad groupings of information systems control activities are **application controls** and **general IT controls** (see later section). |
| Physical controls | Physical security of assets | Only authorised personnel should have access to certain assets (particularly valuable or portable ones).<br><br>For example, ensuring that the inventories store is only open when the store personnel are there and is otherwise locked. |
| | Authorisation for access to computer programs and data files | Passwords over computer programs and data files will ensure only authorised personnel can access them.<br><br>For example, a password over the payroll system prevents unauthorised changes such as creating a fictitious employee. |
| | Periodic counting and comparison with amount shown on control accounts | For example, a physical count of petty cash.<br><br>The balance shown in the cash book should be the same amount as is in the petty cash box. |
| Segregation of duties | Assigning different individuals the responsibilities of authorising transactions, recording transactions and maintaining custody of assets | Segregation makes it more difficult for fraudulent errors to be processed (since a number of people would have to collude in the fraud) and also for accidental errors to be processed (since the more people that are involved, the more checking there can be).<br><br>For example, the same staff should not record transactions and carry out the related reconciliations at the period-end. |

## 2.4.2 Information processing controls

The internal controls in a computerised environment includes both manual procedures and procedures designed into computer programs. Such manual and computer control procedures comprise two types of control.

### Definitions

**Application controls:** Manual or automated procedures that typically operate at a business process level. Application controls can be preventative or detective in nature and are designed to ensure the integrity of the accounting records. Accordingly, application controls relate to procedures used to initiate, record, process and report transactions or other financial data.

**General controls:** Policies and procedures that relate to many applications and support the effective function of application controls by helping to ensure the continued proper operation of information systems.

| Examples of general controls | |
|---|---|
| Development of computer applications | Standards over **systems design, programming and documentation** |
| | Full **testing procedures** using test data (See Chapter 11) |
| | Approval by **computer users** and **management** |
| | **Segregation of duties** so that those responsible for design are not responsible for testing |
| | **Installation procedures** so that data is not corrupted in transition |
| | **Training** of staff in new procedures and availability of adequate documentation |
| Prevention or detection of unauthorised changes to programs | **Segregation of duties** |
| | **Full records** of program **changes** |
| | **Password protection** of programs so that access is limited to computer operations staff |
| | **Restricted access** to **central computer** by locked doors, keypads |
| | **Maintenance of program logs** |
| | **Virus checks** on software: use of anti-virus software and policy prohibiting use of non-authorised programs or files |
| | **Back-up copies** of programs being taken and stored in other locations |
| | **Control copies** of programs being preserved and regularly **compared** with **actual programs** |
| | **Stricter controls** over certain programs (utility programs) by use of **read only memory** |
| Testing and documentation of program changes | Complete **testing procedures** |
| | **Documentation standards** |
| | **Approval** of changes by computer users and management |
| | **Training** of staff using programs |
| Controls to prevent wrong programs or files being used | **Operation controls** over programs |
| | **Libraries** of programs |
| | **Proper job scheduling** |

| | |
|---|---|
| **Controls to prevent unauthorised amendments to data files** | Such as passwords to prevent unauthorised entry, built in controls to permit changes |
| **Controls to ensure continuity of operations** | **Storing extra copies** of programs and data files off-site |
| | **Protection of equipment** against fire and other hazards |
| | **Back-up power sources** |
| | **Emergency procedures** |
| | **Disaster recovery procedures**, eg availability of back-up computer facilities |
| | **Maintenance agreements** and **insurance** |

The auditors will wish to test some or all of the above general controls, having considered how they affect the computer applications significant to the audit.

General controls that relate to some or all applications are usually interdependent controls, ie their operation is often essential to the effectiveness of application controls. As application controls may be useless when general controls are ineffective, it will be more efficient to review the design of **general controls first,** before reviewing the application controls.

The purpose of application controls is to establish **specific control activities** over the accounting applications in order to provide reasonable assurance that all transactions are authorised and recorded, and are processed completely, accurately and on a timely basis. Application controls include the following.

| Examples of application controls | |
|---|---|
| **Controls over input: completeness** | Manual or programmed agreement of control totals |
| | Document counts |
| | One-for-one checking of processed output to source documents |
| | Programmed matching of input to an expected input control file |
| | Procedures over resubmission of rejected data |
| **Controls over input: accuracy** | Programs to check data fields (for example value, reference number, date) on input transactions for plausibility: |
| | • Digit verification (eg reference numbers are as expected) |
| | • Reasonableness test (eg VAT to total value) |
| | • Existence checks (eg customer name) |
| | • Character checks (no unexpected characters used in reference) |
| | • Necessary information (no transaction passed with missing information) |
| | • Permitted range (no transaction processed over a certain value) |
| | Manual scrutiny of output and reconciliation to source |
| | Agreement of control totals (manual/programmed) |
| **Controls over input: authorisation** | Manual checks to ensure information input was |
| | • Authorised |
| | • Input by authorised personnel |
| **Controls over processing** | Similar controls to input must be completed when input is completed, for example, batch reconciliations |
| | Screen warnings can prevent people logging out before processing is complete |

CHAPTER

5

| Examples of application controls | |
| --- | --- |
| Controls over **master files and standing data** | One to one checking of master files to source documents (such as payroll master files to individual employee personal files) |
| | Cyclical reviews of all master files and standing data |
| | Record counts (number of documents processed) and hash totals (for example, the total of all the payroll numbers) used when master files are used to ensure no deletions |
| | Controls over the deletion of accounts that have no current balance |

Control over input, processing, data files and output may be carried out by IT personnel, users of the system, a separate control group and may be programmed into application software. The auditors may wish to test the following application controls.

| Testing of application controls | |
| --- | --- |
| **Manual controls exercised by the user** | If manual controls exercised by the user of the application system are capable of providing reasonable assurance that the system's output is complete, accurate and authorised, the auditors may decide to limit tests of control to these manual controls. |
| **Controls over system output** | If, in addition to manual controls exercised by the user, the controls to be tested use information produced by the computer or are contained within computer programs, such controls may be tested by examining the system's output using either manual procedures or computer assisted audit techniques (CAATs) which will be described in more detail in Chapter 11. Such output may be in the form of magnetic media, microfilm or printouts. Alternatively, the auditor may test the control by performing it with the use of CAATs. |
| **Programmed control procedures** | In the case of certain computer systems, the auditor may find that it is not possible or, in some cases, not practical to test controls by examining only user controls or the system's output. The auditor may consider performing tests of control by using CAATs, such as test data, reprocessing transaction data or, in unusual situations, examining the coding of the application program. |

As we have already noted, general IT controls may have a pervasive effect on the processing of transactions in application systems. If these general controls are not effective, there may be a risk that misstatements occur and go undetected in the application systems. Although weaknesses in general IT controls may preclude testing certain IT application controls, it is possible that manual procedures exercised by users may provide effective control at the **application level**.

Bear in mind that most companies have computerised accounting systems so these controls are important in practice as well as in your assessment.

## 2.5 Monitoring of controls

An entity should review its overall control system to ensure that it still meets its objectives, it still operates effectively and efficiently and that necessary corrections to the system are made on a timely basis. If it does not, then the control system may not be operating optimally. This is often a role undertaken by a company's internal audit department, as we shall see in Chapter 9.

In smaller companies that do not have an internal audit function, the company may make use of auditor feedback to ensure that controls continue to operate efficiently. Auditors will often produce a management report at the end of an audit, outlining any weaknesses they have observed in internal controls. Auditors are also required by ISAs to identify control weaknesses observed to those charged with governance. However, this does not remove the onus from the company itself to monitor its own internal controls.

# 3 Information about controls

**Section overview**

- Auditors will obtain information about internal controls from a variety of sources, including company internal control manuals and observing controls in operation.

- Auditors will record information about internal controls in a variety of ways in their files, including notes, flowcharts and questionnaires.

## 3.1 Information about internal controls

Auditors will obtain information about internal controls from a variety of sources.

The company may have manuals of internal controls and copies of internal controls policies, or minutes of meetings of the risk assessment group. These will be useful documents for the auditors to read. In addition, in recurring audits, the auditors should have a record of what the controls were in previous years and therefore will only be looking for new policies in the current year.

The auditors will also obtain knowledge by talking to the people involved with internal control at all stages and asking them what the controls are and why they have been implemented. Again, where auditors have a record of what the controls were last year, inquiry will be useful in updating the picture to what they are now.

Lastly, an important tool for auditors in determining what internal controls exist in an organisation or whether controls in use in an operation are the same as those stated to be in operation is observation. The auditor will watch operations at a company to identify the control activities being put into action.

## 3.2 Recording of internal controls

Auditors shall record the internal controls that they see.

There are broadly three types of document which are used for recording the understanding of the business:

- Narrative notes
- Questionnaires/checklists and
- Diagrams

**Narrative notes**

These are good for things like:

- Short notes on simple systems
- Background information

They are less good when things get more complex when diagrams tend to take over.

**Questionnaires and checklists**

These are:

- Good as aide memoires to ensure you have all the bases covered

  **but**

- Can lead to a mechanical approach so that an important extra question is never asked

- Tick boxes often get ticked whether the brain is engaged or not

**Diagrams**

Things like:

- Flowcharts
- Organisation charts
- Family trees
- Records of related parties

Organisation charts and family trees are without doubt the best way of recording relationships, reporting lines, etc.

Flow charts of systems are an excellent and comprehensive way of recording systems, but they are time consuming to construct and can be difficult for the reader to assimilate.

### Interactive question 1: Internal control     [Difficulty level: Exam standard]

Which **one** of the following is a reason that organisations have effective systems of control?

To assist the organisation in:

A   Maximising profitability
B   Maximising operating efficiency
C   Reducing time required for the statutory audit
D   Minimising audit risk

See **Answer** at the end of this chapter.

### Interactive question 2: Control activities     [Difficulty level: Exam standard]

The following are examples of internal controls which operate at Searson plc.

For each example, select the **one** type of control activity which it illustrates.

| | Authorisation | Performance review | Information processing | Physical |
|---|---|---|---|---|
| 1   The receivables ledger clerk checks the manually calculated batch total for a batch of sales invoices entered to the sales day book to the computer generated batch total | ☐ | ☐ | ☐ | ☐ |
| 2   The sales director compares monthly budgeted sales figures to actual | ☐ | ☐ | ☐ | ☐ |

See **Answer** at the end of this chapter.

### Interactive question 3: IT controls     [Difficulty level: Exam standard]

Most entities use IT systems for financial reporting and operational purposes. Controls operating in an IT environment can be split into general controls and application controls.

Which **two** of the following are application controls?

☐   Document counts

☐   Digit verification

☐   Passwords

☐   Virus checks

See **Answer** at the end of this chapter.

# Summary and Self-test

## Summary

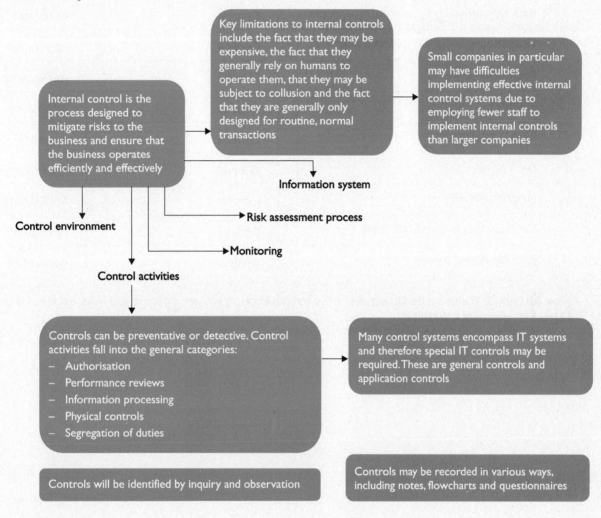

Internal control is the process designed to mitigate risks to the business and ensure that the business operates efficiently and effectively

Key limitations to internal controls include the fact that they may be expensive, the fact that they generally rely on humans to operate them, that they may be subject to collusion and the fact that they are generally only designed for routine, normal transactions

Small companies in particular may have difficulties implementing effective internal control systems due to employing fewer staff to implement internal controls than larger companies

Control environment

Information system

Risk assessment process

Monitoring

Control activities

Controls can be preventative or detective. Control activities fall into the general categories:
- Authorisation
- Performance reviews
- Information processing
- Physical controls
- Segregation of duties

Many control systems encompass IT systems and therefore special IT controls may be required. These are general controls and application controls

Controls will be identified by inquiry and observation

Controls may be recorded in various ways, including notes, flowcharts and questionnaires

## Self-test

Answer the following questions.

1   Complete the definition taking the words given below.

The ............ .............. includes the governance and management functions and the .............., .......... and .......... of those charged with ..............and management concerning the entity's internal .......... and its importance in the entity. It sets the ....... of an organisation, influencing the control ............. of its people.

| attitudes | consciousness | awareness | governance | actions | control |
| control | environment | tone | | | |

2   Name **two key** inherent limitations of an internal control system

1   ...............................................................

2   ...............................................................

3   For each of the following controls, state whether they are general or application:

| | | | |
|---|---|---|---|
| One-to-one checking | ☐ General | ☐ Application | |
| Segregation of duties | ☐ General | ☐ Application | |
| Review of master files | ☐ General | ☐ Application | |
| Back-up copies | ☐ General | ☐ Application | |
| Virus checks | ☐ General | ☐ Application | |
| Passwords | ☐ General | ☐ Application | |
| Training | ☐ General | ☐ Application | |
| Record counts | ☐ General | ☐ Application | |
| Hash totals | ☐ General | ☐ Application | |
| Program libraries | ☐ General | ☐ Application | |
| Controls over account deletions | ☐ General | ☐ Application | |
| Back-up power source | ☐ General | ☐ Application | |

Now go back to the Learning Objectives in the Introduction. If you are satisfied you have achieved these objectives, please tick them off.

# Technical reference

### 1 What is internal control?

- Definition of internal control — ISA 315.4 (UK and Ireland)
- Limitations of internal controls — ISA 315.A53 – A55 (UK and Ireland)

### 2 Components of internal control

- Control environment — ISA 315.14, A76 – A86 (UK and Ireland)
- The entity's risk assessment process — ISA 315.15, A87 (UK and Ireland)
- Information system — ISA 315.18, A89 (UK and Ireland)
- Control activities — ISA 315.20, A96 – 105, Appendix 1, 9 – 10 (UK and Ireland)
- Monitoring of controls — ISA 315.22 – 24 (UK and Ireland)

CHAPTER

5

# Answers to Interactive questions

### Answer to Interactive question 1

B

### Answer to Interactive question 2

1 Information processing
2 Performance review

### Answer to Interactive question 3

Document counts and digit verification

1   Control, environment, attitudes, awareness, actions, governance, control, tone, consciousness

2   Two from:

Human error

Possibility of staff colluding in fraud

Only designed for routine, normal transactions

May be expensive to implement

3

| Application controls | General controls |
|---|---|
| One-to-one checking | Virus checks |
| Hash totals | Program libraries |
| Review of master files | Segregation of duties |
| Record counts | Passwords |
| | Controls over account deletions |
| | Training |
| | Back-up power source |
| | Back-up copies |

# CHAPTER 6

# Revenue system

Introduction

Examination context

**Topic List**

    1   Ordering

    2   Despatch and invoicing

    3   Recording

    4   Cash collection

    5   Deficiencies

Summary and Self-test

Answers to Interactive questions

Answers to Self-test

### Learning objectives

- Identify relevant controls to mitigate risk

- Identify tests of those controls

- Identify risks in a sales system

- Recognise weaknesses in a sales system

Specific syllabus references for this chapter are: 2f, g, h, 3f.

### Syllabus links

You will have learnt about the various books of record in the sales system in Accounting.

### Examination context

As the sales system is an important practical area, your assessment might well include a scenario internal controls question in this area. The sample paper contained one question looking at strengths and weaknesses in a given sales system.

In the assessment, candidates may be required to:

- Show how specific internal controls in a revenue system mitigate risk and state their limitations
- Identify internal controls for an organisation in a given scenario
- Identify internal control strengths and weaknesses in a given scenario
- Determine the extent to which tests of controls should be used in a given set of circumstances

# 1 Ordering

**Section overview**

- Key risks include accepting customers who are a poor credit risk and not fulfilling orders.
- Key controls include authorising credit terms to customers and ensuring orders are matched with production orders and despatch notes.

## 1.1 Risks and control objectives

When considering sales orders, a company might recognise all or some of the following risks:

- Orders may be taken from customers who are not able to pay
- Orders may be taken from customers who are unlikely to pay for a long time
- Orders may not be recorded properly and therefore not fulfilled and customers might be lost

The controls put into place will be designed to mitigate these risks. Hence the objectives of the controls will be to prevent these risks from occurring. Here are the control objectives which might arise from the risks noted above:

- **Goods** and **services** are **only supplied** to **customers** with **good credit ratings**
- **Customers** are encouraged to **pay promptly**
- **Orders** are **recorded correctly**
- **Orders** are **fulfilled**

## 1.2 Controls

Once the company has identified the risks which exist in the sales system, it will try and create controls which mitigate those risks (that is, meet the control objectives outlined above). What controls will be put into place depend on the nature of the company and the specific risks associated with the way it operates, but the following controls can be used as examples of how the above risks can be mitigated.

- **Segregation** of duties; credit control, invoicing and inventory despatch

- **Authorisation** of **credit terms** to customers

    - References/credit checks obtained
    - Authorisation by senior staff
    - Regular review

- **Authorisation** for changes in **other customer data**

    - Change of address supported by letterhead
    - Deletion requests supported by evidence of balances cleared/customer in liquidation

- **Orders** only **accepted** from **customers** who have no credit problems

- **Sequential numbering** of blank pre-printed order documents and subsequent checking of sequence for completeness

- **Correct prices quoted** to **customers**

- **Matching** of **customer orders** with production orders and despatch notes and querying of orders not matched

- **Dealing** with **customer queries**

Worked example: Controls over ordering

Manufacturing Company Ltd (MCL) is a large manufacturing company selling a unique product. It has an established customer base, but as its product is unique, it also receives regular inquiries from potential customers that have not bought products from MCL before. In respect of such new customers, MCL has a significant risk of taking orders from customers who might not be able to pay.

In order to mitigate this risk, MCL should put the following controls into place:

- MCL should have a policy of obtaining credit checks on all new customers from a reputable credit agency, such as Dun and Bradstreet.

- MCL should ensure that it sets limited credit terms for new customers, such as a low credit limit or a short credit period, although these terms could be reviewed once the relationship is established.

- A senior member of staff should sign off on all new customers before orders are accepted. This member of staff should check that appropriate credit references have been obtained and that the credit terms extended are reasonable.

- New customer accounts should be reviewed and followed up for prompt payment until a relationship is established.

MCL is in a strong position to set limited credit terms to new customers as it is the sole source of a product. Other companies might have to balance the risk of customers not paying with the need to encourage new customers to use them rather than their competitors. In this case, companies would concentrate on the credit checks and the authorisation by senior staff.

## 1.3 Tests of controls

The tests that the assurance providers carry out over such controls will obviously also depend on the exact nature of the control and the business. However, again, some general ideas can be generated.

- **Check** that **references** are being **obtained** for **all new customers**

- **Check** that all **new accounts** on the receivables ledger have been **authorised** by senior staff

- **Check** that **orders** are only **accepted** from customers who are **within** their **credit terms** and **credit limits**

- **Check** that **customer orders** are being **matched** with **production orders** and **despatch notes**

Worked example: Tests of controls over ordering

The audit senior at MCL has been asked to test controls over sales, particularly with reference to new customers. There are three controls in particular that he should check – obtaining credit references, setting credit terms and authorisation.

The senior would select a sample of new customers by comparing the current year receivables ledger with the prior year one. He would then ask a member of the sales team for the customer files. These files should contain the details of the credit check, terms and evidence that the customer has been authorised by the sales director and when.

Interactive question 1: Ordering                    [Difficulty level: Exam standard]

MC plc is a company that has had a number of inquiries from potential new customers in recent months. The sales director is excited at this potential sales growth, but the financial controller is concerned that the company could be exposed to the risk of increased bad debts.

Which **two** of the following internal controls will mitigate the risk of bad debts arising from new customers?

| | Obtaining a credit reference for new customers |
| | Matching of customer orders with **despatch** notes |
| | Quoting the correct prices to customers making orders |
| | Authorisation of new customers by a senior staff member |
| | Authorisation for changes in customer data |

See **Answer** at the end of this chapter.

# 2 Despatch and invoicing

**Section overview**

- A key risk is despatching goods to a customer but not invoicing for them.
- A control to mitigate that risk is matching despatch notes to invoices.

## 2.1 Risks and control objectives

When considering despatch and invoicing, a company might recognise all or some of the following risks:

- Goods may be despatched but not recorded so they are lost to the business
- Goods may be despatched but not invoiced for
- Invoices may be raised in error with resulting customer dissatisfaction
- Invoices may be wrongly cancelled by credit notes resulting in loss to the business

These risks lead to the following control objectives:

- All **despatches** of goods are **recorded**
- All **goods and services** sold are **correctly invoiced**
- All **invoices** raised **relate to goods and services supplied** by the business
- **Credit notes** are only given for **valid reasons**

## 2.2 Controls

The following are types of controls which could be put in place to fulfil the above objectives.

- Authorisation of **despatch** of goods

    - Despatch only on sales order
    - Despatch only to authorised customers
    - Special authorisation of despatches of goods free of charge or on special terms

- Examination of goods outwards as to quantity, quality and condition

- Recording of all goods outwards on a despatch note

- Agreement of despatch notes to customer orders and invoices

- Pre-numbering of despatch notes and regular checks on sequence

- Condition of returns checked

- Recording of goods returned on goods returned notes

- Signature of despatch notes by customers

- Preparation of invoices and credit notes

    - Authorisation of selling prices/use of price lists
    - Authorisation of credit notes
    - Checks on prices, quantities, extensions and totals on invoices and credit notes
    - Sequential numbering of blank invoices/credit notes and regular sequence checks

- Inventory records updated

- Matching of sales invoices with despatch notes and sales orders

- Regular review for despatch notes not matched by invoices

### Worked example: Controls over despatch

MCL has experienced a number of requests for credit notes recently as a result of the alleged poor condition of goods when they arrive with customers.

In order to ensure that credits are not being wrongly issued, MCL needs to ensure that it has sufficient control over the despatch of its goods and their receipt by the customer.

MCL should ensure that goods are checked before they leave MCL's premises to ensure that the goods are packaged appropriately and are not damaged when they leave. Evidence of this check could be made by the checker signing a despatch note to accompany the goods to the customer. MCL could try to ensure that goods are not left with the customer until a similar quality check has been carried out by a member of the customer's staff, and similarly evidenced on the despatch note, a copy of which can be left with the customer.

These steps would mean that MCL had more control over the quality of the goods that arrived at the customer and more knowledge about the condition of the goods and whether a credit note was required. If the customer has signed that the condition appeared fine when the goods arrived, customers will have to give further justification to obtain a credit.

## 2.3 Tests of controls

The following tests could be used in relation to the controls noted above.

- Verify details of trade sales or goods despatch notes with sales invoices checking

    - Quantities
    - Prices charged with official price lists
    - Trade discounts have been properly dealt with
    - Calculations and additions
    - Entries in sales day book are correctly analysed
    - VAT, where chargeable, has been properly dealt with
    - Postings to receivables ledger

- Verify details of trade sales with entries in inventory records

- Verify non-routine sales (scrap, non-current assets etc) with:

    - Appropriate supporting evidence
    - Approval by authorised officials
    - Entries in plant register

- Verify credit notes with:

    - Correspondence or other supporting evidence
    - Approval by authorised officials
    - Entries in inventory records

- Entries in goods returned records
- Calculations and additions
- Entries in day book, checking these are correctly analysed
- Postings to receivables ledger

- Test numerical sequence of despatch notes and enquire into missing numbers

- Test numerical sequence of invoices and credit notes, enquire into missing numbers and inspect copies of those cancelled

- Test numerical sequence of order forms and enquire into missing numbers

- Check that despatches of goods free of charge or on special terms have been authorised by management

## Worked example: Tests of controls over invoicing

MCL have recently been the subject of an HMRC enquiry into errors in their invoicing impacting on VAT declared. MCL have asked an assurance provider to review the controls in place over invoicing to see what can be improved in the system.

As a minimum, the assurance providers would expect to see the following controls over invoice preparation:

- Evidence that the sales invoice has been agreed to the goods despatch note to confirm quantities of goods sold

- Evidence that the sales invoice has been agreed to the order to confirm the price of the goods sold

- Evidence that the calculations on the invoice, including the VAT calculation, have been checked

In a large computerised function, these checks are likely to be carried out by a computer program, so could be checked by processing 'dummy' invoices through the system, some of which contain errors, to ensure that the appropriate checks are being made.

In a less complex system, these checks might be made manually by a member of staff. In this case, the checks might be evidenced by signature or initials by that staff member. This is sometimes done by using a pre-printed stamp on the copy of the invoice, such as the following:

| Quantity agreed to despatch note? | NM |
|---|---|
| Price agreed to price list? | NM |
| Calculations checked? | NM |

## Interactive question 2: Despatch and invoicing     [Difficulty level: Exam standard]

Which **three** of the following controls will help to mitigate the risk of goods being despatched but not invoiced?

☐ Pre-numbering of goods despatched notes and regular checks on sequence
☐ Pre-numbering of invoices and regular checks on sequence
☐ Matching of goods despatched notes with orders and invoices
☐ Regular review of despatch notes not matched with invoices

See **Answer** at the end of this chapter.

# 3 Recording

**Section overview**

- A key risk is failure to record sales so that payment is not prompted.
- Controls include various methods of prompting payment, such as statements sent out to customers.

## 3.1 Risks and control objectives

The following risks arise at this stage:

- Invoiced sales might not be properly recorded
- Credit notes might not be properly recorded
- Sales might be recorded in the wrong customer accounts
- Debts might be included on the receivables ledger that are not collectable

These risks lead to the following objectives:

- All sales that have been **invoiced** are **recorded** in the nominal and receivables ledgers
- All **credit notes** that have been **issued** are **recorded** in the nominal and receivables ledgers
- All **entries** in the receivables ledger are **made** to the **correct** receivables ledger **accounts**
- **Cut-off** is applied correctly to the receivables ledger
- Potential **bad debts** are **identified**

## 3.2 Controls

The following controls might be used to fulfil the objectives outlined above:

- **Segregation of duties:** recording sales, maintaining customer accounts and preparing statements
- **Recording** of **sales invoices** sequence and **control** over **spoilt invoices**
- **Matching** of **cash receipts** with **invoices**
- **Retention** of **customer remittance advices**
- **Separate recording** of **sales returns, price adjustments** etc
- **Cut-off procedures** to ensure goods despatched and not invoiced (or *vice versa*) are properly dealt with in the correct period
- Regular **preparation** of **trade receivables statements**
- **Checking** of **trade receivables statements**
- **Safeguarding** of **trade receivables statements** so that they cannot be altered before despatch
- **Review** and **follow-up** of **overdue accounts**
- **Authorisation** of **writing off** for **bad debts**
- **Reconciliation** of **receivables ledger control account**
- **Analytical review** for receivables ledger and profit margins

Worked example: Controls over recording of sales

In the course of the audit of Perkins Limited, a small family owned company, it becomes clear from other testing that invoices which do not appear in the receivables ledger have been paid by customers. This has been caused by a failure in controls over recording of invoices and payments.

Further inquiry has revealed that since the previous receivables ledger clerk left half-way through the accounting year, customers have not been sent statements of their account on a monthly basis as the new clerk has not had time. She has also not matched receipts with particular invoices, but has simply allocated receipts to the customer accounts on the ledger when they have arrived. Some customers are in credit at the end of the year as a result of the problems arising.

Matching receipts with specific invoices on the ledger would have highlighted immediately if there were invoices missing from the ledger. Had statements been sent it is possible that an honest customer might have queried why invoices he had been sent had not been included on the statement.

(It emerges that a batch of invoices raised on the receivables ledger clerk's last day were not posted to the ledger but were instead lost in a pile of papers which the new receivables ledger clerk had put in a drawer.)

## 3.3 Tests of controls

The following tests of control might be appropriate.

**Sales day book**

- **Check entries** with **invoices** and **credit notes** respectively
- **Check additions** and **cross casts**
- **Check postings** to **receivables ledger control account**
- **Check postings** to **receivables ledger**

**Receivables ledger**

- **Check** entries in a **sample of accounts** to sales day book

- **Check additions** and **balances** carried down

- **Note** and **enquire** into **contra entries**

- Check that **control accounts** have been **regularly reconciled** to total of receivables ledger balances

- **Scrutinise accounts** to see if credit limits have been observed

- Check that **trade receivables statements** are **prepared** and **sent out regularly**

- Check that **overdue accounts** have been **followed up**

- Check that **all bad debts written off** have been **authorised** by management

### Worked example: Tests of controls over recording of sales

The audit senior wants to ensure that the above error in invoice recording at Perkins Ltd was isolated. He selects a sample of invoices from each month following the incident and traces them through the receivables ledger. The error appears to be isolated.

However, the fact that the error was not picked up indicates that other controls, such as reconciliations between the receivables ledger and receivables ledger control account have not been carried out. As such, it is unlikely that reliance can be placed on the sales recording system, and alternative substantive procedures should be carried out.

**Interactive question 3: Recording of sales**  [Difficulty level: Exam standard]

The auditor at Icy Limited, a wholesaler of frozen goods, has discovered that the receivables ledger clerk has not matched receipts with invoices when processing receipts onto the ledger.

Which **two** of the following are potential risks arising from this failure?

☐ The clerk could be siphoning off individual receipts and defrauding the company
☐ Old outstanding invoices could be left unpaid
☐ Sales might be recorded in the wrong supplier's accounts
☐ Sales may not be recorded properly in the sales account

See **Answer** at the end of this chapter.

# 4 Cash collection

**Section overview**

• A risk is that cash is misappropriated before recording and/or banking.
• Segregation of duties is very important.

## 4.1 Risks and control objectives

The key risks are that money might be received at the business premises but not be recorded or banked (generally due to fraud but also by simply losing cheques received). This leads to two key objectives:

• All monies received are recorded
• All monies received are banked

## 4.2 Controls

As there is a particular risk of fraud in relation to cash receipts, segregation of duties (the involvement of various people in the process) is particularly important. The following controls may be relevant:

| Controls: Cash at bank and in hand – receipts |
| --- |

**Segregation of duties** between the various functions listed below is particularly important.

| Recording of receipts received by post | • **Safeguards** to **prevent interception of mail** between receipt and opening<br>• Appointment of **responsible person** to supervise mail<br>• **Protection** of **cash and cheques** (restrictive crossing)<br>• **Amounts received listed** when post opened<br>• **Post stamped** with date of receipt |
| --- | --- |
| Recording of cash sales and collections | • **Restrictions** on **receipt of cash** (by cashiers only, or by sales representatives)<br><br>• **Evidencing** of receipt of cash<br><br>  – Serially numbered receipt forms<br>  – Cash registers incorporating sealed till rolls<br><br>• **Emptying** of cash offices and registers<br><br>• **Agreement of cash collections with till rolls**<br><br>• **Agreement of cash collections with bankings and** cash and sales **records**<br><br>• **Investigation** of cash shortages and surpluses |

| | |
|---|---|
| **General controls over recording** | • Prompt maintenance of records (cash book, ledger accounts) |
| | • Limitation of duties of receiving cashiers |
| | • Ensuring that the person who records cash takes holidays (so they do not have absolute control over cash recording) and controls are continued in their absence |
| | • Giving and recording of receipts |
| |     – Retained copies<br>    – Serially numbered receipts books<br>    – Custody of receipt books<br>    – Comparisons with cash records and bank paying in slips |
| **Banking** | • **Daily bankings** |
| | • **Make-up** and **comparison** of **paying-in** slips against initial receipt records and cash book |
| | • **Banking** of receipts **intact**/control of payments |
| **Safeguarding of cash and bank accounts** | • **Restrictions** on **opening new bank accounts** |
| | • **Limitations** on **cash floats** held |
| | • **Restrictions** on **payments** out of **cash received** |
| | • **Restrictions** on **access** to cash registers and offices |
| | • **Independent checks** on cash floats |
| | • **Surprise cash counts** |
| | • **Custody** of **cash** outside **office hours** |
| | • **Custody** over **supply** and issue of cheques |
| | • **Preparation** of **cheques** restricted |
| | • **Safeguards** over **mechanically signed cheques**/cheques carrying printed signatures |
| | • **Restrictions** on issue of **blank** or **bearer** cheques |
| | • **Safeguarding** of **IOUs**, cash in transit |
| | • **Insurance arrangements** |
| | • **Bank reconciliations** |
| |     – Issue of bank statements<br>    – Frequency of reconciliations by independent person<br>    – Reconciliation procedures<br>    – Treatment of longstanding unpresented cheques<br>    – Sequence of cheque numbers<br>    – Comparison with cash books |

## Worked example: Controls over cash receipts

Hampton Hotels plc (HH) owns a number of exclusive hotels in England and Wales. The majority of sales are cash sales made on the day guests check out of the hotel. HH take customer credit card details on arrival and reserve the right to extract full payment in the event of non-payment. Only cashiers are allowed to process cash transactions. Till receipts are maintained and reconciled to daily takings (cash and credit card slips) by the cashier in the presence of a member of staff who is not a cashier. This reduces the chance that cash will be misappropriated. Daily takings are entered in the cashbook after the daily reconciliation. Credit card slips are reconciled to statements from the card companies on a monthly basis. Cash transactions are sufficiently slight on a hotel basis to necessitate banking only on a weekly basis. Cash is kept in locked tills in the reception area. The financial controller reconciles the bank statements for each hotel on a monthly basis.

## 4.3 Tests of controls

The following tests of control may be used:

| Area | Tests of control |
|---|---|
| Receipts received by post | • **Observe procedures** for **post opening** are being followed<br>• **Observe** that **cheques** received by post are immediately **crossed** in the company's favour<br>• For items entered in the rough cash book (or other record of cash, cheques etc received by post), **trace entries** to:<br> – **Cash book**<br> – **Paying-in book**<br> – **Counterfoil** or carbon copy receipts<br>• **Verify amounts entered** as **received** with remittance advices or other supporting evidence |
| Cash sales, branch takings | • For a sample of cash sales summaries/branch summaries from different locations:<br> – **Verify with till rolls** or copy cash sale notes<br> – **Check to paying-in slip** date-stamped and initialled by the bank<br> – **Verify that takings** are banked intact daily<br> – **Vouch expenditure** out of takings |
| Collections | • For a sample of items from the original collection records:<br> – **Trace amounts** to **cash book** via collectors' cash sheets or other collection records<br> – **Check entries** on **cash sheets** or collection records with collectors' receipt books<br> – **Verify** that **goods delivered** to travellers/salesmen have been regularly **reconciled** with sales and inventories in hand<br> – **Check numerical sequence** of collection records |
| Cash receipts cash book | • For cash receipts for several days throughout the period:<br> – **Check to entries in rough cash book**, receipts, branch returns or other records<br> – **Check to paying-in slips** obtained direct from the bank (rather than looking only at client copy of the slip which might have been tampered with), observing that there is no delay in banking monies received<br> – **Check additions** of **paying-in slips**<br> – **Check additions** of **cash book**<br> – **Check postings** to the **receivables ledger**<br> – **Check postings** to the **general ledger**, including control accounts<br>• **Scrutinise the cash book** and **investigate items** of a **special** or **unusual nature** |

## Worked example: Tests of controls over cash receipts

You are a member of the assurance team at Happy Manufacturers Ltd (HM). All of their sales are made on credit terms and they receive cheques daily in the post. In order to ensure that the security over cheques is adequate, you will be observing the post opening, cheque listing and storing procedures. As a minimum, you would expect to see:

- Two people present at post opening (to prevent misappropriation of cheques)

- Cheques received being listed (to prevent misappropriation of cheques after initial receipt but before cheques are passed to accounts department)

- Cheques being put into a safe until banking (to prevent misappropriation of cheques before they are banked – for example, these cheques could be stolen and later cheques allocated to the relevant invoices in the customer account to hide the fraud)

## Interactive question 4: Cash receipts                    [Difficulty level: Exam standard]

An effective system of internal control requires segregation of basic functions. Which **three** of the following functions should ideally be segregated?

| | |
|---|---|
| ☐ Authorisation of orders | ☐ Recording cash receipts on receivables ledger |
| ☐ Invoicing | ☐ Credit control |
| ☐ Reconciliation of receivables ledger with receivables ledger control account | |

See **Answer** at the end of this chapter.

# 5 · Deficiencies

### Section overview

- Identifying the deficiencies of a system is a key exam technique.

Once you can identify control risks in a scenario and are aware of the types of control that will mitigate those risks, you should also be able to identify weaknesses in systems. This is an important area in practice, as auditors must be able to determine whether the control system is capable of operating well and therefore is capable of being relied on by them, and it is also an important exam technique.

## Interactive question 5: Sales system deficiencies        [Difficulty level: Exam standard]

The following describes the sales system in operation at Jinbob Company. For each process indicate whether the process indicates a strength or a deficiency of the system.

| | | |
|---|---|---|
| Written orders are received in the sales office. Orders are processed into the sales system with no further action being taken. | ☐ Strength | ☐ Deficiency |
| The order generates a production note which is forwarded to the production department on the basis of which they fulfil the order. Completed goods are despatched with a delivery note, a copy of which is matched with the production note and sent to the invoicing department. | ☐ Strength | ☐ Deficiency |
| Unfulfilled production notes are placed in a pending file which is reviewed weekly and completed as soon as possible. | ☐ Strength | ☐ Deficiency |

See **Answer** at the end of this chapter.

## Summary

Controls in the sales system are focused on the following key points of the cycle

| Ordering | Despatch & invoicing | Recording | Cash receipts |
|---|---|---|---|
| **Risks:**<br>– Customers cannot pay<br>– Orders may not be fulfilled | **Risks:**<br>– Goods are despatched but not invoiced<br>– Invoices/credits raised in error | **Risks:**<br>– Invoices are not recorded<br>– Invoices are processed to wrong account | **Risks:**<br>– Money received but not recorded<br>– Money received but not banked |

## Self-test

Answer the following questions.

1    For each of the following, state whether it is an objective relating to ordering, despatch and invoicing or recording:

| | | Ordering | Despatch/invoice | Recording |
|---|---|---|---|---|
| (a) | All sales that have been invoiced have been put in the general ledger | ☐ | ☐ | ☐ |
| (b) | Orders are fulfilled | ☐ | ☐ | ☐ |
| (c) | Cut-off is correct | ☐ | ☐ | ☐ |
| (d) | Goods are only supplied to good credit risks | ☐ | ☐ | ☐ |
| (e) | Goods are correctly invoiced | ☐ | ☐ | ☐ |
| (f) | Customers are encouraged to pay promptly | ☐ | ☐ | ☐ |

2    List **five** controls relating to the ordering and granting of credit process.

1    ................................................................
2    ................................................................
3    ................................................................
4    ................................................................
5    ................................................................

Now, go back to the Learning Objectives in the Introduction. If you are satisfied you have achieved these objectives, please tick them off.

# Answers to Interactive questions

### Answer to Interactive question 1

(1) Obtaining a credit reference for new customers
(2) Authorisation of new customers by a senior staff member

### Answer to Interactive question 2

Pre-numbering of invoices helps to ensure that invoices are not sent out and not recorded, but does not necessarily ensure that all goods despatched are invoiced. The other controls all contribute to ensuring that all despatched goods are invoiced.

### Answer to Interactive question 3

The clerk could be siphoning off individual receipts and defrauding the company. (This is a fraud called 'teeming and lading' which can be successful if the outstanding balance on the account does not look unusual and the actions of the receivables ledger clerk are not checked.)

Old outstanding invoices could be left unpaid. This is because if the invoices are not matched then it is not clear which invoices are outstanding, and yet the overall balance outstanding looks reasonable, thus older invoices, which should be being chased up by the company may not be paid and ultimately may be forgotten about.

### Answer to Interactive question 4

Authorisation of orders, invoicing and posting of receipts. If one person was in charge of all these functions, that person would have control over the whole process of making an order and fulfilling it, so that it could make fictitious orders and not invoice for them or invoice for goods but transfer other people's payments to make it look as though the fictitious sale had been paid for.

### Answer to Interactive question 5

Deficiency (because the customer's credit status is not checked before the order is processed)

Strength (because the invoices are generated from goods despatched information)

Strength (because production is kept up to date by weekly review of outstanding orders)

1

| | | Ordering | Despatch/invoice | Recording |
|---|---|---|---|---|
| (a) | All sales that have been invoiced have been put in the general ledger | ☐ Ordering | ☐ Despatch/invoice | ✓ Recording |
| (b) | Orders are fulfilled | ✓ Ordering | ☐ Despatch/invoice | ☐ Recording |
| (c) | Cut-off is correct | ☐ Ordering | ☐ Despatch/invoice | ✓ Recording |
| (d) | Goods are only supplied to good credit risks | ✓ Ordering | ☐ Despatch/invoice | ☐ Recording |
| (e) | Goods are correctly invoiced | ☐ Ordering | ✓ Despatch/invoice | ☐ Recording |
| (f) | Customers are encouraged to pay promptly | ✓ Ordering | ☐ Despatch/invoice | ☐ Recording |

2 Any of:

- **Segregation** of duties; credit control, invoicing and inventory despatch

- Authorisation of credit terms to customers

    - References/credit checks obtained
    - Authorisation by senior staff
    - Regular review

- Authorisation for changes in other customer data

    - Change of address supported by letterhead
    - Deletion requests supported by evidence of balances cleared/customer in liquidation

- **Orders** only **accepted** from **customers** who have no credit problems

- **Sequential numbering** of blank pre-printed order documents

- **Correct prices quoted** to **customers**

- **Matching** of **customer orders** with production orders and despatch notes and querying of orders not matched

- Dealing with customer queries

# CHAPTER 7

# Purchases system

## Learning objectives

- Identify risks in a purchases system

- Identify relevant controls to mitigate risk

- Identify tests of those controls

- Recognise weaknesses in a purchases system

Specific syllabus references for this chapter are: 2f, g, h, 3f.

## Syllabus links

You will have learnt about the various books of record in the purchases system in Accounting.

## Examination context

As purchases is another important practical area, your assessment might well include scenario internal controls questions in this area. The sample paper contained one such scenario question looking at consequences of given weaknesses in a purchases system.

In the assessment, candidates may be required to:

- Show how specific internal controls in a purchases system mitigate risk and state their limitations
- Identify internal controls for an organisation in a given scenario
- Identify internal control strengths and weaknesses in a given scenario
- Determine the extent to which tests of controls should be used in a given set of circumstances

# 1 Ordering

**Section overview**

- Key risks are that purchases might be made for personal use or not made on the most advantageous terms.

- Authorisation is therefore an important control.

## 1.1 Risks and control objectives

When considering purchase orders, a company might recognise one or both of the following risks:

- Unauthorised purchases may be made for personal use
- Goods and services might not be obtained on the most advantageous terms

The controls put into place will be designed to mitigate these risks. Hence the objectives of the controls will be to prevent these risks from occurring. Here are the control objectives which might arise from the risks noted above:

- All **orders for goods and services** are properly **authorised** and duly processed. All orders are for **goods and services** actually **required by** the company

- Orders are only made with **authorised suppliers**

- Orders are made at **competitive prices**

## 1.2 Controls

Once the company has identified the risks which exist in the purchases system, it will try and create controls which mitigate those risks (that is, meet the control objectives outlined above). What controls will be put into place depend on the nature of the company and the specific risks associated with the way it operates, but the following controls can be used as examples of how the above risks can be mitigated.

- **Segregation** of duties; requisition and ordering

- **Central policy** for choice of suppliers

- Evidence required of **requirements** for purchase before purchase authorised (pre-set re-order quantities and re-order levels)

- **Order forms** prepared only when a **pre-numbered purchase requisition** has been **received**

- **Authorisation** of order forms

- **Pre-numbered order forms**

- **Safeguarding** of **blank order forms**

- **Review** for outstanding **orders**

- **Monitoring** of **supplier terms** and taking advantage of favourable conditions (bulk order and prompt payment discounts)

### Worked example: Controls over ordering

Truman Limited buys 'Drox' frequently. Drox is highly marketable and easily portable and the company has a history of theft of inventories of Drox. In order to make sure that only Drox required for business use is purchased in the first place, the directors have decided to put the following controls into operation:

- Simon Radinski, the stores manager, will be in charge of purchase requisitions, which will be made when inventories of Drox have fallen to a pre-set level.

- Orders will only be raised in respect of purchase requisitions made by Simon Radinski, except in periods of Simon's absence, when requisitions may be made by his deputy Cathy Lewis.

- Orders will be authorised by Linda Fairburn, the purchases director.

- Random, occasional spot checks will be carried out by Linda Fairburn on the level of Drox when the requisition is raised.

- Purchase orders will be kept in a locked office in the purchase department.

In addition, in order to control inventories, Drox will only be kept in a locked cupboard in the warehouse.

## 1.3 Tests of controls

The tests that the assurance providers carry out over such controls will obviously also depend on the exact nature of the control and the business. However, again, some general ideas can be generated.

- Review list of suppliers and check a sample to orders made
- Check sequence of pre-numbered order forms
- Check orders are supported by a purchase requisition
- Review security arrangements over blank orders

### Worked example: Tests of controls over orders

The directors of Truman Limited have requested that the auditors review that the new controls over the purchase of Drox are operating effectively. The audit senior has therefore drafted the following plan:

- Spot check on security arrangements over purchase orders

- Request Linda Fairburn notifies the audit team of requisitions for Drox during the audit and attend spot check on re-order level

- Observation of premises for evidence of Drox being stored elsewhere than the locked cupboard

- Review of sample of orders for Drox to ensure that purchase requisition exists and orders were made only by Simon Radinski and were authorised by Linda Fairburn

- If sampled requisitions were made by Cathy Lewis, check absence records for Simon Radinski.

### Interactive question 1: Ordering                    [Difficulty level: Exam standard]

The directors of Lyton Limited (LL) have just uncovered a fraud being perpetrated by the stores manager. He was in charge of ordering, had raised a number of false orders to non-existent suppliers, raised goods received notes in respect of non-existent deliveries and forwarded an invoice to the accounts department, which was then paid.

Which **two** of the following controls could have prevented this fraud?

☐ Approved list of suppliers

☐ Check of goods inward by person other than orderer

☐ Pre-numbered order forms

☐ Blank order forms locked in a safe

See **Answer** at the end of this chapter.

# 2 Goods inward and recording of invoices

## Section overview

- Risks are of accepting goods not ordered or for accepting invoices for poor quality goods.
- Controls include matching goods received with orders.

## 2.1 Risks and control objectives

When considering goods inward and recording of invoices, a company might recognise all or some of the following risks:

- Goods may be misappropriated for private use
- Goods may be accepted that have not been ordered
- Invoices may not be recorded resulting in non-payment
- The company may not take advantage of the full period of credit extended
- The company may not record credit notes resulting in paying invoices unnecessarily

These risks lead to the following control objectives:

- All goods and services received are used for the **company's purposes,** and not private purposes
- Goods and services are **only accepted if** they have been **ordered,** and the **order** has been **authorised**
- All **goods** and **services received** are accurately **recorded**
- **Liabilities** are **recognised** for all **goods and services** that have been **received**
- All **credits** to which the company is entitled are **claimed** and **received**
- **Receipt** of **goods** and **services** is **necessary** for a **liability to be recorded**
- All **credit notes** that are received are **recorded** in the nominal and payables ledgers
- All **entries** in the **payables ledger** are **made** to the **correct payables ledger accounts**
- **Cut-off** is **applied correctly** to the **payables ledger**

## 2.2 Controls

The following are types of controls which could be put in place to fulfil the above objectives.

- **Examination** of goods inwards
  - Quality
  - Quantity
  - Condition
- **Recording arrival** and **acceptance** of goods (pre-numbered goods received notes)
- **Comparison** of **goods received notes** with **purchase orders**
- **Referencing** of supplier invoices; numerical sequence and supplier reference
- **Checking** of **suppliers' invoices**
  - Prices, quantities, accuracy of calculation
  - Comparison with order and goods received note
- **Recording return of goods** (pre-numbered goods returned notes)
- Procedures for **obtaining credit notes** from suppliers
- **Segregation** of **duties:** accounting and checking functions
- Prompt **recording of purchases** and **purchase returns** in day books and ledgers

- Regular maintenance of **payables ledger**

- Comparison of **monthly statements** of account balance from suppliers with **payables ledger balances**

- Review of **classification** of expenditure

- Reconciliation of **payables ledger** control account to total of **payables ledger** balances

- Create a **cut-off** accrual of goods received notes not matched by invoices at year-end

### Worked example: Controls over goods inward

The production department at Manufacturing Company Limited (MCL) works on a just-in-time basis. Orders for necessary materials are dispatched by computer according to pre-set re-order levels. Deliveries are made within 12 hours by the suppliers, who invoice electronically when goods are dispatched. Items are put into production within hours of arriving at MCL's premises.

In this example, it is crucial that controls over goods inward operate effectively. In the first case, it is necessary that the quality of goods being put into production immediately are of appropriate quality or production will be held up. Therefore it is vital that goods inward are checked for quality and quantity on arrival at MCL's premises.

It is also important that goods inwards are recorded, as with the goods being used so quickly it would be more difficult to verify purchase invoices to goods being held in a warehouse.

Therefore MCL have a pre-printed, numbered goods received note (GRN) which contains a number of checks in respect of quality and quantity and on which the warehouse staff note the relevant order number, the time of delivery, and the quantity of goods delivered. A copy of this GRN is forwarded to the accounts department to be matched with the supplier's electronic invoice.

### Worked example: Controls over purchase recording

Stibbe Limited have recently discovered that they have been paying invoices that had been credited because the goods had been returned by the production quality controller due to poor quality.

In order to prevent this occurring, Stibbe Limited should have put the following controls in place:

- Raising purchase return notes
- Copy purchase return notes sent to accounts department by production department
- Review of credit notes before payment run authorised
- Regular comparison of supplier statements with payables ledger accounts

## 2.3 Tests of controls

The following tests could be used in relation to the controls noted above.

- Check invoices for goods are:

    - Supported by goods received notes

    - Entered in inventory records

    - Priced correctly by checking to quotations, price lists to see the price is in order

    - Properly referenced with a number and supplier code

    - Correctly coded by type of expenditure

    - Trace entry in record of goods returned etc and see credit note duly received from the supplier, for invoices not passed due to defects or discrepancy

- For invoices of all types:

  - Check calculations and additions
  - Check entries in purchase day book and verify that they are correctly analysed
  - Check posting to **payables ledger**

- For credit notes:

  - Verify the correctness of credit received with correspondence
  - Check entries in inventory records
  - Check entries in record of returns
  - Check entries in purchase day book and verify that they are correctly analysed
  - Check posting to **payables ledger**

- Check for returns that credit notes are duly received from the suppliers

- Test numerical sequence and enquire into missing numbers of:

  - Purchase requisitions
  - Goods received notes
  - Suppliers' invoices
  - Purchase orders
  - Goods returned notes

- Obtain explanations for items which have been outstanding for a long time:

  - Unmatched purchase requisitions
  - Unmatched purchase orders
  - Unmatched goods received notes
  - Unrecorded invoices

- Verify that invoices and credit notes recorded in the purchase day book are:

  - Initialled for prices, calculations and extensions
  - Cross-referenced to purchase orders, goods received notes etc
  - Authorised for payment

- Check additions

- Check postings to nominal ledger accounts and control account

- Check postings of entries to payables ledger

Payables ledger

- For a sample of accounts recorded in the payables ledger:

  - Test check entries back into books of prime entry
  - Test check additions and carried forward balances
  - Note and enquire into all contra entries

- Confirm control account reconciliation has been regularly carried out during the year

- Examine control account for unusual entries

## Worked example: Tests of controls over goods inward and invoices

The auditor is verifying the controls over goods inward at MCL. He selects a sample of goods received notes and checks that they are in sequence, enquiring into any missing numbers (spoilt copies should be retained) and seeking evidence (initials of relevant staff) that the quality checks have been carried out. These goods received notes would then be checked to purchase invoices to ensure that all invoices had an associated goods received note and also to purchase orders to ensure that the goods were ordered properly.

## Interactive question 2: Goods inward and invoices     [Difficulty level: Exam standard]

Weezy plc is a company that has a large number of deliveries daily.

Which **one** of the following internal controls is most likely to prevent Weezy plc paying for goods that have not been received?

☐   Locked stores

☐   Matching of purchase invoices with goods received notes

☐   Authorisation of invoice payment

☐   Safeguarding of blank order documents

See **Answer** at the end of this chapter.

## Interactive question 3: Purchase recording     [Difficulty level: Exam standard]

Rhonda posts the invoices to the payables ledger.

Which **two** of the following would help prevent suppliers from being overpaid?

☐   Posting invoices to the receivables ledger

☐   Reconciliation of the payables ledger to the control account

☐   Authorisation of payments

☐   Bank reconciliations

See **Answer** at the end of this chapter.

# 3 Payment

### Section overview

- Payments might be made to the wrong person.
- Payments should be authorised.

## 3.1 Risks and control objectives

The following risks arise at this stage of proceedings:

- False invoices are paid in error
- Invoices are paid too soon
- Payment is not correctly recorded
- Credits are not correctly recorded
- Payments are not recorded in the right period

The key risk is that money might be paid out by the business inappropriately. The following objectives arise out of the risks:

- All **expenditure** is for goods that are **received**
- All **expenditure** is **authorised**
- All **expenditure** that is made is **recorded** correctly in the nominal and payables ledgers
- **Payments** are **not made twice** for the same liability

ICAEW

## 3.2 Controls

The arrangements for controlling payments will depend to a great extent on the nature of business transacted, the volume of payments involved and the size of the company.

| | |
|---|---|
| **Cheque and cash payments generally** | The cashier should generally not be concerned with keeping or writing-up books of account other than those recording payments, nor should he have access to, or be responsible for the custody of, securities or title deeds belonging to the company.<br><br>The person responsible for preparing cheques should not himself be a cheque signatory. Cheque signatories in turn should not be responsible for recording payments. |
| **Cheque and bank transfer payments** | • **Cheque and bank transfer requisitions**<br>  – Appropriate supporting documentation (for example, invoices)<br>  – Approval by appropriate staff<br>  – Presentation to cheque signatories (in case of cheques)<br>  – Instigation of bank transfer by appropriate staff<br><br>• **Authority** to sign cheques<br>  – Signatories should not also approve cheque requisitions<br>  – Limitations on authority to specific amounts<br>  – Number of signatories<br>  – Prohibitions over signing of blank cheques<br><br>• **Prompt dispatch** of signed **cheques**<br><br>• **Obtaining** of paid **cheques** from **banks**<br><br>• Payments **recorded promptly** in **cash book** and **nominal** and **payables ledgers** |
| **Cash payments** | • **Authorisation** of **expenditure**<br>• **Cancellation** of **vouchers** to ensure they cannot be paid twice<br>• **Limits** on **payments**<br>• **Rules** on **cash advances** to employees, IOUs and cheque cashing |

### Worked example: Controls over cash payments

Build Co has a large number of suppliers and it takes deliveries most days. Deliveries are noted on goods received notes which are matched with invoices when they arrive. Invoices are entered to the payables ledger system, which is programmed with the credit terms given by each supplier and produces a payment listing each week when the computer prints all the necessary cheques.

Linda, the payments clerk, takes the cheques to the financial controller for authorisation and signature.

ICAEW

## 3.3 Tests of controls

The following controls may be used:

| | |
|---|---|
| **Payments cash book (authorisation)** | • For a sample of payments:<br><br>– Compare with paid cheques to ensure payee agrees<br><br>– Check that cheques are signed by the persons authorised to do so within their authority limits<br><br>– Check that bank transfer was authorised and initiated by appropriate person<br><br>– Check to suppliers' invoices for goods and services. Verify that supporting documents are signed as having been checked and passed for payment and have been stamped 'paid'<br><br>– Check to suppliers' statements<br><br>– Check to other documentary evidence, as appropriate (agreements, authorised expense vouchers, petty cash books etc) |
| **Payments cash book (recording)** | • For a sample of weeks:<br><br>– Check the sequence of cheque numbers and enquire into missing numbers<br><br>– Trace transfers to other bank accounts, petty cash books or other records, as appropriate<br><br>– Check additions, including extensions, and balances forward at the beginning and end of the months covering the periods chosen<br><br>– Check postings to the payables ledger<br><br>– Check postings to the nominal ledger, including the control accounts |

When checking that bank and cash are **secure**, assurance providers should consider the security arrangements over blank cheques. Bank reconciliations are also a very important control and assurance providers should carry out the following tests on these.

| Area | Tests of control |
|---|---|
| **Bank reconciliations** | • For a period which includes a reconciliation date reperform reconciliation (see Chapter 13)<br><br>• Verify that reconciliations have been prepared at regular intervals throughout the year<br><br>• Scrutinise reconciliations for unusual items |
| **Petty cash payments** | • For a sample of payments:<br><br>– Check to supporting vouchers<br><br>– Check whether they are properly approved<br><br>– See that vouchers have been marked and initialled by the cashier to prevent their re-use |

### Worked example: Tests of controls over cash payments

The auditors of Build Co have decided that it is important to check the computer control that ensures that suppliers' credit terms are used and payments are made on time. To do this they will use a computer assisted audit technique (CAAT). They will process a number of 'dummy' invoices from existing suppliers and check that the computer processes the payments at the correct time. CAATs will be covered in more detail in Chapter 11.

### Interactive question 4: Cash payments                      [Difficulty level: Exam standard]

Which **two** of the following control activities are most likely to reduce the risk of payments being made twice for the same liability?

☐ Stamping **'Paid'** on invoices that have been paid

☐ Prompt dispatch of cheques

☐ Authorisation of payments

☐ Checking supplier statements before payments are made

See **Answer** at the end of this chapter.

## 4 Deficiencies

### Section overview

- As outlined in Chapter 6, it is important to be able to identify the deficiencies of systems.

Try the following question.

### Interactive question 5: Deficiencies of the purchases system

[Difficulty level: Exam standard]

The auditor of Sunny plc has identified that there is no procedure to track purchase invoice due dates.

Which **one** of the following is the most likely consequence which might arise as a result of that deficiency?

☐ Prompt payment discounts may not be obtained

☐ Goods not actually received may be paid for

☐ Inferior goods may be purchased

☐ Payments may be made to fictitious suppliers

See **Answer** at the end of this chapter.

## Summary

Controls in the purchases system are focused on the following key points of the cycle

Ordering

Goods inwards and recording of invoices

Cash payments

**Risks:**
- Goods for personal use
- Goods not on most advantageous terms

**Risks:**
- Goods may be misappropriated
- Invoices may be mislaid leading to non-payment
- Invoices are paid at wrong time/amount
- Payments/credits not recorded
- Record in wrong period

**Risks:**
- Payments made inappropriately
- Blank cheques (and therefore cash) stolen

## Self-test

Answer the following questions.

1   For each of the following, state whether it is an objective relating to ordering, recording invoices or payment:

| | | Ordering | Recording invoices | Payment |
|---|---|---|---|---|
| (a) | Orders are only made to authorised suppliers | ☐ | ☐ | ☐ |
| (b) | Liabilities are recognised for all goods and services received | ☐ | ☐ | ☐ |
| (c) | Orders are made at competitive prices | ☐ | ☐ | ☐ |
| (d) | All expenditure is authorised | ☐ | ☐ | ☐ |
| (e) | Cut-off is correctly applied | ☐ | ☐ | ☐ |
| (f) | Goods and services are only accepted if there is an authorised order | ☐ | ☐ | ☐ |

2   List **four** examples of purchase documentation on which numerical sequence should be checked.

1   ........................................

2   ........................................

3   ........................................

4   ........................................

3    Why is numerical sequence on GRNs checked?

4    Give **five** examples of tests to be performed on the cash payments book.

1    .......................................

2    .......................................

3    .......................................

4    .......................................

5    .......................................

Now, go back to the Learning Objectives in the Introduction. If you are satisfied you have achieved these objectives, please tick them off.

### Answer to Interactive question 1

Approved list of suppliers.

Check of goods inward by person other than orderer.

Because the stores manager is entitled to make orders, pre-numbered order forms and safekeeping of order forms would have made no difference in this case.

### Answer to Interactive question 2

Matching of purchase invoices with goods received notes.

### Answer to Interactive question 3

Reconciliation of the payables ledger to the control account.

Authorisation of payments.

### Answer to Interactive question 4

Stamping 'Paid' on invoices that have been paid.

Authorisation of payments.

Although checking supplier statements will help, the timing differences between the statement date and payments made may mean that this method is not foolproof.

### Answer to Interactive question 5

Prompt payment discounts may not be obtained.

1

| (a) | Orders are only made to authorised suppliers | ☑ Ordering | ☐ Recording invoices | ☐ Payment |
|---|---|---|---|---|
| (b) | Liabilities are recognised for all goods and services received | ☐ Ordering | ☑ Recording invoices | ☐ Payment |
| (c) | Orders are made at competitive prices | ☑ Ordering | ☐ Recording invoices | ☐ Payment |
| (d) | All expenditure is authorised | ☐ Ordering | ☐ Recording invoices | ☑ Payment |
| (e) | Cut-off is correctly applied | ☐ Ordering | ☑ Recording invoices | ☐ Payment |
| (f) | Goods and services are only accepted if there is an authorised order | ☐ Ordering | ☑ Recording invoices | ☐ Payment |

2 Four from: (1) purchase requisitions, (2) purchase orders, (3) goods received notes, (4) goods returned notes, (5) suppliers' invoices

3 Sequence provides a control that purchases are completely recorded. Missing documents should be explained, or cancelled copies available otherwise the implication could be that goods have been received but not matched with an invoice and the liability in respect of that invoice is being omitted.

4 For a sample of payments:

- **Compare** with paid cheques to ensure payee agrees

- **Note** that **cheques** are **signed** by the **persons authorised** to do so within their authority limits

- **Check** to **suppliers' invoices** for goods and services. Verify that supporting documents are signed as having been **checked** and **passed for payment** and have been stamped 'paid'

- **Check** to **suppliers' statements**

- **Check** to **other documentary evidence,** as appropriate (agreements, authorised expense vouchers, wages/salaries records, petty cash books etc)

# CHAPTER 8

# Employee costs

# Introduction

## Learning objectives

- Identify risks in a payroll system
- Identify relevant controls to mitigate risk
- Identify tests of those controls
- Recognise weaknesses in a payroll system

Specific syllabus references for this chapter are: 2f, g, h, 3f.

## Syllabus links

You will have learnt about double entries relating to wages and salaries in Accounting.

## Examination context

As payroll is an important practical area, your assessment might well include scenario internal controls questions in this area. The sample paper contained a number of questions focused on payroll controls.

In the assessment, candidates may be required to:

- Show how specific internal controls in a payroll system mitigate risk and state their limitations
- Identify internal controls for an organisation in a given scenario
- Identify internal control strengths and weaknesses in a given scenario
- Determine the extent to which tests of controls should be used in a set of circumstances

# 1 Calculating wages and salaries

> **Section overview**
>
> - A key risk is paying employees too much.
> - A key control is authorisation (of time records or of changes to the payroll for example).

## 1.1 Risks and control objectives

When calculating wages and salaries, a company might recognise the following risks:

- The company may pay employees too much money
- The company may pay employees who have not been at work
- The company may pay employees who have left

The controls put into place will be designed to mitigate these risks. Hence the objectives of the controls will be to prevent these risks from occurring. Here are the control objectives which might arise from the risks noted above:

- **Employees** are **only paid** for **work** that they have **done**
- **Gross pay** has been **calculated correctly** and **authorised**
- Net pay has been calculated correctly

## 1.2 Controls

The following controls may be put into place to mitigate the risks noted above.

- **Staffing** and **segregation of duties**

- **Maintenance of personnel records** and regular checking of wages and salaries to details in personnel records

- **Authorisation**
    - Engagement and discharge of employees
    - Changes in pay rates
    - Overtime
    - Non-statutory deductions (for example pension contributions)
    - Advances of pay

- **Recording** of **changes** in **personnel** and **pay rates**

- **Recording** of hours worked by **timesheets, clocking** in and out arrangements

- **Review** of hours worked

- **Recording** of **advances** of **pay**

- **Holiday pay** arrangements

- **Answering queries**

- **Review** of **wages** against **budget**

### Worked example: Calculating wages

The workforce at CleanCo Limited has negotiated a pay rise through discussions between the union and management. In relation to this pay rise, management will want to ensure that they have the following controls in place to ensure that employees are not paid too much or too little for their work:

- Increases should be authorised on an individual basis by Adrian Lewis, the personnel manager, who is in charge of payroll

- Details of the pay rise should be entered into each employee's personnel file

- As the computer system calculates pay automatically, the new details must be entered into the master file by Adrian Lewis using the private password which allows him to make such changes.

## 1.3 Tests of controls

- Check that the **wages** and **salary summary** is **approved** for payment.

- Confirm that procedures are operating for **authorising changes** in **rates of pay**, overtime, and holiday pay.

- Obtain evidence that staff **only start being paid when they join the company**, and are **removed** from the payroll **when they leave the company**.

- Check that the **engagement** of **new employees** and **discharges** have been **confirmed in writing**.

- Check **calculations** of wages and salaries are being **checked**.

- For wages, check **calculation** of **gross pay** with:

  – Authorised rates of pay

  – Production records. See that production bonuses have been authorised and properly calculated

  – Clock cards, time sheets or other evidence of hours worked. Verify that overtime has been authorised

- For salaries, **verify that gross salaries and bonuses are in accordance with personnel records, contracts of employment** etc and that increases in pay have been properly authorised.

### Worked example: Tests of controls over calculating pay

The auditors at CleanCo want to check that controls over the negotiated pay rise operated properly. They have a copy of the minutes of the meeting where the pay rise was agreed, the pay rise being a 3.25% increase across the board. This minute of agreement indicates that the pay rise was authorised by the directors.

The auditors select a sample of employees and request their personnel files. They recalculate the pay rise as compared to the previous pay rate (which they agree to the previous payroll).

They then review the standing data in the payroll system for each employee sampled to ensure that the computer system contains the correct pay rate. They check that each employee was paid the correct wage in the month following the pay rise.

Lastly, (with permission) the auditors attempt to change the standing data in the computer system to ensure that unauthorised amendments cannot be made.

**Interactive question 1: Calculating pay**                    [Difficulty level: Exam standard]

The following system of time records exists at Shepherd Limited. Staff members are required to fill in a manual timesheet as they arrive, stating the time of arrival and as they leave, stating the time of departure. Staff members are then paid an hourly rate on the basis of this record.

Which **two** of the following outcomes could arise from this system?

☐ Employees may be paid at an inappropriate rate

☐ Employees may be paid for work they have not done

☐ Employees are paid for the hours they have worked

☐ Employee deductions may be inappropriate

See **Answer** at the end of this chapter.

# 2 Recording of wages and salaries and deductions

**Section overview**

* A risk is not recording wages and therefore making incorrect payments.
* The payroll should be prepared, checked and authorised.

## 2.1 Risks and control objectives

When considering recording wages and salaries, the company might recognise the following risks:

* The various elements of pay might not be recorded correctly in the payroll
* Amounts paid to employees might not be reflected in the cash books
* Pay might not be recorded correctly in the general ledger

In addition, the company has a duty to pay over to HMRC the correct amounts in respect of tax and national insurance. If these are calculated wrongly, the company might face a large tax bill in the future of arrears and penalties. The company also has a duty to pay other deductions on behalf of employees, for example, pension deductions. Again, errors might mean future liabilities.

These lead to the following control objectives:

* **Gross** and **net pay** and **deductions** are **accurately recorded** on the payroll
* **Wages and salaries paid** are **recorded correctly** in the **bank** and **cash records**
* **Wages and salaries** are **correctly recorded** in the **general ledger**
* All **deductions** have been **calculated correctly** and are **authorised**
* The **correct amounts** are paid to **HMRC**

## 2.2 Controls

Responsibility for the preparation of payroll should be delegated to a suitable person, and adequate staff appointed to assist him. The extent to which the staff responsible for preparing wages and salaries may perform other duties should be clearly defined. In this connection full advantage should be taken where possible of the division of duties, and checks available where automatic wage accounting systems are in use.

In addition there should be:

* Bases for compilation of payroll (for example, clockcards, overtime records, agreed hours)

* Arrangements for the preparation, checking (reconciling to payroll information) and approval of payroll

* Procedures for dealing with non-routine matters

- Maintenance of separate employees' personnel records

- One for one checking of payroll details back to independently maintained personnel records

- Reconciliation of total pay and deductions between one pay day and the next

- Comparison of actual pay totals with budget estimates or standard costs and the investigation of differences between them

- Agreement of gross earnings and total tax deducted with taxation returns

### Worked example: Preparation of payroll

The system of control over payroll production at Maybury plc operates as follows.

Anne, the payroll clerk, uses a well-known computerised payroll system. She enters the number of hours worked by each employee in the week per their clock cards. The computer then produces the payroll based on the standing data concerning pay rates and deductions. Anne prints off the payroll for the week, checks that the brought forward figures for tax and national insurance agree to the previous payroll and sends it to Sandra, who checks the payroll and authorises it.

Sandra also checks that the brought forward figures agree to the previous payroll and indicates that she has checked by initialling the appropriate column in the payroll. She compares a sample of net pays to the previous payroll and investigates any significant differences. She authorises it by signing it. She prepares the journals that will be posted to the cash books and general ledgers and passes these and the payroll to the finance department, so that the journals may be posted and the cheques prepared.

## 2.3 Tests of controls

A key control assurance providers will be concerned with will be the reconciliation of wages and salaries. For wages, there should have been reconciliations with:

- The **previous week's payroll**
- **Clock cards/time sheets/job cards**
- **Costing analyses, production budgets**

The total of **salaries** should be **reconciled** with the **previous week/month** or the **standard payroll**.

In addition, assurance providers should confirm that important calculations have been checked by the clients and re-perform those calculations.

These include checking for wages for a number of weeks:

- **Additions** of **payroll**
- **Totals** of **payroll detail** selected to summary of payroll
- **Additions** and **cross-casts** of summary
- **Postings** of **summary** to **general ledger** (including control accounts)
- **Net cash column** to cash book

For salaries they include checking for a number of weeks/months:

- **Additions** of **payroll**
- **Totals** of **salaries details** to **summary**
- **Additions** and **cross-casts** of **summary**
- **Postings** of **summary** to **general ledger** (including control accounts)
- **Total** of **net pay column** to cash book

Assurance providers should **check** the **calculations** of **taxation** and **non-statutory deductions**. For PAYE and NI they should carry out the following tests:

- **Scrutinise** the **control accounts** maintained to see **appropriate deductions** have been **made**
- **Check** that the **payments to HMRC** are **correct**

They should check other deductions to appropriate records. For voluntary deductions, they should see the authority completed by the relevant employees.

### Worked example: Test of controls over recording pay

An audit assistant on the audit of Maybury plc has been asked to test controls over the payroll. She has been given the following audit plan.

- Sample four separate weeks of payroll.
- Ensure that Sandra's signature appears, authorising payroll.
- Check for Sandra's initials showing the brought forward figures have been checked.
- Recheck the brought forward figures from the previous payroll.
- Cast a sample of lines in the payroll to ensure it is arithmetically accurate.
- Check the calculations of statutory deductions.
- Obtain journal sheet for posting to ledger and cash book and confirm the postings are correct.
- Trace postings to ledgers to ensure processed correctly.
- Check a sample of hours worked to original clock cards.

### Interactive question 2: Recording pay                [Difficulty level: Exam standard]

Personnel and wages records at Simonston Brothers Limited are maintained by Sam, the wages clerk, on a personal computer. Sam calculates the hours worked by each employee on a weekly basis, based on that employee's clock cards and enters them on the computer. The payroll program, using data from personnel records in respect of wage rates and deductions, produces the weekly payroll and a payslip for each employee.

Sam prepares a cheque requisition for the total net pay for the week, which is sent to the company accountant together with a copy of the payroll. The accountant draws up the cheque, made payable to cash, and has it countersigned by a director. The wages clerk takes the cheque to the bank and uses the cash to prepare the wage packets.

Which **two** of the following are deficiencies which exist in the wages system at Simonston Brothers Limited?

- [ ] Sam records the salaries and organises the pay packets
- [ ] There is no authorisation of the payroll
- [ ] The wages cheque is countersigned by a director
- [ ] The payroll and the time recording system are separate

See **Answer** at the end of this chapter.

# 3 Payment of wages and salaries

### Section overview
- There is a risk that payments are made incorrectly.
- Authorisation should prevent this.

## 3.1 Risks and control objectives

The key risks here are that people who are not employees are paid and those that are employees are not paid. Therefore the overriding control objective is that the correct employees are paid.

## 3.2 Controls

| | |
|---|---|
| **Payment of cash wages** (this is increasingly rare) | • Segregation of duties<br><br>   – Preparing the payroll net pay summary<br>   – Filling of pay packets<br>   – Distribution of wages<br><br>• Authorisation of wage cheque cashed<br><br>• Custody of cash<br><br>   – When the wages cheque is cashed<br>   – Security of pay packets<br>   – Security of transit<br>   – Security and prompt banking of unclaimed wages<br><br>• Verification of identity<br><br>• Recording of distributions |
| **Payment of salaries** | • Preparation and authorisation of cheques and bank transfer lists<br>• Comparison of cheques and bank transfer list with payroll<br>• Maintenance and reconciliation of wages and salaries control account |

### Worked example: Payment of wages

At Pynewood Limited, the bookkeeper calculates the wages, counts out the cash and puts it into envelopes for the staff. This system displays the following weakness:

- There is no segregation of duties between preparing the payroll and making up the pay packets, so that the bookkeeper could easily perpetrate a fraud of paying staff extra or paying non existent staff and keeping the proceeds.

## 3.3 Tests of controls

If wages are paid in cash

- **Arrange to attend** the **pay-out** of wages to confirm that the official procedures are being followed.

- Before the wages are paid **compare payroll** with **wage packets** to ensure all employees have a wage packet.

- **Examine receipts** given by employees; **check unclaimed wages** are recorded in unclaimed wages book.

- **Check** that **no employee receives more than one wage packet.**

- **Check entries** in the **unclaimed wages book** with the entries on the payroll.

- **Check that unclaimed wages** are **banked regularly.**

- **Check** that unclaimed wages books show **reasons** why wages are unclaimed.

- **Check pattern** of **unclaimed wages** in unclaimed wages book; variations may indicate failure to record.

- For salaries, check that comparisons are being made between each month's payroll net pay summary and **examine paid cheques** or a **certified copy** of the **bank list** for employees paid by cheque or bank transfer.

## Worked example: Tests of control over payment of wages

At HyperCo plc, all employees are salaried and are paid by direct transfer to their bank each month. The auditors will test that controls operate properly over this direct transfer by requesting a certified copy of the bank list for the payroll to see how the sum leaving the company's bank account is broken down and checking the individual amounts paid back to the payroll.

## Interactive question 3: Payment of wages                     [Difficulty level: Exam standard]

Which **two** of the following control activities will reduce the risk of employees who have left being made up a pay packet which is collected by the leaver or an accomplice?

☐ Check that each employee only collects one pay packet

☐ Supervision of payout by member of staff who knows all the employees personally

☐ Authorisation of payroll

☐ Comparison of payroll with wage packets to ensure that they match

See **Answer** at the end of this chapter.

# 4 Deficiencies

### Section overview

- Being able to identify the deficiencies of a system an important exam technique.

## Interactive question 4: Deficiencies of a payroll system

[Difficulty level: Exam standard]

The following describes the payroll system in operation at Whistling Co. For each process indicate whether the process indicates a strength or a deficiency of the system.

| | | | |
|---|---|---|---|
| (1) | Employees each have an electronic card to swipe in order to enter and leave the factory premises. This 'swipe' system automatically updates time records in the payroll system. | ☐ Strength | ☐ Deficiency |
| (2) | There is no personnel department. Employees are engaged by department heads with the verbal consent of a director. | ☐ Strength | ☐ Deficiency |
| (3) | On leaving, employees are required to return their swipe cards. | ☐ Strength | ☐ Deficiency |
| (4) | The payroll has a variance function which reports items within the payroll falling outside the expected conventions which must be resolved by an authorised member of staff before the payroll can be finalised. The ability to resolve this report is controlled by a secret password. | ☐ Strength | ☐ Deficiency |

See **Answer** at the end of this chapter.

## Summary

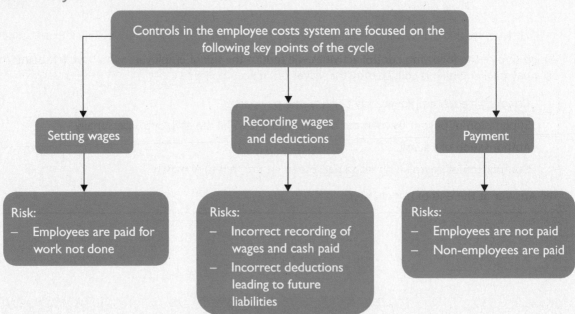

## Self-test

Answer the following questions.

1   List **six** procedures assurance providers should carry out if wages are paid in cash.

    (1)  .......................................

    (2)  .......................................

    (3)  .......................................

    (4)  .......................................

    (5)  .......................................

    (6)  .......................................

2   What are the most important authorisation controls over amounts to be paid to employees?

3   How should assurance providers confirm that wages have been paid at the correct rate to individual employees?

Now, go back to the Learning Objectives in the Introduction. If you are satisfied you have achieved these objectives, please tick them off.

### Answer to Interactive question 1

Shepherd has a simple control over how much work is being done by its employees. Therefore, employees should be being paid for the hours they have worked.

However, it is a very simple control, which relies on the integrity of the employees in recording the correct times they arrived and left the premises. There does not appear to be a supervisory control ensuring that employees are writing the correct times. Nor is there any provision for times when the employees are not working, for example, lunch hour or slack periods. Therefore it is possible that despite the presence of this control, employees may be paid for work they have not done.

### Answer to Interactive question 2

Sam records the salaries and organises the pay packets, there is no authorisation of the payroll.

### Answer to Interactive question 3

Check that each employee only collects one pay packet. Authorisation of payroll.

Comparison of the payroll with the pay packets will only be effective if the payroll has been properly updated for the leaver. Supervision by a member of staff who knows all the staff will be necessary if the employees are not required to show identification to pick up wages, but will not necessarily stop a leaver picking up a wage packet if the supervisor does not know the staff member has left.

### Answer to Interactive question 4

(1) Strength. The fact that employees cannot access the factory to work without updating the time records automatically is a strength in the system.

(2) Deficiency. It appears that the recruitment process is casual and there is not necessarily any written documentation resulting from the appointment of an employee. This could lead to errors in pay rates and payroll production that could be eliminated if written notice of an employee's start was given to the payroll department.

(3) Strength. The fact that employees are required to return their cards when they leave means that they are effectively excluded from the time recording system and in practice cannot continue to be paid after they have left.

(4) Strength. The fact that the payroll has parameters beyond which it seeks authorisation means that mistakes should be corrected before the payroll is finalised. In addition, there are application controls over correction of the payroll, strengthening this control.

1    Any from:

- **Arrange to attend** the **pay-out** of wages to confirm that the official procedures are being followed
- Before the wages are paid **compare payroll** with **wage packets** to ensure all employees have a wage packet
- **Examine receipts** given by employees; **check unclaimed wages** are recorded in unclaimed wages book
- **Check** that **no employee receives more than one wage packet**
- **Check entries** in the **unclaimed wages book** with the entries on the payroll
- **Check that unclaimed wages** are **banked regularly**
- **Check** that unclaimed wages book shows **reasons** why wages are unclaimed
- **Check pattern** of **unclaimed wages** in unclaimed wages book; variations may indicate failure to record
- **Verify** a sample of holiday pay **payments** with the **underlying records** and **check** the **calculation** of the amounts paid

2    The most important authorisation controls over wages and salaries are controls over:

- Engagement and discharge of employees
- Changes in pay rates
- Overtime
- Non-statutory deductions
- Advances of pay

3    Assurance providers should confirm that wages have been paid at the correct rate by checking calculation of gross pay to:

- Authorised rates of pay
- Production records
- Clock cards, time sheets or other evidence of time worked

# CHAPTER 9

# Internal audit

## Learning objectives

- Understand the role that internal audit plays in internal control

- Distinguish between the role of the internal auditor and the external auditor

The specific syllabus reference for this chapter is: 2d.

## Syllabus links

Internal audit will be looked at again in the Business and Finance syllabus, and also in the Audit and Assurance syllabus.

## Examination context

A question on this topic is likely to be included in your assessment as one of the questions on internal controls.

In the assessment, candidates may be required to identify the components of internal control in both manual and IT environments, including internal audit.

In addition, candidates may be required to:

- Identify the role of the internal auditor in internal control
- Identifying activities carried out by the internal auditor
- Identify features which distinguish the internal auditor from the external auditor

# 1 What is internal audit?

**Section overview**

- The internal audit function assists management in achieving corporate objectives, particularly in achieving good corporate governance.

- Although many of the techniques internal and external auditors use are similar, the basis and reasoning of their work is different.

**Definition**

Internal audit function: An appraisal activity established or provided as a service to the entity. Its functions include, amongst other things, examining, evaluating and monitoring the adequacy and effectiveness of internal control.

Internal audit is generally a feature of large companies. It is a function, provided either by employees of the entity or sourced from an external organisation to assist management in **achieving corporate objectives.**

If the internal audit function exists to assist management in achieving corporate objectives, it is important to ask '**what are corporate objectives**?' Obviously, these will vary from company to company, and will be found, for example, in companies' mission statements and strategic plans.

In principle, all companies will want good management, and the internal audit function is a recognised way of ensuring good corporate governance.

The codes of corporate governance that indicate good practice for companies, such as the UK Corporate Governance Code (formerly the 'Combined Code'; mandatory for UK listed companies) highlight the need for businesses to maintain **good systems of internal control** to manage the risks the company faces. **Internal audit** can play a **key role in assessing and monitoring** internal control policies and procedures.

The internal audit function can assist the board in other ways as well:

- By, in effect, acting as auditors for board reports not audited by the external auditors.

- By being the experts in fields such as auditing and accounting standards and assisting in implementation of new standards.

- By liaising with external auditors, particularly where external auditors can use internal audit work and reduce the time and therefore cost of the external audit. In addition, internal auditors can check that external auditors are reporting back to the board everything they are required to under auditing standards.

The UK Corporate Governance Code highlights the importance of internal audit by stipulating that directors of companies that do not have an internal audit department should re-consider the need for one annually.

## 1.1 Distinction between internal and external audit

An external audit is an audit carried out by an external, as opposed to an internal, auditor. Remember that the objective of an external audit of financial statements is to enable auditors to express an opinion on whether the financial statements are prepared (in all material respects) in accordance with the applicable financial reporting framework.

Contrast this with the definition of the internal audit function given at the beginning of this chapter. The external audit is focused on the financial statements, whereas the internal audit function is focused on the operations of the entire business.

The following table highlights the differences between internal and external audit.

| | Internal audit | External audit |
|---|---|---|
| Reason | The internal audit function is an activity designed to add value and improve an organisation's operations. | An exercise to enable auditors to express an opinion on the financial statements. |
| Reporting to | Internal auditors report to the board of directors, or the audit committee, which is a sub committee of the board of directors concerned with financial and audit matters. | The external auditors report to the shareholders of a company on the truth and fairness of the financial statements. |
| Relating to | As demonstrated in the reason for their existence, an internal auditor's work relates to the operations of the organisation. | External audit's work relates to the financial statements. They are concerned with the financial records that underlie these. |
| Relationship with the company | Internal auditors are very often employees of the organisation, although sometimes the internal audit function is outsourced. | External auditors are independent of the company and its management. They are appointed by the shareholders. |

The table shows that although some of the procedures that the internal audit function undertake are very similar to those undertaken by the external auditors, the **whole basis and reasoning of their work is fundamentally different.**

## 2 What does the internal audit function do?

### Section overview

- The internal audit function has two key roles to play in relation to organisational risk management: (i) ensuring the company's risk management system operates effectively (ii) ensuring that strategies implemented in respect of business risks operate effectively.

- Internal auditors undertake operational audits.

- Internal auditors may also undertake special investigations on behalf of the directors.

- However, to preserve objectivity, internal auditors must not get involved in operational decision making matters.

The activities of the internal audit function usually involve:

- Monitoring internal controls (we shall consider this more in sections 2.1 and 2.2)

- Examining financial and operating information (for example, reviewing the accounting system and carrying out tests of detail on transactions and balances in the same way as the external auditor does)

- Review of the economy, efficiency and effectiveness of operations (this would include looking at non-financial controls of the organisation)

- Review of compliance with laws, regulations and other external requirements

- Special investigations, for instance, into suspected fraud

- Identifying and evaluating significant exposures to risk and contributing to the improvement of risk management and control systems

- Assessing the governance process in its accomplishment of objectives on ethics and values, performance management and accountability, communicating risk and control information to appropriate areas of the organisation and effectiveness of communication among those charged with governance, external and internal auditors, and management

## 2.1 Risk

We introduced the concept of the company facing risks in Chapter 5. All companies face risks arising from their activities, which cannot be eliminated, but such risks must be **managed** by the company.

Designing and operating internal control systems is a key part of a company's risk management. This will often be done by employees in their various departments, although sometimes (particularly in the case of specialised computer systems) the company will hire external expertise to design systems.

The internal audit function has a two-fold role in relation to risk management.

- Monitoring the company's overall risk management policy to ensure it operates effectively.
- Monitoring the strategies implemented to ensure that they continue to operate effectively.

## 2.2 Internal controls

The internal audit function is unlikely to assist in the development of systems because its key role will be in **monitoring the overall process** and in **providing assurance** that the **systems** which the departments have designed **meet objectives** and **operate effectively**.

It is important that the internal audit function retains **objectivity** towards these aspects of their role, which is why internal auditors would generally not be involved in the assessment of risks and the design of the system.

The fact that the control system should be monitored was discussed in Chapter 5. If there is an internal audit function, testing (and therefore monitoring) controls is likely to be an important part of their role. The tests that they carry out will be on the same lines as the tests outlined in the previous three chapters that external auditors will carry out. However, as internal auditors are focused on all the operations of the company, they are focusing on all controls, not just ones linked ultimately to the financial statements, so the scope of their testing will be far greater than that of the external auditors.

The work that internal auditors carry out on controls can be termed **operational audits**. These are audits of the operational processes of the organisation. They are also known as management or efficiency audits. Their prime objective is the monitoring of management's performance, ensuring company policy is adhered to.

There are two aspects of an operational assignment:

- Ensure policies are adequate
- Ensure policies work effectively

In terms of adequacy, the internal auditor will have to review the policies of a particular department by:

- Reading them
- Discussion with members of the department

Then the auditor will have to assess whether the policies are adequate, and possibly advise the board of improvement.

The auditor will then have to examine the effectiveness of the controls by testing them, as discussed in the previous few chapters.

## 2.3 Other functions

The internal audit function may also carry out other work for the directors in a company. For instance, they might undertake special investigations in respect of a suspected fraud, or they might carry out traditional financial audits, similar to the exercise carried out by the external auditors.

However, the key issue to remember with regard to the internal audit function is the necessity for the department to retain objectivity in order to carry out its important monitoring role in respect of risk and controls. Therefore internal auditors will not become involved in the operational activities of the company.

## Worked example: Internal audit

Ritzy Hotels plc (RH) is a listed company which owns a number of hotels in the United Kingdom. Each hotel is a subsidiary company of RH, for example, Ritzy Southampton Limited is the hotel in Southampton. RH charges each hotel a management charge, which is determined on a fixed calculation dependent on the number of rooms at the hotel. One of the things this management charge covers is the internal audit function, which is managed centrally by RH.

The internal audit function at RH is required to carry out cyclical operational audits at all the hotels. The London Hotel, which comprises 20% of group income, is audited annually. Other hotels are audited on a rotational basis, with each hotel being audited at least once every three years.

'An audit' comprises a number of elements, all of which have to have been carried out (although not all at the same time) for the full cyclical audit to have been completed. These elements are:

- Surprise cash counts in key cash transactions areas (reception, bar, restaurant)

- Asset inspections, particularly linens and leisure facilities

- Inventory count for certain assets, particularly the larder and bar

- Tests of controls in key systems: sales, purchases, payroll (RH has a systems manual that all hotels are required to follow)

- Health and safety control systems testing

- Review of actual results against budget for the year

In addition, the internal audit function is sometimes required to carry out a special investigation. In 2004, there was a special investigation into VAT errors at one hotel. Currently the directors of RH, concerned at the results of analytical review on bar income at one of the hotels is considering implementing a discrepancy investigation at that hotel.

## Interactive question: Internal audit activities          [Difficulty level: Exam standard]

Lightening plc has an organisational structure which includes accounting, human resources, internal audit and audit committee. Which department should not be involved in determining pay rises?

A  Accounting
B  Human resources
C  Internal audit
D  Audit committee

See **Answer** at the end of this chapter.

## Summary

> The internal audit function is an appraisal activity established or provided as a service to the entity. Its functions include, amongst other things, examining, evaluating and monitoring the adequacy and effectiveness of internal control.

**Monitoring** for **adequacy** and **effectiveness**

Therefore, must stay **objective**. Not involved in operational activities.

## Self-test

Answer the following questions.

1   What is an internal audit function?

2   Name three key differences between external and internal audit.

    (1)   ...................................

    (2)   ...................................

    (3)   ...................................

3   It is possible to buy in an internal audit service from an external organisation.

    ☐   True

    ☐   False

4   As objectivity is a key issue for internal auditors, they are likely to routinely be involved in operational activities.

    ☐   True

    ☐   False

Now, go back to the Learning Objectives in the Introduction. If you are satisfied you have achieved these objectives, please tick them off.

Answer to Interactive question

C    The internal audit function must not become involved in operational activities

1    The internal audit function is an appraisal activity established or provided as a service to the entity

2    (1)   External report to members, internal to directors
       (2)   External report on financial statements, internal on systems, controls and risks
       (3)   External are independent of the company, internal often employed by it

3    True

4    False. The reverse is true

# CHAPTER 10

# Documentation

Introduction

Examination context

**Topic List**

1 Purpose of documentation

2 Form and content of documentation

3 Safe custody and retention of documentation

4 Ownership of and right of access to documentation

Summary and Self-test

Technical reference

Answers to Interactive question

Answers to Self-test

## Introduction

### Learning objectives

Tick off

- Understand the nature of working papers

- Understand the form and content of working papers

- Understand why assurance providers record their work

- Understand why and how assurance providers keep these records

The specific syllabus references for this chapter are: 3a, 1f.

### Syllabus links

One reason for keeping working papers is to protect the assurance provider in the event of a negligence claim. This will be looked at in more detail in Audit and Assurance.

### Examination context

This topic is likely to be examined on a regular basis and questions should be reasonably straightforward if you are well prepared.

There was one question in the sample paper on documentation, looking at the reasons behind preparing particular pieces of documentation and whether these reasons were valid.

In the assessment, candidates may be required to:

- Define audit documentation
- State the reasons for preparing and keeping documentation relating to an assurance engagement
- State the form and content of working papers
- Identify the advantages of automated working papers
- State the content of a permanent audit file and a current audit file

# 1   Purpose of documentation

**Section overview**

- Assurance providers should document the work they have done.

- This should be a record of the procedures performed, the evidence obtained and the conclusions reached.

- This provides evidence that the engagement was performed in accordance with any relevant standards, law or regulatory requirements.

- A record of work done also assists the team to plan and direct work, facilitates review by senior staff, provides accountability for work, provides a record of matters that are relevant to future engagements and enables experienced auditors to carry out any additional reviews necessary.

All assurance work must be documented: the working papers are the tangible evidence of the work done in support of the conclusion.

Audit documentation or working papers provides:

(a) Evidence for the auditor's basis for a conclusion about the achievement of the overall objectives of the auditor; and

(b) Evidence that the audit was planned and performed in accordance with ISAs and applicable legal and regulatory requirements.

They must be prepared on a timely basis. Documentation prepared after the audit work has been performed is likely to be less accurate than timely documentation.

**Definition**

Audit documentation (working papers): is the record of procedures performed, relevant evidence obtained and conclusions the auditor reached.

---

In addition, particularly in relation to audit, assurance providers record their work to:

- Assist the audit team to plan and perform the audit

- Assist relevant members of the team to direct and supervise work

- Enable the audit team to be accountable for its work (and to prove adherence to ISAs in a litigious situation)

- Retain a record of matters of continuing significance to future audits

- Enable an experienced auditor to carry out quality control reviews

- Enable an experienced auditor to conduct external inspections in accordance with applicable legal, regulatory or other requirements

Auditors may find it helpful to include in the audit documentation a summary of all significant matters arising during the audit and how these were addressed. This summary will facilitate effective and efficient reviews of the audit documentation. Additionally, it may assist the auditor's consideration of significant matters and help the auditor to consider if any individual ISA objectives have not been met.

# 2 Form and content of documentation

## Section overview

- Working papers should be headed in a certain way and contain certain information.
- They may be automated.

Working papers should be sufficiently complete and detailed to provide an overall understanding of the engagement.

However, assurance providers cannot record everything they consider. Therefore judgement must be used as to the extent of working papers, based on the following general rule (given in an audit context):

'Documentation that is sufficient to enable an experienced auditor, having no previous connection with the audit, to understand the nature, timing and extent of audit procedures performed to comply with the ISAs and applicable legal and regulatory requirements, the results of audit procedures performed and the audit evidence obtained, and significant matters arising during the audit, the conclusions reached thereon and significant professional judgements made in reaching those conclusions.'

The form and content of working papers are affected by matters such as:

- The **size** and **complexity** of the entity

- The **nature** of the audit procedures to be performed

- The **identified risks** of material misstatement

- The **significance** of the audit evidence obtained

- The **nature and extent** of **exceptions** identified

- The **need to document** a conclusion or the **basis for a conclusion not readily determinable** from the documentation of the work performed or audit evidence obtained

- The **audit methodology** and tools used

## Worked example: Audit file

An audit file will normally contain the following working papers:

- Information obtained in understanding the entity and its environment, including its internal control, such as the following:

  - Information concerning legal documents, agreements and minutes

  - Extracts from, or copies of, important legal documents, agreements and minutes

  - Information concerning the industry, economic and legislative environment within which the entity operates

  - Extracts from the entity's internal control manual

- Evidence of the planning process including audit plans and any changes thereto

- Evidence of the auditor's consideration of the work of the internal audit function and conclusions reached

- Analyses of transactions and balances

- Analyses of significant ratios and trends

- The identified and assessed risks of material misstatements

- A record of the nature, timing, extent and results of audit procedures

- Evidence that the work performed by assistants was supervised and reviewed

- An indication as to who performed the audit procedures and when they were performed

- Details of audit procedures applied regarding components whose financial statements are audited by another auditor

- Copies of communications with other auditors, experts and other third parties

- Copies of letters or notes concerning audit matters communicated to or discussed with management, including the terms of the engagement and material weaknesses in internal control

- Written representations received from the entity (these are covered in Chapter 12)

- Conclusions reached by the auditor concerning significant aspects of the audit, including how exceptions and unusual matters, if any, disclosed by the auditor's procedures were resolved or treated

- Copies of the financial statements and auditor's reports

- Notes of discussions about significant matters with management and others

- In exceptional circumstances, the reasons for departing from a basic principle or essential procedure of an ISA and how the alternative procedure performed achieved the audit objective

---

Working papers should show:

- The name of the client
- The reporting date
- The file reference of the working paper
- The name of the preparer
- The date of preparation
- The subject of the working paper
- The name of the reviewer
- The date of the review
- The objective of the work done
- The source of information

- How any sample was selected
- The sample size determined
- The work done
- A key to any audit ticks or symbols
- Appropriate cross-referencing
- The results obtained
- Analysis of errors
- Other significant observations
- The conclusions drawn
- The key points highlighted

## Worked example: Working paper

Client: Example Ltd (1)

Subject: Payables (6)

Year end: 31 December 20X3 (2)

Prepared by
(4) pc
Date: 16.2.X4 (5)

Reviewed by
(7) AD
(8) Date: 3.3.X4

(3) E³/₁

| | | | | | | |
|---|---|---|---|---|---|---|
| (9) **Objective** | To ensure payables ledger balances fairly stated. | | | | | |
| (11) **Work done** | | | | | | (10) |
| | Selected a sample of trade payables as at    31 December and reconciled the supplier's statement to the year end payables ledger balance. Vouched any reconciling items to source documentation. | | | | | |
| | (10) | | | | | |
| (13) **Results** | See E³/₂ | | | | | |
| | One credit note, relating to Woodcutter Ltd, has not been accounted for. An adjustment is required. | | | | | (14) |
| | DEBIT | Trade payables | | £4,975 | | |
| | CREDIT | Purchases | | | £4,975 | H1/2 |
| | One other error was found, which was immaterial, and which was the fault of the supplier. | | | | | |
| | (14) | | | | | |
| | In view of the error found, however, we should recommend that the client management checks supplier statement reconciliations at least on the larger accounts. Management letter point. | | | | | |
| (15) **Conclusion** | | | | | | |
| | After making the adjustment noted above, payables ledger balances are fairly stated as at 31 December 20X3. | | | | | |

ICAEW

Client: Example Ltd

Subject: Payables

Year end: 31 December 20X3

| Prepared by | Reviewed by |
|---|---|
| PC | AD |
| Date: 16.2.X4 | Date: 3.3.X4 |

E ³/₂

| Client | | Payables ledger £ | | Supplier statement £ | | Difference £ | | Agreed | | Reconciling item £ | | |
|---|---|---|---|---|---|---|---|---|---|---|---|---|
| A Ltd | ⌄ | 300 | 00 | 300 | 00 | - | | ✓ | | - | | |
| B Ltd | ⌄ | 747 | 00 | 732 | 00 | 15 | 00 | ✗ | | 15 | 00 | • |
| | | | | | | | | | | | | |
| | | | | | | | | | | | | |
| | | | | | | | | | | | | |
| | | | | (12) | | Key | | | | | | |
| | | | | | | | | | | | | |
| | | | | | | ✓ | Agreed | | | | | |
| | | | | | | ✗ | Not agreed | | | | | |
| | | | | | | ⌃ | Adds checked | | | | | |
| | | | | | | ⌄ | Agreed to payables ledger | | | | | |
| | | | | | | • | Vouched to credit note | | | | | |
| | | 1,047 | 00 | | | | | | | | | |
| | | ⌃ | | | | | | | | | | |

KEY

① The **name** of the **client**
② The reporting **date**
③ The **file reference** of the working paper
④ The **name** of the **person** preparing the working paper
⑤ The **date** the working paper was **prepared**
⑥ The **subject** of the working paper
⑦ The **name** of the person **reviewing** the working paper
⑧ The **date** of the **review**
⑨ The **objective** of the work done
⑩ The **sources of information**
⑪ The **work done**
⑫ A **key** to any audit ticks or symbols
⑬ The **results obtained**
⑭ **Analysis** of **errors** or other significant observations
⑮ The **conclusions drawn**

The auditor shall record the identifying characteristics of specific items or matters being tested.

## 2.1 Automated working papers

**Automated** working paper packages have been developed which can make the documenting of audit work much easier. Such programs aid preparation of working papers, lead schedules, trial balance and the financial statements themselves. These are automatically cross referenced, adjusted and balanced by the computer.

The **advantages** of automated working papers are as follows.

- The risk of errors is reduced.

- The working papers will be neater and easier to review.

- The time saved will be substantial as adjustments can be made easily to all working papers, including working papers summarising the key analytical information.

- Standard forms do not have to be carried to audit locations.

- Audit working papers can be emailed or faxed for review.

These days most documents can be scanned and stored electronically rather than in paper form.

## 2.2 Filing working papers

Firms should have standard referencing and filing procedures for working papers, to facilitate their review.

For recurring audits, working papers may be split between permanent and current audit files, although this distinction is fading as audit files become automated, and 'permanent' documents can be scanned and carried in computer files year on year.

**Permanent audit files** (contain any information of continuing importance to the audit). These may contain:

- Engagement letters
- New client questionnaire
- The memorandum and articles of association
- Other legal documents such as prospectuses, leases, sales agreements
- Details of the history of the client's business
- Board minutes of continuing relevance
- Previous years' signed accounts and analytical procedures
- Accounting systems notes, previous years' control questionnaires

**Current audit files** (contain any information of relevance to the current year's audit). These should be compiled on a timely basis after the completion of the audit and should contain (amongst other things):

- Financial statements
- Accounts checklists
- Management accounts details
- Reconciliations of management accounts and financial statements
- A summary of unadjusted errors
- Report to partner including details of significant events and errors
- Review notes
- Audit planning memorandum
- Time budgets and summaries
- Written representations from management
- Notes of board minutes
- Communications with third parties such as experts or other auditors

They also contain working papers covering each audit area. These should include the following:

- A lead schedule including details of the figures to be included in the accounts
- Problems encountered and conclusions drawn
- Audit plans
- Risk assessments
- Sampling plans
- Analytical procedures
- Details of tests of detail and tests of control

# 3 Safe custody and retention of documentation

**Section overview**

- Assurance providers should retain documents for a certain period of time.
- Documents must be kept secure during this period due to confidentiality requirements.

Judgement may have to be used in deciding the duration of holding working papers, and further consideration should be given to the matter before their destruction. The ICAEW requires all firms should have a document retention policy and Registered Auditors to keep all audit working papers required by auditing standards for at least six years from the end of the accounting period to which they relate.

Given that assurance work must be kept confidential (as we shall see in Chapter 16), it is important that firms have good security procedures over their retained working papers. Paper documents must be kept securely, in locked premises. Electronic documents should be protected by electronic controls.

# 4 Ownership of and right of access to documentation

**Section overview**

- Working papers belong to the assurance providers.
- The report, once issued, belongs to the client.
- Assurance providers must keep working papers confidential.
- They may show working papers to the client at their discretion.
- They should obtain client permission before showing working papers to third parties.

ICAEW regulations, standards and guidance (available at http://www.icaew.com/en/members/regulations-standards-and-guidance) provides members with assistance in relation to documents and records: ownership, lien and rights of access.

Working papers are the property of the assurance providers. They are not a substitute for, nor part of, the entity's accounting records. However, the report becomes the property of the client once it has been issued.

Assurance providers must follow ethical guidance on the confidentiality of working papers. As working papers belong to the firm, the assurance providers are not required to show them to the client. However, the firm may show working papers to the client at their discretion, so long as the assurance process is not prejudiced.

Information should not be made available to third parties without the permission of the client. An example of when working papers might be shared with a third party is when a new firm is taking over an audit from the existing auditors.

## Interactive question: Documentation

[Difficulty level: Exam standard]

The auditor will prepare documentation in relation to the fieldwork carried out on an assurance engagement.

Indicate whether the following are, or are not, valid reasons for preparing such documentation.

| | | | |
|---|---|---|---|
| (i) | To comply with the law. | ☐ Valid | ☐ Not valid |
| (ii) | To provide a record of matters of continuing significance to future audits. | ☐ Valid | ☐ Not valid |
| (iii) | To facilitate review by senior staff. | ☐ Valid | ☐ Not valid |
| (iv) | To prove adherence to ISAs in a litigious situation. | ☐ Valid | ☐ Not valid |

See **Answer** at the end of this chapter.

The table shows how the ownership of documents depends on the nature of the work being carried out.

| Nature of work | Type of document | Who has ownership? |
|---|---|---|
| *Auditing* | | |
| Preparation of auditor's report whether carried out under statutory provisions or not | Any documents prepared by member solely for purpose of carrying out his duties as auditor | Member |
| | Auditor's Report | Client |
| *Accountancy* | | |
| Preparation of accounting records | Accounting Records | Client |
| Preparation of financial statements from client's records | Financial statements | Client |
| | Draft/office copy of financial statements | Member |
| | Correspondence with third parties | Member |

## Summary

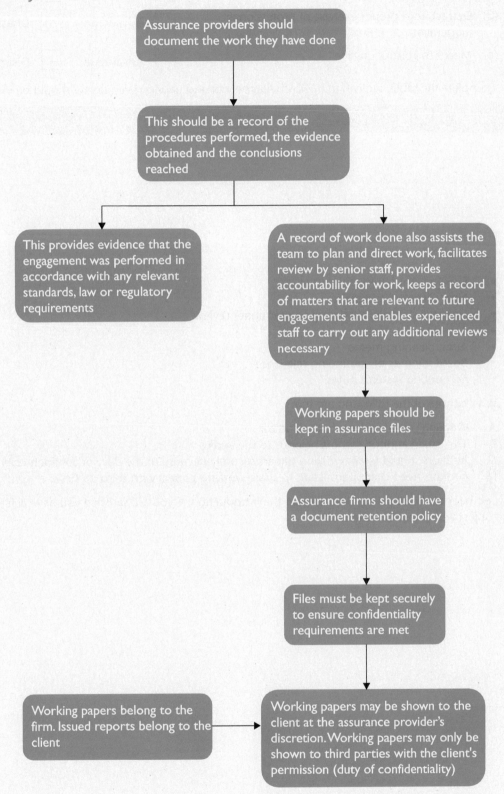

Assurance providers should document the work they have done

This should be a record of the procedures performed, the evidence obtained and the conclusions reached

This provides evidence that the engagement was performed in accordance with any relevant standards, law or regulatory requirements

A record of work done also assists the team to plan and direct work, facilitates review by senior staff, provides accountability for work, keeps a record of matters that are relevant to future engagements and enables experienced staff to carry out any additional reviews necessary

Working papers should be kept in assurance files

Assurance firms should have a document retention policy

Files must be kept securely to ensure confidentiality requirements are met

Working papers belong to the firm. Issued reports belong to the client

Working papers may be shown to the client at the assurance provider's discretion. Working papers may only be shown to third parties with the client's permission (duty of confidentiality)

ICAEW

## Self-test

Answer the following questions.

1   State whether the following are advantages or disadvantages of standardised audit working papers:

(a)  Facilitate the delegation of work  ☐ Advantage  ☐ Disadvantage

(b)  Detract from proper exercise of professional judgement  ☐ Advantage  ☐ Disadvantage

(c)  Means to control quality  ☐ Advantage  ☐ Disadvantage

2   Complete the table, indicating in which file the working papers given below should be included.

| Current audit file | Permanent audit file |
| --- | --- |
|  |  |
|  |  |
|  |  |
|  |  |

- Engagement letters
- New client questionnaire
- Financial statements relating to year under review
- Accounts checklists
- Audit planning memo
- Board minutes of continuing relevance
- Accounting systems notes

3   Which **three** of the following are true?

A   Working papers belong to the auditor
B   The issued auditor's report belongs to the auditor
C   Auditors should retain working papers securely because of the duty of confidentiality
D   Auditors need client permission to share working papers with third parties

Now, go back to the Learning Objectives in the Introduction, if you are satisfied you have achieved these objectives, please tick them off.

# Technical Reference

CHAPTER

10

## Answer to Interactive question

(i)   Not valid. It is not a legal requirement for the auditor to prepare working papers
(ii)  Valid
(iii) Valid
(iv)  Valid

1   (a)   Advantage
    (b)   Disadvantage
    (c)   Advantage

2

| Current audit file | Permanent audit file |
|---|---|
| Financial statements relating to year under review | Engagement letters |
| Accounts checklists | New client questionnaire |
| Audit planning memo | Board minutes of continuing relevance |
|  | Accounting systems notes |

3   A, C, D

CHAPTER

10

ICAEW

# CHAPTER 11

# Evidence and sampling

Introduction

Examination context

**Topic List**

## Learning objectives

- Understand the procedures for obtaining evidence

- Identify when tests of controls and substantive procedures will be used

- Recognise the strengths and weaknesses of particular forms of evidence

- Understand how much evidence to obtain

- Recognise when sufficient appropriate evidence has been obtained such that a conclusion can be drawn

Specific syllabus references for this chapter are: 3b, c, d, e, g.

## Syllabus links

In Audit and Assurance you will focus on the drawing conclusions part of evidence, based on the collection of evidence that we focus on in this Assurance manual.

## Examination context

This is a very important part of your syllabus and the issues discussed here and previously in Chapter 4 underpin the following two chapters as well. You can expect a number of practical and theoretical questions in the assessment covering audit evidence.
In the assessment, candidates may be required to:

- Distinguish between tests of controls and substantive procedures

- Identify and evaluate procedures used to obtain evidence

- Select the appropriate means of obtaining evidence in a given scenario

- Determine whether an audit test would be a test for overstatement or understatement in a given scenario

- Identify factors affecting sample sizes

- Identify weaknesses in methods of obtaining evidence

# 1 Evidence

**Section overview**

- Evidence must be sufficient and appropriate.

- Evidence is obtained in the form of substantive procedures and/or tests of controls.

- Evidence can be obtained by inspection, observation, inquiry and confirmation, recalculation, reperformance and analytical procedures.

- Substantive procedures will test for evidence of understatement or overstatement of account balances.

## 1.1 Overview of evidence from Chapter 4

You studied the basic principles of evidence in Chapter 4. These are the key points:

Evidence includes all the information contained within the accounting records underlying the financial statements, and other information gathered by the assurance providers, such as confirmations from third parties. Evidence is obtained in relation to the financial statement assertions which were set out in Chapter 4. There are two types of test; tests of controls (which we have looked at in detail in Chapters 5 to 9) and substantive procedures (which we will look at in more detail in Chapters 12 and 13).

ISA 500 states that evidence must be sufficient and appropriate.

- **Sufficiency** is the measure of the **quantity** of audit evidence.
- **Appropriateness** is the measure of the **quality** or relevance and **reliability** of the audit evidence.

We will look at the quantity of evidence obtained in section 2 below.

There are some general principles relating to the quality of evidence which were set out in Chapter 4.

| Quality of evidence | |
|---|---|
| External | Evidence from **external sources** is more reliable than that obtained from the entity's records |
| Auditor | Evidence obtained **directly by assurance providers** is more reliable than that obtained indirectly or by inference |
| Entity | Evidence obtained from the entity's records is more reliable when related **control systems operate effectively** |
| Written | Evidence in the form of **documents (paper or electronic)** or **written representations** are more reliable than oral representations |
| Originals | Original documents are more reliable than photocopies, or facsimiles |

## 1.2 Procedures to obtain evidence

Assurance providers obtain evidence by one or more of the following procedures outlined in ISA 500.

| Procedures | Explanation | Strengths and weaknesses |
|---|---|---|
| **Inspection of tangible assets** | Inspection (physical examination) of tangible assets that are recorded in the accounting records confirms existence, but does not confirm rights and obligations or valuation. For example, machinery recorded in asset register can be inspected by assurance providers.<br><br>Confirmation that assets seen are recorded in accounting records gives evidence of completeness. However, this is limited to assets assurance providers can see – if assets have been taken off site (hidden) they might not be picked up. | Inspection of assets is a good procedure, particularly in the case of assets that the entity could not function without (for example its production plant), but the weakness associated with inspection is that assets not used in daily production could be hidden from the assurance providers and not included in financial statements. |
| **Inspection of documentation** | Inspection of documents involves examining records or documents, for example, looking at a sales contract or a share certificate.<br><br>What inspection of documents achieves depends on the nature of the document. For example, looking at a share certificate gives evidence of the existence of the investment. Looking at source documents (eg sales invoices) and tracing to financial statements gives evidence of completeness (eg of revenue).<br><br>Inspection also provides evidence of valuation (for example, a purchase invoice gives evidence of the cost of inventory), rights and obligations (for example, a hire purchase agreement gives evidence in relation to ownership of non-current assets) and the nature of items (presentation and disclosure). It can also be used to compare documents (and hence test consistency of audit evidence) and confirm authorisation. | The strength of this procedure depends on what is being inspected to give evidence. For instance, inspection of a purchase invoice gives better quality evidence than inspection of sales invoice, because a purchase invoice is created by a third party. |
| **Observation** | This involves watching a procedure being performed (for example, post opening). | This procedure is relatively weak, as it only confirms that the procedure is being performed correctly when the assurance provider is watching. |
| **Inquiry** | This involves seeking information from client management or staff or external sources and evaluating responses. | The strength or weakness of this procedure will depend on of whom the inquiry is being made – a member of client staff could misrepresent matters to the assurance provider if they misunderstand the nature of the question, or they are seeking to conceal a misstatement or fraud. |

| Procedures | Explanation | Strengths and weaknesses |
|---|---|---|
| External confirmation (a particular form of inquiry) | This involves seeking confirmation from a third party, eg confirmation from bank of bank balances. | This can be a very strong procedure but there may be instances where the third party is motivated to misrepresent, for example an understated receivables balance might be confirmed because it favoured the customer. |
| Recalculation | Checking mathematical accuracy of client's records, for example, adding up ledger accounts. | Recalculation is evidence created by the assurance provider so is strong evidence. |
| Reperformance | Independently executing procedures or controls, either manually or through the use of computer assisted audit techniques (covered below). | Again, the fact that the assurance provider carries out the performance of a control himself makes it strong evidence. |
| Analytical procedures | Evaluating and comparing financial and/or non-financial data for plausible relationships and investigating unexpected fluctuations. | Evidence here is limited by the strength or weakness of the underlying accounting system. However, this can be a strong procedure if comparison is made to items that do not rely on the same accounting system or that the assurance provider can corroborate outside the accounting system. |

Often these procedures will be used in conjunction with one another to provide a greater quality of evidence. For example, an assurance provider might observe controls in operation and then reperform the control himself to confirm that it operates as he has observed. Auditors will gather detailed evidence but other assurance providers may need less evidence.

## 1.3 Computer assisted audit techniques

With so many accounting systems now held on computer, the assurance provider may wish to make use of computer assisted audit techniques (CAATs). These have been mentioned before in your Study Manual, particularly in Chapter 5. There are two main types of CAAT that can be used:

- Test data
- Audit software

### 1.3.1 Test data

Under this test of control, the assurance provider supervises the process of running data through the client's system. The stages in the use of test data are as follows:

- Note controls in client's system

- Decide upon test data, the options include:

    - Dummy data (the assurance provider must be very careful to reverse all effects)
    - Real data (the data may not contain all the errors necessary to test the controls rigorously)
    - Dummy data against a verified copy of the client's system (much safer)

- Run the test data

- Compare results with those expected

- Conclude on whether controls are operating properly

### Worked example: Test data

Test data makes use of the client's own system. To carry out such a test the assurance provider identifies a control (or series of controls) in the client's system. The assurance provider then predicts the system's reaction to the test data. For example:

- An invoice which does not cast should be rejected when entered in the system
- An invoice with an invalid supplier code should be rejected
- Dates outside the current year should be rejected
- Valid data should be posted to the correct account

The assurance provider then runs the test data through the client's system (or a copy thereof) and compares the results with those expected. The results tell the assurance provider whether the controls within the system are operating correctly; the test is therefore a test of control.

---

### 1.3.2 Audit software

Audit software makes use of the assurance providers' own specialised software. There are a number of off-the-shelf packages available, or the assurance provider could have a tailormade system. Audit software works on the basis of interrogating the client's system and extracting and analysing information. It can therefore carry out a whole range of substantive procedures, across all sorts of different data.

Examples of what audit software can do include:

- Extract a sample according to specified criteria:

    - Random
    - Over a certain amount
    - Below a certain amount
    - At certain dates

- Calculate ratios and select those outside set criteria (eg more than five per cent different from last year)

- Check calculations and casts performed by the system

- Prepare reports (eg comparison of actual against budgeted figures)

- Follow items through a system and flag where they are posted

The procedures listed above are mostly substantive procedures, because they are substantiating the figures in the accounts. To generate more procedures that can be done using audit software, just think of the substantive tests that you may wish to carry out, and consider whether the information is held on the client's computer (you can normally assume that it is). If the test does not require judgement, then it can almost certainly be carried out by audit software.

## 1.4 Analytical procedures

ISA 520 (UK and Ireland) *Analytical Procedures* gives more detail on the use of analytical procedures as substantive procedures (optional) and at the overall review stage (compulsory) of an audit. The use of analytical procedures in planning (compulsory) is included in ISA 315 and was covered in Chapter 3. These ISAs apply to audits only, but all assurance providers may be able to use analytical procedures (indeed, they will be an important tool where less detailed evidence is required) and will need to consider the same general principles.

ISA 520 describes how the **auditor** must decide whether using substantive analytical procedures will be effective and efficient in **reducing audit risk** to an acceptably low level. Auditors may find it effective to use analytical data prepared by the entity's management, provided they are satisfied that it has been properly prepared.

There are a number of factors that the auditors should consider when using analytical procedures as substantive procedures:

- Objective of the analytical procedures (for example analytical procedures may be good at indicating whether a population is complete)

- Suitability of analytical procedures

- Reliability of the data

| Factor | Issues to consider |
| --- | --- |
| Suitability | <ul><li>Generally analytical procedures are more applicable to large volumes of transactions that tend to be predictable (for example, payroll)</li><li>It depends on the purpose of the test – for example, some analytical procedures will provide persuasive evidence and others will provide corroboration of other tests</li><li>Other audit tests directed to the same assertions</li><li>The auditor must decide if analytical procedures are suitable given the nature of the assertion and the assessment of risk associated with it</li></ul> |
| Reliability of the data | <ul><li>The source of the information used (third party or internal, for example)</li><li>The comparability of the information (for example, an industry standard may not be useful if the company is unusual within the industry)</li><li>Nature and relevance of the information used (for example, if comparing something to budget, is the budget realistic or more of a target?)</li><li>Whether there are controls over the production of the information used to ensure completeness, accuracy, validity</li></ul> |
| Precision | <ul><li>The accuracy with which results in test area can be predicted (for example, compare gross margin with a less predictable item, for example, advertising)</li><li>The extent to which information can be disaggregated(for example, by division)</li><li>Availability of required information</li></ul> |
| Acceptable difference | This is influenced by materiality and the desired level of assurance. As assessed risk rises, the amount of difference from expected results considered acceptable without investigation will reduce. |

When analytical procedures identify significant fluctuations or relationships that are inconsistent with other relevant information, or that are not the results that were expected, this must be investigated further.

The auditor shall make inquiries of management about the inconsistency or unexpected result and then corroborate those replies with other evidence.

If management responses cannot be corroborated or are unavailable, the auditor shall perform other audit procedures as necessary.

The auditor may consider testing the operating effectiveness of controls, if any, over the **preparation** of **information** used in applying analytical procedures. When such controls are effective, the auditor generally has greater confidence in the reliability of the information, and therefore in the results of analytical procedures.

The operating effectiveness of **controls** over **non-financial information** may often be tested in conjunction with other tests of controls. For example, in establishing controls over the processing of sales invoices, a business may include controls over the recording of sales units. In these circumstances the auditor may test the operating effectiveness of controls over the recording of unit sales in conjunction with tests of the operating effectiveness of controls over the processing of sales invoices.

The suitability of a particular analytical procedure will depend upon the auditor's assessment of how effective it will be in detecting a misstatement that may cause the financial statements to be materially misstated.

The ISA states that 'the auditor shall design and perform analytical procedures near the end of the audit that assist the auditor when forming an overall conclusion as to whether the financial statements are consistent with the auditor's understanding of the entity'.

The conclusions from these analytical procedures should corroborate the conclusions formed from other audit procedures on parts of the financial statements. This assists the auditor to draw reasonable conclusions on which to base the audit opinion. However, these analytical procedures may identify a previously unrecognised risk of material misstatement. In such circumstances the auditor is required to revise the auditor's assessment of the risks of material misstatement and modify the further planned audit procedures accordingly.

As we have discussed, analytical procedures should be used at the risk assessment stage. Possible sources of information about the client include:

- Interim financial information
- Budgets
- Management accounts
- Non-financial information
- Bank and cash records
- Sales tax returns
- Board minutes
- Discussions or correspondence with the client at the year end

Auditors may also use specific industry information or general knowledge of current industry conditions to assess the client's performance.

As well as helping to determine the nature, timing and extent of other audit procedures, such analytical procedures may also indicate aspects of the business of which the auditors were previously unaware. Auditors are looking to see if developments in the client's business have had the expected effects. They will be particularly interested in changes in audit areas where problems have occurred in the past.

## 1.5 Directional testing

For any item in the final statements which is being tested there are two possibilities. It could be fairly stated or misstated.

If it is misstated there are again two possibilities. It could be:

- Overstated; or
- Understated

When testing for overstatement (or existence/occurrence) a different approach is used from testing for understatement (or completeness).

Worked example: Two invoices

Imagine two invoices, each for £1,000.

Invoice 1 is a fraudulent purchase invoice and should not have been posted. As a result, purchases are overstated by £1,000. To find this misstatement the auditor can either:

- Look at all the purchase invoices and try to identify the fraudulent one

- Look at the figure for purchases in the financial statements and gradually follow the audit trail until arriving at persuasive supporting evidence

One might think that either of these approaches would work. If the fraudulent invoice had been suppressed in some way, however, it would be impossible to find it by looking through the invoices. It follows therefore that, when testing for overstatement, the auditor should start with the figures given, and follow the audit trail until coming to the supporting documentation.

To summarise, the pattern for overstatement testing is as follows.

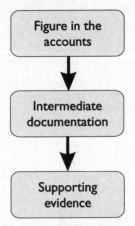

Now consider invoice 2, a sales invoice which has been omitted resulting in an understatement of revenue by £1,000. In this case, selecting a sample from the final revenue figure in the financial statements will be no use. As the item has been omitted, it will be impossible to select it and test it.

So in order to test for understatement the auditor will have to select from a population which will give the chance of selecting omitted items. Such a population has been described as "a reciprocal population". For invoice 2, that population would be the entity's dispatch notes, provided that the auditor is satisfied that all despatches are 'captured' on dispatch notes at the point of dispatch.

A reciprocal population for **accounts payable** is more difficult to arrive at. Paragraph A27 of ISA 500 suggests that when testing accounts payable for understatement, such a population could be:

- Subsequent disbursements
- Unpaid invoices
- Suppliers' statements
- Unmatched receiving reports

The pattern for understatement (or completeness) testing can be summarised as follows.

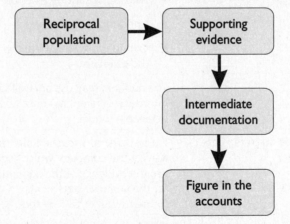

Traditionally directional testing has been used as a mechanism for reducing the amount of testing done. If in a double entry bookkeeping system there is a debit for every credit, the trial balance balances and all debit entries (expenses and assets) are tested for overstatement, and all credit entries (revenue, liabilities, equity and reserves) are tested for understatement, it is possible to draw the conclusion that, if no misstatements are found, all items are fairly stated.

The "normal" approach adopted, therefore, is to test debits for overstatement and credits for understatement.

However, note that the majority of high profile corporate scandals (including Enron) have involved the overstatement of income rather than its understatement. Money laundering schemes would also tend to show similar characteristics. It is important therefore to assess the true risks, rather than automatically apply a formula.

### Interactive question 1: Evidence

[Difficulty level: Exam standard]

In respect of an assurance engagement, which one of the following is the least persuasive method of gathering evidence?

A Inspection of a purchase invoice
B Inspection of a sales invoice
C Inspection of inventory by the auditor
D Reperformance of a supplier statement reconciliation undertaken by the client

See **Answer** at the end of this chapter.

## 1.6 Audit of accounting estimates

The auditor often has to audit estimated figures, such as those for product warranties, depreciation, inventory or receivables provisions, where the values included in the financial statements are not the result of transactions with third parties (which are fairly reliable) but result from judgements made by management. Yet these figures can have a very significant effect on reported profits.

There is a risk that management may be biased in the judgements it makes when calculating estimated figures. The auditor must therefore approach these values with professional scepticism regarding the judgements made.

The audit approach required is set out in ISA 540 (UK and Ireland) *Auditing Accounting Estimates, Including Fair Value Accounting Estimates, and Related Disclosures*. Essentially, if risk assessment procedures have identified a risk of material misstatement due to accounting estimates, the auditor can respond by undertaking one or more of the following methods.

| Method | Example |
|---|---|
| Test the process that management used to estimate the figure and the data on which it is based | Management may use a formula to calculate the provision for doubtful accounts receivable. The auditor can test this by:<br><br>• Looking at past experience<br><br>• Checking the calculation<br><br>• Considering if anything this year is likely to have changed the estimate |
| Use a point estimate | The auditors may use an available or proprietary model, or introduce different assumptions, or engage a specialist to develop a model. |
| Review events occurring up to the date of the auditor's report | If a settlement is reached after the year end regarding a claim against the company which requires a provision, the auditor can use the evidence of the agreement to establish the correct figure for the financial statements. In this case there is usually no need to use the other two methods. |
| Test the operating effectiveness of controls over how management made the accounting estimate, with associated substantive procedures | If there are strong controls over the estimation, and the estimate is derived from the routine processing of data by the entity's accounting system. |

Having done the detailed work on the accounting estimate, the auditor checks the reasonableness of the figure and then reaches a conclusion about whether it is fairly stated.

This sort of work is clearly needed in an audit assignment, where estimates such as provisions required for damages in a lawsuit might be required, but the work is also very relevant to a number of other types of assurance engagement. Reports on a business plan often require an accounting estimate to be checked. The techniques used in these assignments will be the same as for audit assignments.

# 2 Selecting items to test

## Section overview

- Assurance providers usually seek evidence from less than 100% of items of the balance or transaction being tested.

- Every item in the population of items being sampled must have an equal chance of being selected in the sample.

- The greater the risk of the area being sampled, the higher the sample size will be.

- When drawing conclusions from sampling, the auditor must identify which discovered misstatements affect the overall balance.

## 2.1 The concept of sampling

Assurance providers do not normally examine all the information available to them; it would be impractical to do so and using sampling will produce valid conclusions provided it is carried out properly.

ISA 530 (UK and Ireland) *Audit Sampling* states that 'the objective of the auditor, when using audit sampling, is to provide a reasonable basis for the auditor to draw conclusions about the population from which the sample is selected'. Remember that the ISA relates specifically to audits, but all assurance providers may use sampling.

## Definitions

Audit sampling: The application of audit procedures to less than 100% of items within a population of audit relevance such that all sampling units have a chance of selection in order to provide the auditor with a reasonable basis on which to draw conclusions about the entire population.

Population is the entire set of data from which a sample is selected and about which an auditor wishes to draw conclusions.

Some testing procedures do **not** involve sampling, such as:

- **Testing all** items in a population (100% examination)
- Testing all items with a **certain characteristic**, as selection is not representative

Assurance providers are unlikely to test 100% of items when carrying out tests of control, but 100% examination may be appropriate for certain substantive procedures. For example, if the population is made up of a small number of high value items and there is a high risk of material misstatement then 100% examination may be appropriate.

The ISA requires distinguishes between **statistical sampling** and **non-statistical methods**.

### Definitions

**Statistical sampling:** An approach to sampling that has the following characteristics:

(i)   Random selection of the sample items; and

(ii)  The use of probability theory to evaluate sample results, including measurement of sampling risk.

**Non-statistical sampling:** A sampling approach that does not have characteristics (i) and (ii) is considered non-statistical sampling.

---

The auditor may alternatively select certain items from a population because of specific characteristics they possess. The results of items selected in this way cannot be projected onto the whole population but may be used in conjunction with other audit evidence concerning the rest of the population.

- **High value or key items.** The auditor may select high value items or items that are suspicious, unusual or prone to error.

- **All items over a certain amount.** Selecting items this way may mean a large proportion of the population can be verified by testing a few items.

- **Items to obtain information** about the client's business, the nature of transactions, or the client's accounting and control systems.

## 2.2   Design of the sample

When designing the sample, ISA 530 requires the auditor to 'consider the **purpose** of the audit procedure and the **characteristics of the population** from which the sample will be drawn', and to consider the sampling and selection methods.

When designing an audit sample, the auditor's consideration includes the specific purpose to be achieved and the combination of audit procedures that is likely to best achieve that purpose. The auditor also needs to consider the nature and characteristics of the audit evidence sought and possible deviation or misstatement conditions. This will help them to define **what constitutes a deviation or misstatement** and **what population to use** for sampling.

### Definitions

**Misstatement:** a difference between the amount, classification, presentation, or disclosure of a reported financial statement item and the amount, classification, presentation, or disclosure that is required for the item to be in accordance with the applicable financial reporting framework. Misstatements can arise from error or fraud.

**Error:** an unintentional misstatement in financial statements, including the omission of an amount or a disclosure.

---

The population from which the sample is drawn must be **appropriate and complete** for the specific audit objectives. Auditors must **define** the **sampling unit** in order to obtain an efficient and effective sample to achieve the particular audit objectives.

### Definition

**Sampling units** are the individual items constituting a population.

---

## Worked example: Sampling units

- Cheques listed on deposit slips
- Credit entries on bank statements
- Sales invoices
- Receivables balances
- A monetary unit (an example of monetary unit sampling is given in section 2.3)

ISA 530 requires that the auditor 'shall select items for the sample in such a way that each sampling unit in the population has a chance of selection'. This requires that **all items** in the population have an opportunity to be selected.

As we saw above, in obtaining evidence, the auditor should use professional judgement to assess audit risk and design audit procedures to ensure this risk is reduced to an acceptably low level. In determining the sample size, the auditor shall determine a sample size sufficient to reduce sampling risk is reduced to an acceptably low level.

## Definitions

Sampling risk is the risk that the auditor's conclusion based on a sample may be different from the conclusion if the entire population were subjected to the same audit procedure.

Non-sampling risk is the risk that the auditor reaches an erroneous conclusion for any reason not related to sampling risk. For example, the use of inappropriate procedures, or misinterpretation of audit evidence and failure to recognise a misstatement or deviation.

### 2.2.1    Factors influencing sample sizes

ISA 530 gives examples of factors which influence sample sizes for tests of controls and tests of details:

| Tests of controls | |
| --- | --- |
| Factor | Effect on sample size |
| An increase in the extent to which the auditor's risk assessment takes into account relevant controls | INCREASE |
| An increase in the tolerable rate of deviation | DECREASE |
| An increase in the expected rate of deviation of the population to be tested | INCREASE |
| An increase in the auditor's desired level of assurance that the tolerable rate of deviation is not exceeded by the actual rate of deviation in the population | INCREASE |
| An increase in the number of sampling units in the population | NEGLIGIBLE EFFECT |

| Tests of details | |
| --- | --- |
| Factor | Effect on sample size |
| An increase in the auditor's assessment of the risk of material misstatement | INCREASE |
| An increase in the use of other substantive procedures directed at the same assertion | DECREASE |
| An increase in the auditor's desired level of assurance that tolerable misstatement is not exceeded by actual misstatement in the population | INCREASE |
| An increase in tolerable misstatement | DECREASE |
| An increase in the amount of misstatement the auditor expects to find in the population | INCREASE |

| Tests of details | |
| --- | --- |
| Factor | Effect on sample size |
| Stratification of the population when appropriate | DECREASE |
| The number of sampling units in the population | NEGLIGIBLE EFFECT |

The greater the auditor's desired level of assurance that the results of the sample are in fact indicative of the actual misstatement in the population, the larger sample sizes have to be. In other words, if the auditor is placing a great deal of relevance on this (it is not corroborating other evidence, for example) the higher the sample size will have to be.

## Definitions

**Tolerable misstatement** is a monetary amount set by the auditor in respect of which the auditor seeks to obtain an appropriate level of assurance that the monetary amount set by the auditor is not exceeded by the actual misstatement in the population.

**Tolerable rate of deviation** is a rate of deviation from prescribed internal control procedures set by the auditor in respect of which the auditor seeks to obtain an appropriate level of assurance that the rate of deviation set by the auditor is not exceeded by the actual rate of deviation in the population.

Tolerable misstatement is considered during the planning stage and, for substantive procedures, is related to the auditor's judgement about materiality. The smaller the tolerable misstatement, the greater the sample size will need to be.

(a) For tests of controls, the auditor makes an assessment of the **expected rate of deviation** based on the auditor's understanding of the relevant controls or on the examination of a small number of items from the population. If the expected rate of deviation is unacceptably high, the auditor will normally decide not to perform tests of controls.

(b) For tests of details, the auditor makes an assessment of the **expected misstatement** in the population, If the expected misstatement is high, 100% examination or use of a large sample size may be appropriate when performing tests of details.

The level of sampling risk that the auditor is willing to accept affects the sample size required. The lower the risk the auditor is willing to accept, the greater the sample size will need to be.

## Worked example: Designing the sample

Sarah is planning the audit of receivables at Manufacturing Company Limited (MCL). MCL makes all its sales on credit, and the receivables ledger is extensive. However, Sarah has adjudged the area to be low risk as most customers pay their debts promptly and controls over the receivables ledger and credit control are good. In previous years, testing has revealed that few misstatements are discovered. She therefore applies a low sample number.

During the course of testing, Sarah discovers a much higher number of misstatements than she was expecting. She therefore increases her sample and extends her test.

In practice, most auditing firms use computer programs to set sample sizes, based on risk assessments and materiality.

## 2.3 Selecting the sample

There are a number of selection methods available.

(a) **Random selection** ensures that all items in the population have an equal chance of selection, eg by use of random number tables or computerised generator.

(b) **Systematic selection** involves selecting items using a constant interval between selections, the first interval having a random start. When using systematic selection assurance providers must ensure that the population is not structured in such a manner that the sampling interval corresponds with a particular pattern in the population.

(c) **Haphazard selection** may be an alternative to random selection provided assurance providers are satisfied that the sample is representative of the entire population. This method requires care to guard against making a selection that is biased, for example towards items that are easily located, as they may not be representative. It should not be used if assurance providers are carrying out statistical sampling.

(d) **Sequence or block selection.** Sequence sampling may be used to check whether certain items have particular characteristics. For example, an auditor may use a sample of 50 consecutive cheques to check whether cheques are signed by authorised signatories rather than picking 50 single cheques throughout the year. Sequence sampling may, however, produce samples that are not representative of the population as a whole, particularly if misstatements only occurred during a certain part of the period, and hence the misstatements found cannot be projected onto the rest of the population.

(e) **Monetary Unit Sampling (MUS).** This is a selection method that ensures that every £1 in a population has an equal chance of being selected for testing. The advantages of this selection method are that it is easy when computers are used, and that every material item will automatically be sampled. Disadvantages include the fact that if computers are not used, it can be time consuming to pick the sample, and that MUS does not cope well with errors of understatement (as the computer cannot select a £ which is not there) or negative balances.

## Worked example: MUS

You are auditing trade accounts receivable. Total trade account receivables is £500,000 and materiality is £50,000. You will select the balances containing each 50,000th £1 from the following ledger.

| CUSTOMER | BALANCE | CUMULATIVE TOTAL | SELECTED |
|---|---|---|---|
| A | 30,000 | 30,000 | |
| B | 35,000 | 65,000 | Yes |
| C | 45,000 | 110,000 | Yes |
| D | **52,000** | **162,000** | Yes |
| E | 13,000 | 175,000 | |
| F | **50,000** | **225,000** | Yes |
| G | 23,000 | 248,000 | |
| H | 500 | 248,500 | |
| I | 41,500 | 290,000 | Yes |
| J | 47,000 | 337,000 | Yes |
| K | **54,000** | **391,000** | Yes |
| L | 17,000 | 408,000 | Yes |
| M | **80,000** | **488,000** | Yes |
| N | 12,000 | 500,000 | Yes |
| | 500,000 | | |

Material items are shown **in bold** and have all automatically been selected. The cumulative column shows you when the next 50,000th £1 has been reached.

**Interactive question 2: Factors affecting sample size**

[Difficulty level: Exam standard]

When determining a sample size for tests of detail there are a number of factors that an auditor should take into account.

For each of the following factors, select whether it would cause the sample size to increase or decrease.

(i) Decrease in the assessed level of tolerable misstatement.

☐ Increase ☐ Decrease

(ii) Increase in the assessed risk level.

☐ Increase ☐ Decrease

(iii) Discovery of more misstatements than were anticipated during testing.

☐ Increase ☐ Decrease

See **Answer** at the end of this chapter.

# 3 Drawing conclusions from sampling

**Section overview**

- The purpose of sampling a set of items was to enable the auditors to project the conclusion to the whole population.

- Auditors must consider the nature of the misstatement and whether it is fair to project that misstatement.

- If the projected misstatement exceeds tolerable misstatement then sampling risk must be reassessed and further audit procedures must be considered.

When the auditors have tested a sample of items, they must then draw conclusions from that sample. The purpose of audit sampling is to enable conclusions to be drawn from an entire population on the basis of testing a sample drawn from it.

To begin with, the auditors must consider whether the items in question are **true misstatements**, as they defined them before the test. For example, when testing receivables, a sampled misposting between customer accounts will not affect whether the auditors conclude the valuation of total receivables is true and fair.

When the expected audit evidence regarding a specific sample item cannot be found, the auditor shall perform the procedure on a replacement item. In such cases, the item is not treated as a misstatement.

The **qualitative** aspects of misstatements are also considered, including the **nature and cause** of the misstatement. Auditors must also consider any possible effects the misstatement might have on **other parts of the audit** including the general effect on the financial statements and on the auditors' assessment of the accounting and internal control systems.

Where common features are discovered in misstatements, the auditors may decide to identify all items in the population that possess the common feature (eg location), thereby producing a sub-population. Audit procedures could then be extended in this area

On some occasions the auditor may decide that the misstatement is an anomaly.

**Definition**

Anomaly: a misstatement or deviation that is demonstrably not representative of misstatements or deviations in a population.

To be considered anomalous, the auditors have to be certain that the misstatements are not representative of the population. Extra work will be required to prove that a misstatement is an anomaly.

The auditors must project the misstatement results from the sample onto the relevant population. The auditors will **estimate the probable misstatement** in the population by extrapolating the misstatements found in the sample.

For substantive tests, auditors will then **estimate any further misstatement** that might not have been detected because of the imprecision of the technique (in addition to consideration of the qualitative aspects of the errors).

Auditors must also consider the effect of the projected misstatement on other areas of the audit. The auditors should compare the projected population misstatement (net of adjustments made by the entity in the case of substantive procedures) to the tolerable misstatement taking account of other relevant audit procedures.

If the projected population misstatement **exceeds** or is close to tolerable misstatement, then the auditors must re-assess sampling risk. If it is unacceptable, they shall consider extending auditing procedures or performing alternative procedures. However, if after alternative procedures the auditors still believe the actual misstatement rate is higher than the tolerable misstatement rate, they should re-assess control risk if the test is a test of controls; if the test is a substantive test, they should consider whether the financial statements need to be adjusted.

## Worked example: Drawing conclusions from sampling

Adrian carried out a supplier statement reconciliation on Peabody Ltd. This means that he compared the statements sent by suppliers to Peabody Ltd to the details on Peabody's own payables ledger. Tolerable misstatement has been set at £10,000. The sample was 10 payables ledger balances totalling £35,024 out of a total of £375,297. Adrian found that of these, 8 reconciliations proved that the balance on the ledger was correct, one showed that an invoice had been misposted to a different supplier's account and one showed that an invoice had not been posted at all.

When considering the results of his sample, Adrian decided that he can disregard the misposting, as, although it means that two accounts were individually misstated, the overall balance was not affected by this mistake. In the case of the invoice that had simply been omitted in error however, Adrian had to conclude that this misstatement of £250, which does impact the overall total balance, could be repeated in the overall population with the potential for causing material misstatement. Adrian projected the total population misstatement based on the sample and compared the outcome to tolerable misstatement. In this case he found that the projected misstatement of £2,679 was considerably below the tolerable misstatement of £10,000 and concluded that no further action was required. He concluded from his testing that the trade payables balance in the financial statements was fairly stated.

## Interactive question 3: Drawing conclusions from sampling

[Difficulty level: Exam standard]

Danielle has carried out a receivables circularisation on Donothing plc to gain evidence about the receivables balance stated in the draft statement of financial position. Identify whether the following conclusions drawn by her are correct or not.

(a) An amount disagreed by Lazy Limited because an invoice had been paid two days before the year end and cleared shortly after the year end, did not constitute a misstatement for the purposes of drawing a conclusion for the whole population.
☐ True   ☐ False

(b) An amount disagreed by Sloth Limited because a credit note had been issued by Donothing plc a month before the year end did not constitute a misstatement for the purposes of drawing a conclusion for the whole population.
☐ True   ☐ False

(c) An amount disagreed by Busy Limited because they had paid the balance some time earlier, which further enquiry revealed had been posted to a different customer account, did constitute a misstatement for the purposes of drawing a conclusion for the whole population.
☐ True   ☐ False

See **Answer** at the end of this chapter.

# 4 Evaluation of misstatements

### Section overview

- ISA 450 (UK and Ireland) *Evaluation of Misstatements Identified during the Audit* requires the auditor to evaluate the effect of identified misstatements on the audit and evaluate the effect of any uncorrected misstatements on the financial statements.

- All non-trivial misstatements must be communicated to management and if uncorrected, to those charged with governance.

The auditor is required to **evaluate the effect of identified misstatements on the audit** in ISA 450 (UK and Ireland) *Evaluation of Misstatements Identified during the Audit*. Under this ISA, the auditor must also **evaluate the effect of any uncorrected misstatements on the financial statements.**

During the audit, auditors must accumulate any non-trivial misstatements identified and determine whether the audit plan or overall audit strategy need to be revised based on these. Additional audit procedures shall be performed where management has examined and corrected balances at the auditor's request.

The auditor is required to communicate all misstatements on a timely basis to the appropriate level of management and request that management corrects the misstatements. The auditor is required to request a written representation from management whether they believe the effects of uncorrected misstatements to be immaterial to the financial statements as a whole. If management have corrected material misstatements, then doing this may help them to fulfil their governance responsibilities, including reviewing the effectiveness of internal control.

If management refuses to correct some or all of the misstatements then the auditor shall:

- Obtain an understanding of management's **reasons** for not making the corrections

- Determine whether uncorrected misstatements are **material** individually or in aggregate

- **Communicate** individual uncorrected misstatements to those charged with governance and request that these be corrected, mentioning any effect on the opinion in the auditor's report

- Request a **written representation** from management (and if appropriate those charged with governance) that they believe the effects of the uncorrected misstatements are immaterial, individually and in aggregate, to the financial statements as a whole

In determining whether uncorrected misstatements are material, the auditor must consider the **size** and **nature** of the misstatements, along with the particular **circumstances** of their occurrence. Certain circumstances may cause the auditor to evaluate misstatements as material, even if they are lower than materiality for the financial statements as a whole. Examples of circumstances include, but are not limited to, the extent to which the misstatement:

- Affects compliance with regulatory requirements

- Affects compliance with debt covenants or other regulatory requirements

- Masks a change in earnings or other trends

- Affects ratios used to evaluate the entity's financial position, results of operations or cash flows

- Increases management's compensation, for example by ensuring the requirements for the award of bonuses are met

## Interactive question 4: Material misstatements          [Difficulty level: Exam standard]

Which TWO of the following should be determined as material uncorrected misstatements?

A    An isolated misposting between two supplier accounts which is below materiality
B    A misstatement which is below materiality and results in director's bonus targets being met
C    An immaterial misstatement of assets which results in a debt covenant not being breached
D    The monthly bank reconciliation was not prepared in August as the cashier was on holiday

See **Answer** at the end of this chapter.

Summary

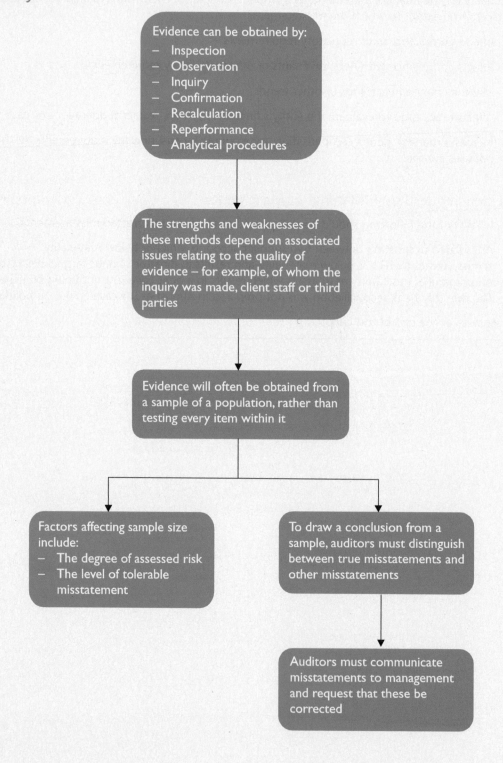

Evidence can be obtained by:
- Inspection
- Observation
- Inquiry
- Confirmation
- Recalculation
- Reperformance
- Analytical procedures

The strengths and weaknesses of these methods depend on associated issues relating to the quality of evidence – for example, of whom the inquiry was made, client staff or third parties

Evidence will often be obtained from a sample of a population, rather than testing every item within it

Factors affecting sample size include:
- The degree of assessed risk
- The level of tolerable misstatement

To draw a conclusion from a sample, auditors must distinguish between true misstatements and other misstatements

Auditors must communicate misstatements to management and request that these be corrected

## Self-test

Answer the following questions.

1    Which **one** of the following procedures would give the most persuasive evidence that a control operated as the assurance providers had been advised?

   A    Inspection of the controls handbook
   B    Inquiry of the staff operating the control
   C    Observation of the staff operating the control
   D    Reperformance of the control by audit staff

2    Indicate the purpose of the primary test for each type of account in directional testing.

   (a)  Assets          ☐ Overstatement          ☐ Understatement

   (b)  Liabilities     ☐ Overstatement          ☐ Understatement

   (c)  Income          ☐ Overstatement          ☐ Understatement

   (d)  Expense         ☐ Overstatement          ☐ Understatement

3    Identify the significant relationships in the list of items below.

   (a)  Payables        (b)  Interest        (c)  Purchases        (d)  Revenue

   (e)  Amortisation    (f)  Loans           (g)  Receivables      (h)  Intangibles

4    Identify whether the following statements are true or false.

|  |  | True | False |
|---|---|---|---|
| (i) | The risk that the auditor's conclusion, based on a sample, may be different from the conclusion if the entire population were subjected to the same audit procedure is sampling risk. | ☐ | ☐ |
| (ii) | The risk that the auditor might use inappropriate procedures or might misinterpret audit evidence and thus fail to recognise a misstatement or deviation is non-sampling risk. | ☐ | ☐ |

5    Identify whether the following examples of sample selection are random, haphazard or systematic.

|  |  | Random | Haphazard | Systematic |
|---|---|---|---|---|
| (a) | Barry is selecting a sample from the list of receivables balances. He selects the second, and thereafter every 7th balance. | ☐ | ☐ | ☐ |
| (b) | Carol is selecting a number of purchase invoices to carry out a directional test. She selects them by flicking through the files and selecting an invoice occasionally. | ☐ | ☐ | ☐ |

Now, go back to the Learning Objectives in the Introduction. If you are satisfied you have achieved these objectives, please tick them off.

# Technical reference

## 1 Evidence

- Procedures to obtain evidence     ISA 500.A14 – A25 (UK and Ireland)
- Analytical procedures     ISA 520 + ISA 315.6 (UK and Ireland)
- Accounting estimates     ISA 540.13 (UK and Ireland)

## 2 Selecting items to test

- The concept of sampling     ISA 500.A54 + ISA 530.4 – 5 (UK and Ireland)
- Design of the sample     ISA 530.5 – 8, Appx 2, Appx 3
- Selecting the sample     ISA 530 Appx 1 (UK and Ireland)

## 3 Drawing conclusions from sampling     ISA 530.14, A18 – A23 (UK and Ireland)

## 4 Evaluation of misstatements     ISA 450.5 – 15 + ISA 450.A16 (UK and Ireland)

### Answer to Interactive question 1

B   A sales invoice is an internally generated document and therefore provides a poor source of evidence. It would be better to obtain information about sales from the customers.

### Answer to Interactive question 2

They would all cause the sample size to increase.

### Answer to Interactive question 3

(a)   True – this is just a timing difference.

(b)   False – this indicates that the credit note may not have been processed to the receivables ledger, which would be an error that could also be true of other potential credits due on the ledger.

(c)   False – this error does not affect the overall balance on the ledger.

### Answer to Interactive question 4

B, C Although these two items are below materiality, the particular circumstances surrounding their occurrence make them material misstatements. D relates to a test of controls.

# Answers to Self-test

1    D    Reperformance by the auditor would give the strongest evidence of this being the case.

2    (a)   Overstatement
      (b)   Understatement
      (c)   Understatement
      (d)   Overstatement

3    (a) and (c)
      (b) and (f)
      (d) and (g)
      (e) and (h)

4    (i)    True
      (ii)   True

5    (a)   Systematic
      (b)   Haphazard

# CHAPTER 12

# Written representations

Introduction

Examination context

**Topic List**

Summary and Self-test

Technical reference

Answers to Interactive question

Answers to Self-test

### Learning objectives

- Understand the purpose and nature of written representations from management

- Understand when oral representations should be confirmed in writing

- Understand how reliable these written representations are as a form of assurance evidence

The specific syllabus reference for this chapter is: 3h.

### Syllabus links

You will need to understand the purpose, content and reliability of written representations as assurance evidence when you go on to draw assurance conclusions and look at assurance reports in Audit and Assurance.

### Examination context

There was one question on the sample paper, relating to written representations, dealing with their purpose. You should not expect more than one or two questions on this area in your assessment.

In the assessment, candidates may be required to:

- Identify the purposes of a written representation letter
- Identify the circumstances in which written representations may be sought

# 1 Written representations as assurance evidence

**Section overview**

- The auditor shall request management to provide certain general written representations: that it has prepared the financial statements in accordance with the applicable financial reporting framework, that it has provided the auditor with all relevant information and access, and that all transactions have been recorded and reflected in the financial statements.

- Some ISAs require the auditor to request written representations. In addition to this, the auditor may decide that it needs more. These written **representations from management** should be restricted to one or more specific assertions in the financial statements.

- Any written representations should be **compared** with other evidence and their **sufficiency** assessed.

Assurance providers receive many representations during the engagement, both unsolicited and in response to specific questions. Some of these representations may be critical to obtaining sufficient appropriate evidence.

ISA 580 (UK & Ireland) *Written Representations* deals with the auditor's responsibility to obtain written representations from management and, where appropriate, those charged with governance in an audit of financial statements. The principles of the ISA (outlined in this section) are also valid for other assurance work.

## Definition

**Management** is the person(s) with executive responsibility for the conduct of the entity's operations. For some entities in some jurisdictions, management includes some or all of those charged with governance, for example, executive members of a governance board, or an owner-manager.

In ISA 580 references to management also include those charged with governance where this is appropriate.

Written confirmation of oral representations avoids confusion and disagreement. Such matters should be discussed with those responsible for giving the written confirmation, to ensure that they understand what they are confirming. Written confirmations are normally required of senior management.

## 1.1 General matters

Written representations are required for general matters; for example, that the accounting records have been made fully available to the auditors.

There are a number of elements that ISA 580 requires auditors to confirm in writing, namely that management (usually the directors in the UK, who have statutory duties in respect of financial statements) has:

- Fulfilled its responsibility for the preparation of the financial statements in accordance with the applicable financial reporting framework, including where relevant their fair presentation, as set out in the terms of the audit engagement

- Provided the auditor with all relevant information and access as agreed in the terms of the audit engagement

- Recorded and reflected all transactions in the financial statements

The confirmation with regard to responsibility and approval of the financial statements is normally done when the auditors receive a signed copy of the financial statements, which incorporate a relevant statement of responsibilities.

The written representations are dated as near as possible, but not after, the date of the auditor's report on the financial statements.

## 1.2 Other written representations

In addition to general written representations about management's responsibilities, the auditors are required to request specific written representations by other ISAs and also where the auditor determines they are necessary to support other audit evidence.

Written representations cannot be used instead of other (better) evidence which the auditors expect to exist.

# 2 When other written representations are required

**Section overview**

- Specific written representations may be required in a variety of situations.

- If written representations do not agree with other audit evidence, other audit procedures should be performed and the implications considered.

Other written representations may include the following matters.

- Whether the selection and application of accounting policies are appropriate

- Whether matters such as the following, where relevant under the applicable financial reporting framework, have been recognised, measured, presented or disclosed in accordance with that framework

    - Plans or intentions that may affect the carrying value or classification of assets and liabilities

    - Liabilities, both actual and contingent

    - Title to assets, the liens on assets, and assets pledged as collateral

    - Aspects of laws, regulations and contractual agreements that may affect the financial statements, including non-compliance

- Whether all deficiencies in internal control of which management is aware have been communicated to auditors

- Specific written representations required by other ISAs

- Support for management's judgement or intent in relation to a specific assertion

### Worked example: Other written representations required

Keira is working on the audit of Prejudiced plc. In the prior year, there had been a large amount of obsolete inventory at the year end due to a decision by management to amend the design of their major product to improve the safety of the product. Keira has been asked to ensure that management provide written representation that they have no intention of making any similar amendments to their products this year that would impact on existing inventory in this way. This representation would be corroborated by reviewing minutes of management meetings.

There may be occasions when there are doubts over the **reliability** of written representations. If the auditor has concerns over the competence, integrity, ethical values or diligence of management, the auditor shall determine the effect that such concerns may have over the reliability of representations (oral and written) and audit evidence in general.

If written representations are **inconsistent with other audit evidence**, the auditor shall perform audit procedures in an attempt to resolve the matter. If the matter remains unresolved, the auditor shall reconsider its assessment of management and determine the effect that this may have on the reliability of representations (oral or written) in general.

# 3 Example of a written representation letter

- Here is an example of a written representation letter from management.

(Entity Letterhead)

(To Auditor) (Date)

This representation letter is provided in connection with your audit of the financial statements of ABC Company for the year ended December 31, 20X1 for the purpose of expressing an opinion as to whether the financial statements are presented fairly, in all material respects, (or give a true and fair view) in accordance with International Financial Reporting Standards.

We confirm that (to the best of our knowledge and belief, having made such inquiries as we considered necessary for the purpose of appropriately informing ourselves):

Financial Statements

- We have fulfilled our responsibilities, as set out in the terms of the audit engagement dated [insert date], for the preparation of the financial statements in accordance with International Financial Reporting Standards; in particular the financial statements are fairly presented (or give a true and fair view) in accordance therewith.

- Significant assumptions used by us in making accounting estimates, including those measured at fair value, are reasonable. (ISA 540)

- Related party relationships and transactions have been appropriately accounted for and disclosed in accordance with the requirements of International Financial Reporting Standards. (ISA 550)

- All events subsequent to the date of the financial statements and for which International Financial Reporting Standards require adjustment or disclosure have been adjusted or disclosed. (ISA 560)

- The effects of uncorrected misstatements are immaterial, both individually and in the aggregate, to the financial statements as a whole. A list of the uncorrected misstatements is attached to the representation letter. (ISA 450)

- Any other matters that the auditor may consider appropriate.

Information provided

- We have provided you with:

    – Access to all information of which we are aware that is relevant to the preparation of the financial statements such as records, documentation and other matters;

    – Additional information that you have requested from us for the purpose of the audit; and

    – Unrestricted access to persons within the entity from whom you determined it necessary to obtain audit evidence.

- All transactions have been recorded in the accounting records and are reflected in the financial statements.

- We have disclosed to you the results of our assessment of the risk that the financial statements may be materially misstated as a result of fraud. (ISA 240)

- We have disclosed to you all information in relation to fraud or suspected fraud that we are aware of and that affects the entity and involves:

    – Management;

    – Employees who have significant roles in internal control; or

    – Others where the fraud could have a material effect on the financial statements. (ISA 240)

- We have disclosed to you all information in relation to allegations of fraud, or suspected fraud, affecting the entity's financial statements communicated by employees, former employees, analysts, regulators or others. (ISA 240)

- We have disclosed to you all known instances of non-compliance or suspected non-compliance with laws and regulations whose effects should be considered when preparing financial statements. (ISA 250A)

- We have disclosed to you the identity of the entity's related parties and all the related party relationships and transactions of which we are aware. (ISA 550)

- Any other matters that the auditor may consider necessary.

.................................                    .................................
Management                                          Management

---

**Interactive question: Written representations**                    [Difficulty level: Exam standard]

Which **two** of the following are purposes of a written representation letter from management?

[ ] Confirmation that management has received the signed audit report

[ ] Confirmation that management has fulfilled its responsibility for the preparation of the financial statements

[ ] Confirmation of all representations made by management in the course of the audit

[ ] Confirmation that management has recorded and reflected all transactions in the financial statements

[ ] Confirmation that management understands the terms of the engagement

See **Answer** at the end of this chapter.

## Summary

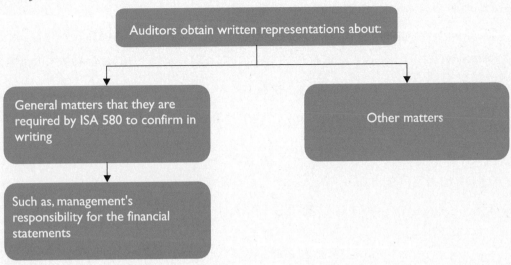

Auditors obtain written representations about:

General matters that they are required by ISA 580 to confirm in writing

Other matters

Such as, management's responsibility for the financial statements

## Self-test

Answer the following questions.

1   Written representations include a statement that management has provided the auditor with all relevant information.

☐   True

☐   False

2   All written representations are in the form of a representation letter addressed to the shareholders.

☐   True

☐   False

3   Which **two** of the following statements are correct?

☐   Written representations must include a statement that the selected accounting policies are appropriate.

☐   Written representations should be corroborated with other sources of evidence.

☐   Written representations are an appropriate source of evidence when other evidence does not exist because it has been accidentally destroyed.

☐   The written representation should be dated on or before the date of the auditor's report.

Now, go back to the Learning Objectives in the Introduction. If you are satisfied you have achieved these objectives, please tick them off.

# Technical reference

1 Written representations as assurance evidence

ISA 580.10 – 11 (UK and Ireland)

2 When other written representations are required

- Other representations

ISA 580.A10 – A12 (UK and Ireland)

- Reliability

ISA 580.16 – 18 (UK and Ireland)

3 Example of a written representation letter

ISA 580 Appx 2 (UK and Ireland)

## Answer to Interactive question

Confirmation that management has fulfilled its responsibility for the preparation of the financial statements.

Confirmation that management has recorded and reflected all transactions in the financial statements.

1    True

2    False – the representation letter is addressed to the auditor

3    Written representations should be corroborated with other sources of evidence.

The written representation should be dated on or before the date of the auditor's report.

# CHAPTER 13

# Substantive procedures – key financial statement figures

### Learning objectives

- Understand the nature of tests on balances carried out by assurance providers and the objectives of those tests

- Identify suitable tests in a given business scenario

- Understand when a matter should be referred to a senior member of staff

Specific syllabus references for this chapter are: 3f, i.

### Syllabus links

The results of the tests outlined here will be the basis for the drawing conclusions part of your Audit and Assurance paper.

### Examination context

Questions about assurance evidence could be set in the context of any balances outlined in this chapter.

In the assessment, candidates may be required to:

- Select appropriate audit procedures for a given financial statement assertion
- Identify the features of external confirmation requests
- Identify why the results of a physical inventory count may differ from inventory records
- Identify the procedures which should be undertaken to confirm the existence of cash at bank
- Evaluate the results of audit work and identify issues that should be referred to a senior colleague

# 1 Non-current assets

**Section overview**

- Key areas when testing tangible non-current assets are:

    - Confirmation of ownership (rights and obligations)
    - Inspection of non-current assets (existence and valuation)
    - Valuation, preferably by third parties (valuation)
    - Adequacy of depreciation rates (valuation)

- Key areas when testing intangible non-current assets are:

    - Confirmation that 'assets' exist
    - Confirmation of appropriate valuation

- Key areas when testing investments are:

    - Confirmation of existence
    - Confirmation of ownership

## 1.1 Tangible non-current assets

You should be aware of the major classes of tangible non-current assets from your Accounting studies. Examples of tangible non-current assets include land, buildings, plant, vehicles, fittings and equipment.

The major risks of the tangible non-current asset balances in the financial statements being misstated are due to:

- The company not actually owning the assets (rights and obligations assertion)

- The assets not actually existing or having been sold by the company (existence assertion)

- Omission of assets owned by the company (completeness assertion)

- The assets being overvalued, either by inflating cost or valuation, or by undercharging depreciation (valuation assertion)

- The assets being undervalued, by not including an appropriate revaluation in a policy of revaluation or by overcharging depreciation (valuation assertion)

- The assets being incorrectly presented in the financial statements (presentation and disclosure assertion)

The objective of assurance tests in respect of non-current assets is therefore to prove that these assertions about the assets are correct. There are several sources of information about non-current assets that can be used (you should consider the strengths and weaknesses of all the sources of evidence listed in this chapter according to the criteria we set out in Chapter 11):

- The non-current asset register (which many companies maintain as a control over the assets they own)

- Purchase invoices for assets purchased within the year

- Sales invoices for assets sold within the year

- Registration documents or other documents of title such as title deeds for property

- Valuations carried out by employees or third party valuers

- Leases or hire purchase documentation in respect of assets

- Physical inspection of the assets themselves by the auditor

- Depreciation records or calculations (these are often kept with the asset register)

### Worked example: Non-current asset assurance engagement

Peter is carrying out a non-current asset assurance engagement at Manufacturing Company Limited (MCL). MCL owns the property from which it operates. It has a lot of fixed plant, which it replaced three years ago, and owns several industrial vehicles for moving inventory between locations at its premises. It also owns a number of cars, which its staff have as company cars, and a great deal of office furniture, fittings and computers in the office complex attached to the factory.

Peter is concerned with concluding that the non-current assets declared in the financial statements are complete, exist, are owned by the company and are valued appropriately.

*Completeness*

Peter will:

- Obtain a schedule of non-current assets from the client

- Agree the figures per the schedule to the financial statements and accounting records (nominal ledger)

- Compare the schedule to the asset register to ensure that the schedule reflects all the assets owned by the company

- Select a number of assets physically present on site and ensure that they are contained in the asset register

- Confirm the additions on the schedule are correct

*Existence*

Peter will:

- Select a sample of assets contained in the asset register and verify that they are physically present on site

*Rights and obligations*

Peter will:

- Select a sample of assets in the asset register and vouch them to the registration documents available for those assets (vehicles – registration documents (although these indicate who is the 'registered keeper', who is not necessarily the owner), building – title deeds, plant and fixtures – purchase invoice, ensuring that it is not a lease)

- Review sales invoices for sold assets to ensure that ownership has been transferred

*Valuation*

Peter will:

- Confirm the cost or valuation of a sample of assets to purchase invoices or valuation certificates

- Confirm the brought forward depreciation levels of those assets (if relevant) to prior year audit files or by reviewing the brought forward asset register files

- Confirm the annual depreciation in respect of those assets is appropriate (by reference to the accounting policy on depreciation published in the financial statements), and correctly calculated (by recalculation or by using analytical procedures)

- Review to ensure that depreciation has been correctly calculated on disposed assets, and recalculate profit or loss on sale of those assets

*Presentation and disclosure*

- Peter will review the financial statements to ensure that the disclosure requirements relating to non-current assets have been met

*Other matters*

- Peter is likely to focus asset testing on asset additions, as these will comprise a large proportion of the cost of non-current assets as they will have been depreciated the least.

- Peter will use sampling on some classes of assets and not others. For example, in this instance, property is likely to be a material balance and therefore will be vouched 100%. Other classes of assets are likely to be sampled as the overall total contains a large number of assets.

## Worked example: Self-constructed assets

Katie is working on the audit of Quickshop plc, a large supermarket chain. She has been allocated the audit of non-current assets. One aspect of this audit is the fact that the company has built four new superstores during the year, which have been capitalised into non-current assets. The key objectives she is working on are that all the relevant costs have been capitalised (completeness) and that the self-built stores are valued correctly at cost (valuation).

*Completeness*

Katie will:

- Obtain architect's certificates for the stores, certifying that the work is complete.

- Obtain a schedule of all the costs capitalised into the stores; this is also likely to have been verified by the contractor, giving comfort that the costs are complete.

*Valuation*

Katie will:

- Vouch a sample of costs to appropriate sources of evidence, for example, labour costs to payroll records or contractor bills, materials costs to purchase invoices or contractor bills, finance costs to statements from lenders (for example, bank statements).

- In respect of finance costs, Katie will review bank statements to ensure that all relevant finance costs have been included.

## Interactive question 1: Non-current assets          [Difficulty level: Exam standard]

Which **three** of the following might an auditor vouch when testing the rights and obligations of a company in respect of a vehicle?

☐ A purchase invoice

☐ A registration document

☐ A hire-purchase agreement

☐ An asset register

See **Answer** at the end of this chapter.

## 1.2 Intangible non-current assets

Examples of intangible assets include licences, development costs and purchased brands.

The major risks of misstatement of the intangible non-current asset balances in the financial statements are due to:

- Expenses being capitalised as non-current assets inappropriately (existence assertion)

- Intangible assets being carried at the wrong cost or valuation due to inflating the cost or valuation (valuation assertion)

- Intangible assets being carried at the wrong cost or valuation due to charging inappropriate amortisation, wrongly amortising or not amortising (valuation assertion)

- Intangible assets being carried at the wrong cost or valuation due to impairment reviews not being carried out appropriately (valuation assertion)

The objective of tests in respect of intangible non-current assets is therefore to prove that these assertions about the assets are correct. The following sources of information can be used:

- Accounting standards/auditor's knowledge of accounting standards for what constitutes an intangible asset

- Purchase invoices or documentation (particularly for, say, purchased intangibles)

- Client calculations and schedules

- Specialist valuations

- Auditor understanding of the entity for signs of impairment factors

# 2 Inventory

### Section overview

- Key areas when testing inventory are:
    - Attending an inventory count (existence)
    - Valuation at the lower of cost and net realisable value (valuation)
    - In some cases, confirmation of ownership (rights and obligations)

The major risks of misstatement of the inventory balance in the financial statements are due to:

- Inventory that does not exist being included in the financial statements (existence)

- Not all inventory that exists being included in the financial statements (completeness)

- Inventory being included in the financial statements at full value when it is obsolete or damaged (valuation)

- Inventory being included in the financial statements at the wrong value, whether due to miscalculation of cost or the fact that cost has been used although net realisable value is lower than cost (valuation)

- Inventory that actually belongs to third parties being included in the financial statements (rights and obligations)

- Inventory which has actually been sold is included in the financial statements (cut-off)

The objective of assurance tests in respect of inventory is therefore to prove that these assertions about the assets are correct. The following sources of information can be used:

- The company's controls over inventory counting
- The auditors' attendance at the annual inventory count
- Confirmations with third parties holding inventory or having inventory stored for them by the company
- Purchase invoices for inventory
- Work-in-progress records for inventory
- Post-year-end sales invoices for inventory
- Post-year-end price lists for inventory
- Post-year-end sales orders

Inventory may lend itself to analytical review as there is a relationship between inventory, revenue and purchases.

## 2.1 Inventory count

Attendance at an inventory count can be very important. In order to confirm the amount of inventory in existence, rather than undertake a count itself, assurance providers usually rely on the controls that a company has in operation over its inventory or its annual inventory count.

It is important that the assurance provider is satisfied that controls are such that it can be concluded that the count, or the overall inventory controls, are capable of ensuring the correct amount of inventory is reflected in the financial statements.

In terms of inventory counts, the assurance provider will be looking for the following sorts of controls.

| REVIEW OF INVENTORY COUNT INSTRUCTIONS | |
|---|---|
| Organisation of count | **Supervision** by senior staff, including senior staff not normally involved with inventory |
| | **Tidying** and **marking** inventory to help counting |
| | **Restriction** and **control** of the production process and inventory movements during the count |
| | **Identification of damaged, obsolete, slow-moving, third party** and **returnable** inventory |
| Counting | **Systematic counting** to ensure all inventory is counted |
| | Teams of **two counters,** with one counting and the other checking, or two **independent counts** |
| Recording | **Serial numbering, control** and **return** of all inventory sheets |
| | Inventory sheets being **completed** in **ink** and **signed** |
| | **Information** to be recorded on the **count records** (location and identity, count units, quantity counted, conditions of items, stage reached in production process) |
| | Recording of **quantity, conditions** and **stage of production** of **work-in-progress** |
| | Recording of last numbers of **goods inwards** and **outwards** records and of internal transfer records |
| | **Reconciliation** with **inventory records** and **investigation** and correction of any **differences** |

Some companies have better day-to-day controls over inventories than others and many have complex systems of perpetual counting rendering an annual year-end count unnecessary. In order to rely on such a system of perpetual counting, the assurance provider needs to confirm that the controls over this system are strong.

If perpetual inventory counting is used, assurance providers will check that management:

(a) Ensures that all inventory lines are counted at least once a year.

(b) Maintains **adequate inventory records** that are kept up-to-date. Assurance providers may compare sales and purchase transactions with inventory movements, and carry out other tests on the inventory records, for example checking casts and classification of inventory.

(c) Has **satisfactory procedures** for **inventory counts** and **test-counting**. Assurance providers should confirm the inventory count arrangements and instructions are as rigorous as those for a year-end inventory count by reviewing instructions and observing counts. Assurance providers will be particularly concerned with **cut-off**; that there are no inventory movements whilst the count is taking place, and inventory records are updated up until the time of the inventory counts.

(d) **Investigates** and **corrects** all **material differences**. Reasons for differences should be recorded and any necessary corrective action taken. All corrections to inventory movements should be **authorised** by a manager who has not been involved in the detailed work; these procedures are necessary to guard against the possibility that inventory records may be adjusted to conceal shortages.

| AUDIT PLAN: PERPETUAL INVENTORY COUNT |
| --- |
| Attend one of the inventory counts (to observe and confirm that instructions are being adhered to) |
| **Follow up** the **inventory counts attended** to compare quantities counted by the assurance providers with the inventory records, obtaining and verifying explanations for any differences, and checking that the client has reconciled count records with book records |
| **Review** the **year's counts** to confirm the extent of counting, the treatment of discrepancies and the overall accuracy of records (if matters are not satisfactory, assurance providers will only be able to gain sufficient assurance by a full count at the year-end) |
| Assuming a full count is not necessary at the year-end, **compare** the **listing of inventory with the detailed inventory records**, and carry out other procedures (**cut-off, analytical review**) to gain further comfort |

## 2.2 Cost v NRV

Management should **compare cost and net realisable value** for each item of inventory. Where this is impracticable, the comparison may be done by group or category.

Net realisable value is likely to be less than cost when there has been:

- An **increase in costs** or a fall in selling price
- **Physical deterioration**
- **Obsolescence** of products
- A **marketing decision** to manufacture and sell products at a loss
- **Errors in production or purchasing**

For work in progress, the **ultimate selling price** should be **compared** with the **carrying value** at the year-end plus **costs** to be **incurred** after the year-end to bring work in progress to a finished state. The example below shows the test carried out to identify whether NRV is lower than cost.

Worked example: Audit of inventory

Rajeev is carrying out the audit of inventory at Icket Ltd. Icket produces various lines of tableware on behalf of high street stores. It also sells tableware to wholesalers and has a small retail outlet. Icket is not entitled to sell branded products to wholesalers and it makes approximately 10% more inventory of branded products than ordered to ensure it meets quality control standards of the stores. This 10% is therefore obsolete once sales of a line to a store are finished. Each high street store has an allocated sales manager at Icket who keeps records of what sales have been made of each line and when the line is coming to an end. One high street store customer, Argus, maintains a store of approved inventory at Icket's premises, which it calls off as required. Icket carried out an annual inventory count at the year-end.

The key issues for Rajeev when auditing inventory are:

- To ensure that obsolete inventory is not included at full cost in the financial statements

- To ascertain that inventory included in the financial statements exists and that all existing and valuable inventory is included, including the inventory held at the retail outlet

- To ensure that inventory belonging to Argus is not included in the financial statements

- To ensure that inventory is held at the appropriate value in the financial statements

*Existence*

Rajeev will:

- Obtain a copy of the count instructions issued to employees of Icket and review them to assess whether controls over the count appear strong enough to ensure that the correct amount of inventory will be reflected in the financial statements.

- Assess the key issues arising at the count; for instance, what the high value inventory is, what the risks are (outlined above), or whether there are any specific issues that will make counting complex (not in this case).

- Plan his count attendance, including sample sizes and target inventory lines.

- Attend the inventory count, at which he will carry out sample counts to ensure that the counters are counting properly, the instructions are being adhered to, procedures for obsolete and damaged inventory are being followed, Argus inventory is properly separated and noted, and to gain an overall impression of the level and state of the inventories and conclude whether the count has been carried out properly.

- Trace a sample of items on the final inventory sheets back to original count documents and ensure all count documents are reflected in the final sheets.

*Completeness*

Rajeev will:

- Follow up items sampled at the inventory count to ensure that they are included in the final inventory sheets, and therefore the financial statements.

- Follow up Argus items sampled at the inventory count to ensure that they are not included in the final inventory sheets, and therefore the financial statements.

- Carry out a 'cut-off' test, ensuring that year-end deliveries and sales have not been double counted or not counted (for example, by including an item in inventory and in sales, or by excluding a consignment of goods received from inventory and purchases). This will be done by selecting the goods inwards and outwards notes on either side of the year-end and tracing them to invoices, ledgers and inventory sheets to ensure they are recorded correctly.

*Rights and obligations*

Rajeev will:

- Send a confirmation letter to Argus, asking them to confirm the level of inventory held at Icket on the year-end date.

- Compare the answer to this letter to Icket's records, and, if necessary, reconcile any differences, liaising with Icket's Argus sales manager. If there are any substantial differences, this could indicate a problem with controls over this area of which Rajeev should inform a senior audit team member.

*Valuation*

Rajeev will:

- Check that the calculations of valuation on the final inventory sheets have been made correctly.

- Select samples of raw materials, work in progress and finished goods from Icket's final inventory sheets.

- Ascertain the accounting policy for inventory cost from the financial statements (for example, FIFO) and confirm it is reasonable and appropriate.

- Trace the cost of the raw materials sample to purchase invoices to ensure cost has been recorded correctly and on the right basis.

- In addition, for work in progress and finished goods samples, ensure that an appropriate level of raw material has been costed, by reviewing production records.

- Confirm labour costs allocated to work in progress and finished goods by reference to production records and payroll.

- Review Icket's overhead allocation to ensure only appropriate costs are included (for example, not idle time) and perform analytical procedures comparing overhead allocation to previous years.

- Compare valuation of cost for finished goods sample to post-year end selling prices, by reference to sales orders or invoices, to ensure inventory is held at the lower of cost and NRV.

- Follow up items noted as obsolete or damaged at the inventory count to ensure that valuation has been appropriately adjusted to reflect NRV.

- For branded goods in excess of customer requirements, ensure that valuation has been entered as zero (these goods should be identifiable from sales manager's records).

---

### Interactive question 2: Inventory                    [Difficulty level: Exam standard]

Which **one** of the following procedures should be undertaken to confirm the existence of inventory?

☐ Attendance at inventory count

☐ Follow up of inventory count sheets to final inventory sheets

☐ Trace items of inventory to purchase invoices

☐ Cast the final inventory sheets

See **Answer** at the end of this chapter.

---

# 3 Receivables

### Section overview

- Key areas when testing receivables are:

  - Confirming debt owed by customers with customers (existence, rights and obligations)
  - Confirming debt is still likely to be collected (valuation)

The major risks of misstatement of the receivables balance in the financial statements are due to:

- Debts being uncollectable (valuation)
- Debts being contested by customers (existence, rights and obligations)

The objective of assurance tests in respect of receivables is therefore to prove that these assertions about the assets are correct. The following sources of information can be used:

- Receivables ledger information
- Confirmations from customers
- Cash payments received after the year end

If the company makes a similar number of sales annually to a fairly established customer base then analytical procedures may give good results.

## 3.1 Confirmations from customers

When it is reasonable to expect customers to respond, the assurance providers should ordinarily plan to obtain direct confirmation of receivables to individual entries in an account balance. Direct confirmation of receivables in an audit is covered by ISA 505 (UK and Ireland) *External Confirmations*. External confirmations are not compulsory in an audit of financial statements.

The verification of trade receivables by external confirmation is a means of providing relevant and reliable audit evidence to satisfy the objective of checking whether customers exist and owe *bona fide* amounts to the company (**existence** and **rights and obligations**).

Confirmation should take place immediately after the year end and hence cover the year end balances to be included in the balance sheet. If this is not possible it may be acceptable to carry out the confirmation **prior to the year end** provided that the auditor obtains further evidence relating to the remainder of the period.

Confirmation is essentially an act of the **client**, who alone can authorise third parties to divulge information to the auditor. If the client refuses to allow the auditor to send a confirmation request, the auditor shall inquire as to management's reasons for the refusal and evaluate the implications on the auditor's risk assessment. Alternative audit procedures must be performed. If these do not generate relevant and reliable audit evidence or the auditor concludes that management's refusal is unreasonable, the auditor must communicate with those charged with governance and determine the implications for the auditor's opinion.

When confirmation is undertaken the method of requesting information from the customer may be either 'positive' or 'negative'.

- Under the **positive** method the customer is requested to give the balance or to confirm the accuracy of the balance shown or state in what respect he is in disagreement.

- Under the **negative** method the customer is requested to reply only if the amount stated is disputed. This method generally provides less reliable audit evidence than the positive method as a lack of response could mean that the customer does not dispute the balance, or it could mean that the customer did not receive the confirmation request, or ignored it.

The positive method is generally preferable as it is designed to encourage definite replies from those contacted. The risk that customers might reply without actually confirming the balance can be mitigated by not providing the balance for confirmation and requesting that the customer fills the balance in. However, this approach can lead to a lower response rate as it involves more work on the part of the customer. The negative method should only be used when:

- Assessed risk of material misstatement is low
- The relevant controls are operating effectively
- A large number of small balances is involved
- A substantial number of errors is not expected
- The auditor has no reason to believe that customers will disregard the request

The statements will normally be prepared by the client's staff, from which point the assurance providers, as a safeguard against the possibility of fraudulent manipulation, must maintain strict control over the checking and despatch of the statements.

Precautions must also be taken to ensure that undelivered items are returned, not to the client, but to the assurance providers' own office for follow up by them.

MANUFACTURING CO LIMITED

15 South Street

London

Date

Messrs (customer)

In accordance with the request of our auditors, Messrs Arthur Daley & Co, we ask that you kindly confirm to them directly your indebtedness to us at (insert date) which, according to our records, amounted to £.......... as shown by the enclosed statement.

If the above amount is in agreement with your records, please sign in the space provided below and return this letter direct to our auditors in the enclosed stamped addressed envelope.

If the amount is not in agreement with your records, please notify our auditors directly of the amount shown by your records, and if possible detail on the reverse of this letter full particulars of the difference.

Yours faithfully,

For Manufacturing Co Limited

Reference No: ...........................

...................................................................................................................................

(Tear off slip)

The amount shown above is/is not * in agreement with our records as at (insert date)

Account No ............................... Signature      ...............................

Date ............................... Title or position      ...............................

* The position according to our records is shown overleaf.

Notes

- The letter is on the client's paper, signed by the client.
- A copy of the statement is attached (although that will not always be the case).
- The reply is sent directly to the auditor in a pre-paid envelope.

---

Assurance providers will normally only contact a sample of customers although it must be based upon a complete list of all customers. In addition, when constructing the sample, the following classes of account should receive special attention:

- **Old unpaid accounts**
- **Accounts written off** during the period under review
- **Accounts with credit balances**
- **Accounts settled by round sum payments**

Similarly, the following should not be overlooked:

- **Accounts with nil balances**
- **Accounts** that have been **paid** by the date of the examination

Assurance providers will have to carry out further work in relation to those receivables who:

- **Disagree** with the **balance stated** (positive and negative confirmation)
- **Do not respond** (positive confirmation only)

In the case of disagreements, where the customer balance was stated, the customer response should have identified specific amounts that are disputed.

There is a **dispute** between the client and the customer. The reasons for the dispute would have to be identified, and specific allowances for receivables made if appropriate against the debt.

**Cut-off problems** exist, because the client records the following year's sales in the current year or because goods returned by the customer in the current year are not recorded in the current year. Cut-off testing may have to be extended.

The customer may have sent the **monies before** the year-end, but the monies were **not recorded** by the client as receipts until **after** the year-end. Detailed cut-off work may be required on receipts.

Monies received may have been posted to the **wrong account** or a cash-in-transit account. Assurance providers should check if there is evidence of other misposting. If the monies have been posted to a cash-in-transit account, assurance providers should ensure this account has been cleared promptly.

Customers who are also suppliers may **net off balances** owed and owing. Assurance providers should check that this is allowed.

**Teeming and lading** (**stealing** monies and **incorrectly posting** other receipts so that no particular customer is seriously in debt), is a fraud that can arise in this area. If assurance providers suspect teeming and lading has occurred, detailed testing will be required on cash receipts, particularly on prompt posting of cash receipts.

When the positive request method is used the assurance providers must follow up by all practicable means those customers who **fail to respond**. Second requests should be sent out in the event of no reply being received within two or three weeks and if necessary this may be followed by telephoning the customer, with the client's permission.

After two, or even three, attempts to obtain confirmation, a list of the outstanding items will normally be passed to a responsible company official, preferably independent of the sales accounting department, who will arrange for them to be investigated.

Where their confirmation is carried out before the year end, assurance providers will have to reconcile the balance agreed to the year-end balance by reviewing ledger records, invoices and receipts.

All confirmations, regardless of timing, must be properly recorded and evaluated. All **balance disagreements** and **non replies** must be **followed up** and their effect on total receivables evaluated.

**Differences** arising that merely represent **invoices** or **cash in transit** (normal timing differences) generally do not require adjustment, but disputed amounts, and errors by the client, may indicate that further substantive work is necessary to determine whether material adjustments are required.

## 3.2 Alternative procedures to verify existence/rights and obligations

If it proves impossible to get confirmations from individual customers, alternative procedures must be performed which may include the following.

**Check receipt of cash** after date

**Verify valid purchase orders**, although these will not necessarily have led to an invoice

**Examine the account** to see if the balance outstanding represents specific invoices and **confirm** their **validity** to despatch notes

**Obtain explanations** for **invoices remaining unpaid** after subsequent ones have been paid

**Check** if the **balance** on the account is **growing**, and if so, why

**Test company's control** over the issue of **credit notes** and the **write-off of irrecoverable receivables**

## 3.3 Irrecoverable receivables

A significant test of irrecoverable receivables will be reviewing the **cash received after** date. This will provide evidence of collectability of debts (and hence **valuation**). It also provides some evidence of correctness of title (**rights and obligations**), although ideally it should be carried out as well as a receivables confirmation (the main test on rights and obligations as outlined above).

## 3.4 Other receivables

A company may also have other receivables, such as royalties. It should be possible to verify such items to third party evidence, such as correspondence from the relevant partner, or by cash received after date.

### Worked example: Audit of receivables

Sajeeda is working on the audit of General Stationery plc (GSP), a company that sells a large range of standard stationery items to businesses by mail order. GSP has a large receivables ledger. Although GSP has many established clients, it also receives a number of one-off or short-term customers, as some companies tend to shop around for the best deals on stationery at the time. GSP's controls over new customers and sales orders are good in principle, but controls testing has revealed weaknesses in their operation. In addition, some problems with goods despatch and invoicing were also discovered during controls testing. It has been concluded that substantial tests of detail are required in this area with quite a large sample of customer accounts being taken.

The major risks of misstatement of GSP's receivables balance arise from:

- Customers disputing the balances due to requested credits and general problems with recording sales on customer accounts.

- There being a high instance of irrecoverable receivables.

*Completeness*

Sajeeda will:

- Obtain a listing of receivables, and ensure that it casts correctly and agrees with the receivables balance in the financial statements and the sales ledger control account total in the nominal ledger.

- Check a sample of customers on the list against the individual sales ledger accounts.

*Rights and obligations/existence*

Sajeeda will:

- Select a sample of receivables balances and carry out confirmation procedures at the year end, using the positive approach, providing a statement of the customer's account.

- Follow up replies appropriately depending on their content.

*Valuation*

Sajeeda will:

- Obtain an analysis of aged debt at the year end from receivables ledger records and review it for debt in excess of GSP's published credit terms.

- Carry out an analysis of after-date receipts to observe whether any old debt remains outstanding at audit date.

- If so, collate a list of old debt as yet unpaid and compare the results of any confirmation replies that are covered by the list.

- Cross-refer her list to any list of debt written off in the financial statements.

- Discuss old debts not written off with the credit controller to see what steps GSP has taken to recover the debt.

- Consider whether any of the debt requires writing off in the financial statements. This amount should be entered on a list of potential adjustments. If material, it should be referred to senior audit team members.

It is the middle of the final audit visit to GSP. Sajeeda has received 54 out of 56 replies to her confirmation requests. Of these replies, 30 agree the balance stated and 24 dispute the balance. Customers who have not yet replied have been sent three reminders each.

Sajeeda will:

- Pass the two outstanding requests to a senior official unconnected with sales for further follow up.

- Perform reconciliations on the 24 disputed balances, using the information given on the reply and the information available in the sales and receipts records of GSP.

Of the 24 disputes, Sajeeda finds that 10 relate to timing differences with regard to receipts. She confirms that all of these receipts clear GSP's bank within reasonable time after the year end by checking the paying in records and bank statements. She can conclude that these 10 accounts are fairly stated.

The remaining 14 have differences resulting from requested credits, for damaged goods (some going back over six months), for invoices in relation to which there were no goods delivered and for invoices relating to different customers.

Sajeeda will:

- Discuss the requested credits with the appropriate sales manager to determine why credits have not been issued and form an opinion as to whether these debts and related sales may need writing off.

- Trace invoices disputed due to lack of goods delivered, try and trace back to despatch notes to ascertain whether GSP states the goods were delivered and form an opinion as to whether these debts and related sales may need writing off.

- Consider the implications in terms of inventory movements if goods are being invoiced but not delivered – is inventory overstated; is a fraud being carried out where goods are being stolen?

- Refer to copy invoices to confirm whether invoices were in fact sent to the wrong customers. These errors, while indicating a lack of control over invoicing, do not affect the overall total of receivables, as they are genuine sales to other customers.

Sajeeda should:

- Highlight to senior audit team members that substantive testing has confirmed conclusions that controls in the area have been ineffective and proved that there is a problem with the receivables balance, and that the sample may have to be extended and further substantive tests carried out in this area.

Interactive question 3: Audit of receivables                [Difficulty level: Exam standard]

Which one of the following procedures should be undertaken to confirm the rights and obligations of trade receivables?

☐ Review of cash received after date

☐ Tests of controls over ordering

☐ Receivables external confirmation

☐ Recalculation of specific allowance for doubtful debts

See **Answer** at the end of this chapter.

# 4 Bank

**Section overview**

- Key areas when testing the balance sheet bank figure are:

    - Confirming bank balances directly with the bank (existence, valuation, rights and obligations)

    - Confirming reconciling differences calculated by the client are reasonable (completeness, valuation)

    - Confirming any material cash balances held at the client are correctly stated (valuation)

The major risks of misstatement of the bank and cash balance in the financial statements are due to:

- Not all bank balances owned by the client being disclosed (rights and obligations/existence)

- Reconciliation differences between bank balance and cash book balance being misstated (valuation)

- Material cash floats being omitted or misstated (completeness/existence)

The objective of tests in respect of bank is therefore to prove that these assertions about the assets are correct. The following sources of information can be used:

- Cash book
- Confirmation from the bank
- Bank statements
- Bank reconciliation carried out by the client

## 4.1 Direct confirmation with bank

Testing of bank balances will need to cover **completeness, existence, rights and obligations and valuation**. All of these elements can be tested directly through the device of obtaining third party confirmations from the client's banks and reconciling these with the accounting records, having regard to cut off. The assurance providers should update details of bank accounts held.

The form and content of a confirmation request letter (bank letter) will depend on the purpose for which it is required and on local practices.

The most commonly requested information is in respect of balances due to or from the client entity on **current, deposit, loan and other accounts**. The request letter should provide the account description number and the type of currency for the account.

It may also be advisable to request information about **nil balances** on accounts, and accounts which were closed in the twelve months prior to the chosen confirmation date. The client entity may ask for confirmation not only of the balances on accounts but also, where it may be helpful, other information, such as the maturity and interest terms, unused facilities, lines of credit/standby facilities, any offset or other rights or encumbrances, and details of any collateral given or received.

The client entity and its assurance providers are likely to request confirmation of **contingent liabilities**, such as those arising on guarantees, comfort letters, bills and so on.

Banks often hold **securities** and other items in safe custody on behalf of customers. A request letter may thus ask for confirmation of such items held by the confirming bank.

The procedure is simple but important.

(a)  The banks will require **explicit written authority** from their client to disclose the information requested.

(b)  The **assurance providers' request** must **refer** to the **client's letter** of authority and the date thereof. Alternatively it may be countersigned by the client or it may be accompanied by a specific letter of authority.

(c)  In the case of joint accounts, **letters of authority** signed by all **parties** will be necessary.

(d)  Such **letters** of **authority** may either **give permission** to the bank to disclose information for a specific request or grant permission for an indeterminate length of time.

(e)  The request should **reach** the **branch manager** at least **two weeks in advance** of the client's **year-end** and should state both that year-end date and the previous year-end date.

(f)  The **assurance providers** should themselves **check** that the bank response covers all the information in the standard and other responses.

## 4.2   Bank reconciliation

Care must be taken to ensure that there is no **window dressing**, by checking **cut off** carefully. Window dressing in this context is usually manifested as an attempt to overstate the liquidity of the company by:

(a)  Keeping the cash book open to take credit for **remittances actually received** after the year-end, thus enhancing the balance at bank and reducing receivables, as cash is more liquid than debt.

(b)  **Recording cheques paid** in the period under review which are not actually despatched until after the year-end, thus decreasing the balance at bank and reducing payables. This can contrive to present an artificially healthy looking current ratio.

With the possibility of (a) above in mind, where lodgements have not been cleared by the bank until the new period, the **assurance providers** should **examine the paying in slip** to ensure that the amounts were actually paid into the bank on or before the balance sheet date.

As regards (b) above, where there appears to be a particularly **large number of outstanding cheques** at the year-end, the **assurance providers** should check whether these were **cleared within** a **reasonable time** in the new period. If not, this may indicate that despatch occurred after the year-end.

## 4.3   Cash count

Planning is an essential element of cash counts, for it is an important principle that all cash balances are counted at the same time as far as possible. Cash in this context may include unbanked cheques received, IOUs and credit card slips, in addition to notes and coins. Often such cash balances are unlikely to be material, but in certain businesses they may be.

As part of their planning procedures the **assurance providers** will hence need to determine the **locations** where cash is held and which of these locations (if any) warrant a count.

Planning decisions will need to be recorded on the current audit file including:

*   The **precise time** of the count(s) and location(s)
*   The **names** of the **audit staff** conducting the counts
*   The **names** of the **client staff** intending to be present at each location

Where a location is not visited it may be expedient to obtain a letter from the client confirming the balance.

The following matters apply to the count itself.

*   All cash/petty **cash books** should be **written up** to date in ink (or other permanent form) at the time of the count.

*   All **balances** must be **counted** at the **same time**.

*   At **no time** should the **assurance providers** be left **alone** with the cash and negotiable securities.

*   **All cash counted** must be **recorded** on working papers subsequently filed on the current audit file. Reconciliations should be prepared where applicable (for example imprest petty cash float).

## Worked example: Audit of bank

Tracey is working on the audit of the bank reconciliation at IT Limited (ITL), a computer systems company. She has obtained the following bank reconciliation.

BANK RECONCILIATION AT 31 DECEMBER 20X6

| | £ | £ |
|---|---|---|
| Balance per bank statement | | 79,938 |
| Less: Unpresented cheques | | |
| Cheque number | | |
| 13539 | (24,933) | |
| 13540 | (54,388) | |
| 13542 | (64,420) | |
| 13543 | (3,492) | |
| 13544 | (1,849) | |
| 13545 | (53,944) | |
| 13546 | (940) | |
| | | (203,966) |
| | | (124,028) |
| Bal c/f | | (124,028) |
| Add: Outstanding lodgements | | |
| Date in cash book | | |
| 27.12 | 355 | |
| 28.12 | 103,344 | |
| 31.12 | 39,455 | |
| 31.12 | 5,301 | |
| | | 148,455 |
| Balance per financial statements | | 24,427 |

The bank letter confirmed the balance per bank given in the bank reconciliation.

Tracey will:

- Trace unpresented cheques to bank statements after the year end to confirm what date they cleared the bank.

- Review paying in books and bank statements in respect of the lodgements, to see what date they were paid into the bank.

- Enquire why a substantial lodgement remained unbanked for three days prior to the year end.

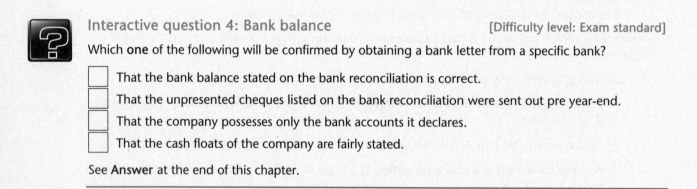

## Interactive question 4: Bank balance                    [Difficulty level: Exam standard]

Which **one** of the following will be confirmed by obtaining a bank letter from a specific bank?

☐ That the bank balance stated on the bank reconciliation is correct.

☐ That the unpresented cheques listed on the bank reconciliation were sent out pre year-end.

☐ That the company possesses only the bank accounts it declares.

☐ That the cash floats of the company are fairly stated.

See **Answer** at the end of this chapter.

# 5 Payables

**Section overview**

- Key areas when testing payables are:
    - Ensuring that all liabilities are included (completeness)
    - Confirming that all liabilities are *bona fide* owed by the company (rights and obligations)

The major risks of misstatements of payables in the financial statements are due to:

- The entity understating its liabilities in the financial statements (completeness)
- Cut-off between goods inward and liability recording being incorrect (cut-off)
- (More rarely) non-existent liabilities being declared (existence, rights and obligations)

The objective of tests in respect of payables is therefore to prove that these assertions about the liabilities are correct. The following sources of information can be used:

- Payables ledger records
- Confirmations from suppliers

Analytical procedures could point to understatement if the account balance is inexplicably reduced from previous years.

## 5.1 Supplier statements

The most important test when considering **trade payables** is comparison of suppliers' statements with payables ledger balances.

When selecting a sample of payables to test, assurance providers must be careful not just to select suppliers with large year-end balances. Remember, it is errors of **understatement** that assurance providers are primarily interested in when reviewing payables, and errors of understatement could occur equally in payables with low or nil balances as with high.

When comparing **supplier statements** with **year-end payables ledger balances**, assurance providers should include within their sample payables with nil or negative **payables ledger** balances. Assurance providers should be particularly wary of low balances with major suppliers. Remember the client has no incentive to record liabilities before being invoiced. The sample should be selected from the client's list of suppliers, not the payables ledger.

You may be wondering, as we normally carry out a circularisation confirmation of receivables, whether we would also circularise suppliers. The answer is generally no.

The principal reason for this lies in the nature of the purchases cycle: third party evidence in the form of suppliers' invoices and, even more significantly, **suppliers' statements**, are part of the standard documentation of the cycle. The assurance providers will hence concentrate on these documents when designing and conducting their tests.

In the following circumstances the assurance providers may, however, determine that a confirmation is necessary. In these cases confirmation requests should be sent out and processed in a similar way to accounts receivable confirmation requests. 'Positive' replies will be required where:

- **Suppliers' statements** are, for whatever reason, **unavailable** or **incomplete**.

- **Weaknesses in internal control** or the nature of the client's business make possible a material misstatement of liabilities that would not otherwise be picked up.

- It is thought that the **client** is **deliberately** trying to **understate payables**.

- The **accounts** appear to be **irregular** or if the nature or size of balances or transactions is abnormal.

## 5.2 Other payables/accrued expenses

Companies may have other **payables** and the tests carried out on them will vary according to what the nature of that account is. Remember that you are primarily testing for understatement. Consider if you can obtain third party evidence about the balance. You may have to think laterally about the specific balance.

## Worked example: Audit of payables

Ugo is working on the audit of payables at Seriously Dodgy Limited (SDL). He has carried out analytical procedures on the payables balance, comparing it with prior years, month by month balance owing levels, levels of purchases during the year and the change in inventory levels from beginning to end of the year.

Ugo has enquired about obtaining supplier statements at the year-end, and the **payables ledger** clerk has directed him to a file where they are kept. She tells him that not all the suppliers send statements, so they only reconcile the ones they get. Ugo confirms this with the audit file from the previous year. On examination of the file, however, Ugo notes that at least three suppliers which sent statements last year have apparently not sent statements this year. In addition, SDL has started major accounts with three new suppliers in the year, none of which has sent a statement.

As a result of this, and the results of his analytical procedures, which indicate that there may be a discrepancy between the level of purchases and the published payables at the year end, he suspects that SDL may be trying to understate payables.

Ugo therefore alerts senior audit staff members to his suspicions and makes a recommendation that a supplier circularisation be carried out as a one-off exercise.

## Interactive question 5: Audit of payables          [Difficulty level: Exam standard]

Indicate whether the following statements are true or false.

|  | True | False |
| --- | --- | --- |
| (i) Supplier statements are a strong source of evidence as they are third party evidence; however, as the assurance provider receives them through the medium of the client, the assurance provider must treat supplier statements with professional scepticism. | ☐ | ☐ |
| (ii) Payables may be tested by cash payments after date as these give an indication that debts were owed and the value of those debts has not been understated. | ☐ | ☐ |

See **Answer** at the end of this chapter.

# 6 Long-term liabilities

### Section overview

- Risks include failure to make correct disclosures and miscalculation of interest.
- There should be third party evidence from lender.

We are concerned here with long-term liabilities comprising debentures, loan stock and other loans **repayable** at a date **more than one year after the year-end**. The major risks of misstatement of long-term liabilities are:

- That not all long-term liabilities have been disclosed (completeness)

- That interest payable has not been calculated correctly and included in the correct accounting period (accuracy and cut-off)

- That disclosure is incorrect (presentation and disclosure)

A complication for the assurance provider is that debenture and loan agreements frequently contain conditions with which the company must comply, including restrictions on the company's total borrowings and adherence to specific borrowing ratios.

The following sources of information exist:

- Schedule of loans/prior year audit file information
- Statutory books, such as register of debentures, articles of association
- Loan agreements
- Bank letter and direct confirmations from other lenders
- Cash book
- Board minutes
- Client schedules and calculations
- Accounting policies in the financial statements

## PLAN: LONG-TERM LIABILITIES

**Obtain/prepare schedule of loans** outstanding at the balance sheet date showing, for each loan: name of lender, date of loan, maturity date, interest date, interest rate, balance at the end of the period and security

**Compare opening balances** to previous year's working papers

**Test the clerical accuracy** of the analysis

**Compare balances** to the **nominal ledger**

**Check name** of **lender** etc, to **register** of **debenture holders** or equivalent (if kept)

**Trace additions** and **repayments** to **entries** in the **cash book**

**Confirm repayments** are in accordance with **loan agreement**

**Examine cancelled cheques** and **memoranda of satisfaction** for **loans repaid**

**Verify** that **borrowing limits** imposed either by Articles or by other agreements are **not exceeded**

**Examine signed Board minutes** relating to **new borrowings/repayments**

**Obtain direct confirmation** from **lenders** of the amounts outstanding, accrued interest and what security they hold

**Verify interest charged** for the period and the adequacy of accrued interest

**Confirm assets charged** have been **entered** in the **register of charges** and **notified** to the **Registrar**

**Review restrictive covenants** and provisions relating to default:
- **Review** any **correspondence** relating to the loan
- **Review confirmation** replies for non-compliance
- If a **default appears** to exist, **determine** its **effect**, and schedule findings

**Review minutes, cash book** to **check** if all **loans have been recorded**

# 7 Income statement items

**Section overview**

- A key area when testing income statement items is completeness.

## 7.1 Revenue

It was stated in Chapter 6 that revenue will often be tested by testing controls. Subsequent testing on revenue will usually involve analytical procedures, as revenue is the area of the business the company is most likely to have information and analysis about. In addition, revenue has predictable relationships with other items in the financial statements, notably receivables, about which it is possible to obtain strong third party evidence as outlined above.

Revenue can also be tested by vouching individual transactions. If the major risk with revenue at a particular client is that it is overstated, this would involve selecting individual items of revenue recorded in the nominal ledger and tracing back to source documents, such as sales invoice, then despatch notes.

## 7.2 Purchases

As noted in Chapter 7, purchases are often tested by testing controls in that area. Additional or alternative substantive procedures will often include the use of analytical procedures due to the strong relationships that purchases has with other items in financial statements, notably inventory and payables.

In addition, individual transactions can be tested, commencing with goods received notes and tracing transactions through the system to ensure completeness.

## 7.3 Payroll costs

Analytical procedures are often carried out on payroll costs as there are strong relationships between numbers of staff, pay rates and overall costs and also tax/NI rates and pay.

Tests of details to verify if payroll costs might include checking for a sample of payroll records that time worked has been correctly included (to clockcards), employees exist (personnel records) and are being paid at the correct rate (contracts/personnel records) and that the payroll is calculated correctly (by reperforming calculations).

Payments from the payroll to staff and tax authorities can be verified to bank statements. Postings from the payroll to the nominal ledger should also be checked.

## 7.4 Interest paid/received

Interest paid/received can usually be tested by inspecting bank statements, or confirmations from other lenders.

## 7.5 Expenses

Other expenses in the income statement can be tested by analytical procedures, and also by vouching specific transactions to purchase invoices.

## Summary

### Non-current assets

Key issues:
Existence, rights and obligations, completeness, valuation

Sources of information:
Third party valuations, invoices, auditor inspection (strong)
Client schedules and calculations (not so strong)

### Inventory

Key issues:
Existence, valuation

Sources of information:
Auditor attendance at count, invoices, third party confirmations (strong)
Client controls over count, client production schedules (not so strong)

### Receivables

Key issues:
Rights and obligations, valuation

Sources of information:
Third party confirmations, cash payments after date (strong)

### Payables

Key issue:
Completeness

Sources of information:
Supplier statements (strong, but open to tampering by client)

### Bank

Key issues:
Completeness, existence, rights and obligations, valuation

Sources of information:
Confirmation from bank, bank statements (strong)
Client schedules, reconciliations (not so strong)

### Long-term liabilities

Key issues:
Completeness, accuracy, disclosure

Sources of information:
Loan documentation, statutory books, confirmations from lenders (strong)
Client schedules, board minutes, client calculations (not so strong)

### Income statement

Key issue:
Completeness

## Self-test

Answer the following questions.

1  Complete the table, showing which tests on tangible non-current assets are designed to provide evidence about which financial statement assertion.

| Completeness | Existence |
|---|---|
| Valuation | Rights and obligations |

(a)  Inspect assets

(b)  Verify to valuation certificate

(c)  Refer to title deeds

(d)  Compare assets in ledger to non-current asset register

(e)  Review depreciation rates

(f)  Verify material on self-constructed assets to invoices

(g)  Examine invoices after the year end

(h)  Review repairs in nominal ledger

2  Should the following inventory counting tests take place before, during or after the count?

| | Before | During | After |
|---|---|---|---|
| (a)  Check client staff are following instructions | ☐ | ☐ | ☐ |
| (b)  Review previous year's inventory count arrangements | ☐ | ☐ | ☐ |
| (c)  Assess method of accounting for inventories | ☐ | ☐ | ☐ |
| (d)  Trace counted items to final inventory sheets | ☐ | ☐ | ☐ |
| (e)  Check replies from 3rd parties re inventory held for them | ☐ | ☐ | ☐ |
| (f)  Conclude whether count has been properly carried out | ☐ | ☐ | ☐ |
| (g)  Gain an overall impression of levels/values of inventory | ☐ | ☐ | ☐ |
| (h)  Consider the need for expert help | ☐ | ☐ | ☐ |

3  Which of the following is not a reason why NRV of inventory should be lower than cost?

A  An increase in costs or a fall in selling price
B  Physical deterioration
C  A marketing decision to manufacture and sell products at a loss
D  Errors in recording or counting

4  The negative method of receivables' external confirmation should only be used if the client has a good internal control and a small number of large receivables accounts.

☐  True

☐  False

5    Complete these two sentences of the audit tests performed to verify the bank reconciliation.

(a)    Trace cheques shown as outstanding on the ..................................... to the ...................
..................... prior to the year end and ................................................................
.................................

(b)    Obtain satisfactory explanations for all items in the ........................................... for which
there is no corresponding entry in the ............................................. and .....................
.................................

6    At which **two** of the following locations would auditors expect to see more substantial cash floats?

☐    Hotels

☐    Retail outlets

☐    Manufacturing company

☐    Solicitor's practice

7    Nil balances should not be included in a supplier statement test.

☐    True

☐    False

Now, go back to the Learning Objectives in the Introduction. If you are satisfied you have achieved
these objectives, please tick them off.

## 1 Receivables

* **Confirmations from customers**                                    ISA 505 (UK and Ireland)

### Answer to Interactive question 1

A purchase invoice, a registration document and a hire-purchase agreement

### Answer to Interactive question 2

Attendance at inventory count

### Answer to Interactive question 3

Receivables external confirmation

### Answer to Interactive question 4

That the bank balance stated on the bank reconciliation is correct. The others are incorrect for the following reasons:

- That the unpresented cheques listed on the bank reconciliation were sent out pre year-end. (These will not be accounted for in the bank's year-end balance; only post-balance sheet bank statements will indicate whether these may have been held back.)

- That the company possesses only the bank accounts it declares. (As the company may have bank accounts with a different bank.)

- That the cash floats of the company are fairly stated. (As cash floats at the company are not within the scope of the bank letter.)

### Answer to Interactive question 5

(i) True. Assurance providers must always behave with professional scepticism, not assuming that documents such as supplier statements have been tampered with, but bearing in mind that it is a possibility if indications arise supporting that suggestion.

(ii) False. Cash payments after date do not prove that the balance is not understated, as the client may control the payments it makes and conceal correspondence from suppliers requesting full payment.

1

| Completeness | Existence |
|---|---|
| (d) Compare assets in ledger to non-current asset register | (a) Inspect assets |
| (h) Review repairs in nominal ledger | |
| **Valuation** | **Rights and obligations** |
| (b) Verify to valuation certificate | (c) Refer to title deeds |
| (e) Review depreciation rates | (g) Examine invoices after the year end |
| (f) Verify material on self-constructed assets to invoices | |

2  (a) During    (b) Before    (c) Before    (d) After
    (e) After     (f) During    (g) During    (h) Before

3  D    Errors in recording or counting

4  False

5  (a) Bank reconciliation, cash book, after date bank statements

   (b) Bank statements, cash book, bank reconciliation

6  Hotels and retail outlets

7  False

# CHAPTER 14

# Codes of professional ethics

Introduction

Examination context

**Topic List**

Summary and Self-test

Answers to Interactive question

Answers to Self-test

ICAEW

# Introduction

## Learning objectives

- Be aware of the key ethical codes to which ICAEW members are subject and the sources that influence them

- Understand the difference between principles and rules based systems

- Understand why ethics are important to accountants

- Know the key features of IFAC and ICAEW Codes

- Know the fundamental principles of IFAC and ICAEW Codes

Specific syllabus references for this chapter are : 4a, b, c, d, e.

## Syllabus links

You will build on the principles of professional ethics you learn here in your Audit and Assurance paper.

## Examination context

Ethics is 20% of the syllabus, and therefore in the sample paper, there were ten questions on ethics. These were a combination of questions about general ethical concepts and principles, which we shall look at in this chapter, and more detailed ethical threats and safeguards, which we shall look at in the next two chapters.

In the assessment, candidates may be required to:

- State the role of ethical codes and their importance to the profession

- Recognise the differences between a rules based ethical code and one based upon a set of principles

- Identify the key features of the system of professional ethics adopted by IFAC and ICAEW

- Identify the fundamental principles underlying the IFAC and the ICAEW Code of Ethics

# 1 Professional ethics

**Section overview**

- Accountants require an ethical code because they hold positions of trust, and people rely on them.

- Accountants work in the public interest, which extends beyond clients to people associated with those clients and the general community.

- ICAEW members are subject to ICAEW guidance (influenced by IFAC guidance) and FRC standards.

- Guidance tends to be issued in the form of principles rather than hard and fast rules.

## 1.1 Need for ethics

Professional accountants have a responsibility to consider the public interest and maintain the reputation of the accounting profession. Personal self-interest must not prevail over these duties. The IFAC and ICAEW Codes of Ethics help accountants to meet these obligations by setting out ethical guidance to be followed.

Acting in the public interest involves having regard to the legitimate interests of clients, government, financial institutions, employees, investors, the business and financial community and others who rely upon the objectivity and integrity of the accounting profession to support the propriety and orderly functioning of commerce.

In summary, then, the key reason accountants need to have an ethical code is that **people rely on them and their expertise**. It is important to note that this reliance extends beyond clients to the general community.

Accountants deal with a range of issues on behalf of clients. They often have access to confidential and sensitive information. Auditors (and other assurance providers) claim to give an independent view. It is therefore critical that accountants (particularly those giving assurance) are independent.

Compliance with a shared set of ethical guidelines gives protection to accountants as well, as they cannot be accused of behaving differently from (that is, less well than) other accountants.

## 1.2 Sources of ethical guidance

ICAEW members (and trainees) and employees of member firms are subject to the ICAEW Code of Ethics. This is influenced by the guidance of IFAC (the International Federation of Accountants, of which ICAEW is a member), which is actually issued by the IESBA (a body of IFAC) as the IESBA Code of Ethics for Professional Accountants. This is referred to here as the IFAC Code of Ethics. You should already be aware of this body as it is the same body that issues International Standards on Auditing, which we have been studying in this Study Manual.

UK auditors are also subject to the FRC's Ethical Standards for Auditors. The FRC is the Financial Reporting Council in the UK, which also issues auditing standards (adopted from IFAC, which creates them). These ethical standards were originally developed and published under the former APB and you may still see them referred to as such.

## 1.3 Rules or principles-based guidance?

The ethical guidance we shall look at tends to be in the form of a principles-based framework. It contains some rules (as we shall see in the next chapter), but in the main it is flexible guidance. It can be seen as being a framework of principles rather than a set of rules. There are a number of advantages of a framework of principles over a system of ethical rules, which are outlined in the following table.

| Factor | Explanation |
| --- | --- |
| Active consideration and demonstration of conclusions | A framework of principles places the onus on the accountant to actively consider independence for every given situation, rather than just agreeing a checklist of forbidden items. It also requires him to demonstrate that a responsible conclusion has been reached about ethical issues. |
| Broad interpretation of ethical situations | A principles-based framework prevents auditors interpreting legalistic requirements narrowly to get around ethical requirements. There is an element to which rules engender deception whereas principles encourage compliance. |
| Individual situations covered | A principles-based framework allows for the variations that are found in individual situations. Each situation is likely to be different. |
| Flexible to changing situation | A principles-based framework can accommodate a rapidly changing environment, such as the one that assurance providers are involved in. |
| Can incorporate prohibitions | However, a principle-based framework can contain certain prohibitions where these are necessary. |

# 2 IFAC Code

**Section overview**

- The IFAC Code contains a number of fundamental principles.

- It also gives guidance on the meaning of independence and the approach accountants should take to ethical questions.

- The IFAC Code sets out a number of general threats to independence and categories of safeguards.

The IFAC Code (also known as the 'IESBA Code' – the International Ethics Standards Board for Accountants (IESBA) is the ethics body of IFAC) contains a number of fundamental principles. It then goes on to outline key issues of ethics, such as independence, and highlight general and specific threats to independence and the safeguards that can be implemented to reduce those threats. A key issue to remember is that if it is impossible to reduce a threat to an acceptable level, the threat must be avoided (for example, by not accepting an engagement).

## 2.1 Fundamental principles

The fundamental principles are:

- **Integrity.** To be straightforward and honest in all professional and business relationships.

- **Objectivity.** To not allow bias, conflict of interest or undue influence of others to override professional or business judgements.

- **Professional competence and due care.** To maintain professional knowledge and skill at the level required to ensure that a client or employer receives competent professional service based on current developments in practice, legislation and techniques, and act diligently and in accordance with applicable technical and professional standards.

- **Confidentiality.** To respect the confidentiality of information acquired as a result of professional and business relationships and, therefore, not disclose any such information to third parties without proper and specific authority, unless there is a legal or professional right or duty to disclose, nor use the information for the personal advantage of the professional accountant or third parties.

- **Professional behaviour.** To comply with relevant laws and regulations and avoid any action that discredits the profession.

## 2.2 Independence

**IFAC Code**

'It is in the public interest and, therefore, required by this Code of Ethics, that members of assurance teams and firms be independent of assurance clients and that any threats that the firm has reason to believe are created by a network firm's interests and relationships be evaluated.'

The Code discusses independence in the light of the wider term 'assurance engagements' and separately in relation to audits.

The guidance states its purpose in a series of steps. It aims to help firms and members:

### Step 1
**Identify threats** to independence

### Step 2
**Evaluate** whether the threats are insignificant

### Step 3
**Apply safeguards**, when necessary, to eliminate the threats or reduce them to an acceptable level.

It also recognises that there may be occasions **where no safeguard is available**. In such a situation, it is only appropriate to

- **Eliminate the interest** or activities causing the threat;
- **Decline the engagement**, or discontinue it.

### Definitions

Independence of mind: The state of mind that permits the expression of a conclusion without being affected by influences that compromise professional judgement, allowing an individual to act with integrity, and exercise objectivity and professional scepticism.

Independence in appearance: The avoidance of facts and circumstances that are so significant that a reasonable and informed third party would be likely to conclude, weighing all the specific facts and circumstances, that a firm's, or a member of the assurance team's, integrity, objectivity or professional scepticism has been compromised.

The degree of independence required is highest for an audit engagement, with less stringent requirements for non-audit engagements at an audit client, and engagements at non-audit clients.

## 2.3 Threats and safeguards

The following general points are made in the Code. We shall look at more specific guidance in the following chapters.

There are five general sources of threat identified by the Code. The FRC's Ethical Standard 1 identifies a sixth threat (the management threat):

- **Self-interest** threat (for example, having a financial interest in a client)

- **Self-review** threat (for example, auditing financial statements prepared by the firm)

- **Advocacy** threat (for example, promoting the client's position by dealing in its shares)

- **Familiarity** threat (for example, an audit team member having family at the client)

- **Intimidation** threat (for example, threats of replacement due to disagreement)

- **Management** threat (for example, doing work that should be carried out by management, such as the design and implementation of IT systems)

There are two general categories of safeguard identified by the Code:

- Safeguards created by the profession, legislation or regulation
- Safeguards within the work environment

Examples of safeguards created by the profession, legislation or regulation:

- Educational training and experience requirements for entry into the profession
- Continuing professional development requirements
- Corporate governance regulations
- Professional standards
- Professional or regulatory monitoring and disciplinary procedures
- External review by a legally empowered third party of the reports, returns, communication or information produced by a professional accountant

Examples of safeguards in the work environment:

- Involving an additional professional accountant to review the work done or otherwise advise as necessary
- Consulting an independent third party, such as a committee of independent directors, a professional regulatory body or another professional accountant
- Rotating senior personnel
- Discussing ethical issues with those in charge of client governance
- Disclosing to those charged with governance the nature of services provided and extent of fees charged
- Involving another firm to perform or re-perform part of the engagement

The team and the firm should be independent **during the period of the engagement.**

The period of the engagement is from the commencement of work until the signing of the final report being produced. For a **recurring audit**, independence may only cease on **termination of the contract** between the parties.

# 3 ICAEW Code

## Section overview

- The ICAEW Code is relevant to professional accountants in all of their professional and business activities.
- The ICAEW Code incorporates the IFAC Code of Ethics, but also contains additional rules deemed appropriate by the ICAEW.

The ICAEW Code states that 'professional accountants are expected to follow the guidance contained in the fundamental principles in all of their professional and business activities whether carried out with or without reward and in other circumstances where to fail to do so would bring discredit to the profession.'

Therefore the Code may apply not only to the job of the professional accountant but also to the life of the professional accountant, particularly if he is involved in matters relevant to his profession, such as keeping the books for a private club of which he is a member.

The Code also states that professional accountants are required to follow the spirit as well as the letter of the guidance. In other words, a specific matter being excluded from the guidance does not mean that the accountant does not have to think about it; rather he must determine if the spirit of the guidance would also apply to that situation.

The ICAEW Code implements the IFAC Code above so that following it ensures compliance with the IFAC Code.

# 4 FRC Ethical Standards for Auditors

## Section overview

- The FRC has issued ethical standards with which UK auditors must comply when carrying out audits.

- The ethical standards were drafted with the IFAC Code of Ethics in mind.

As noted above, the FRC has issued ethical standards for Auditors (ESs), with which UK auditors must comply when carrying out UK audits. They are as follows:

- ES 1 *Integrity, Objectivity and Independence*
- ES 2 *Financial, Business, Employment and Personal Relationships*
- ES 3 *Long Association with the Audit Engagement*
- ES 4 *Fees, Remuneration and Evaluation Policies, Litigation, Gifts and Hospitality*
- ES 5 *Non-Audit Services Provided to Audit Clients*

There is also an ES with provisions available for smaller entities, which is not examinable. This offers exemptions and special rules to the auditors of smaller entities.

These standards were developed with regard to the IFAC Code of Ethics and also the EC Recommendation on the independence of statutory audits.

### Interactive question: Ethical codes         [Difficulty level: Exam standard]

There are two main approaches to a code of professional ethics: a rules based ethical code and a code based on a set of principles.

Indicate whether the following statements are true or false.

| | | | | | |
|---|---|---|---|---|---|
| (a) | A code based on a set of principles rather than rules is more flexible in a rapidly changing environment. | ☐ | True | ☐ | False |
| (b) | ICAEW's Code of Ethics is principles based. | ☐ | True | ☐ | False |
| (c) | A code based on a set of rules requires accountants to evaluate and address threats to independence. | ☐ | True | ☐ | False |

See **Answer** at the end of this chapter.

## Summary

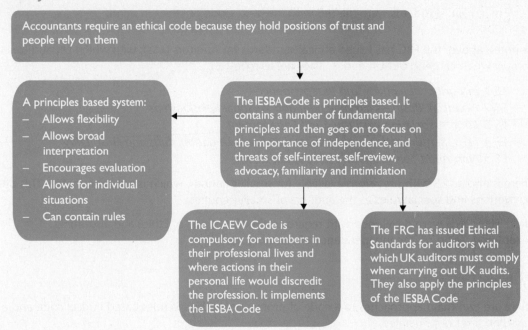

Accountants require an ethical code because they hold positions of trust and people rely on them

A principles based system:
- Allows flexibility
- Allows broad interpretation
- Encourages evaluation
- Allows for individual situations
- Can contain rules

The IESBA Code is principles based. It contains a number of fundamental principles and then goes on to focus on the importance of independence, and threats of self-interest, self-review, advocacy, familiarity and intimidation

The ICAEW Code is compulsory for members in their professional lives and where actions in their personal life would discredit the profession. It implements the IESBA Code

The FRC has issued Ethical Standards for auditors with which UK auditors must comply when carrying out UK audits. They also apply the principles of the IESBA Code

## Self-test

Answer the following questions.

1    Which **two** of the following statements are correct?

    (a)    Accountants must have ethical codes because people rely on accountants.

        ☐ Yes

        ☐ No

    (b)    A set of ethical principles gives protection to accountants as it means they are all working to the same guidelines.

        ☐ Yes

        ☐ No

    (c)    Rules-based codes provide better protection to users of accountancy services because every potential situation arising is covered by them.

        ☐ Yes

        ☐ No

2   Are the following statements true or false?

   (a)   The principle of integrity can be defined as the accountant not allowing bias, conflict of interest or undue influence of others to override his choice of actions.

<br>

     ☐  True

     ☐  False

   (b)   Accountants may use information obtained during the course of their professional work for personal use so long as they do not disclose it to others in breach of their duty of confidentiality.

     ☐  True

     ☐  False

   (c)   Professional accountants should be technically up to date so as to give appropriate advice to clients.

     ☐  True

     ☐  False

3   The following are examples of which types of general threats to independence?

   (a)   The financial statements of Dropdown Ltd have been prepared by Glazer Brothers, their audit firm.

   (b)   Know how plc has intimated to the audit firm that if they do not receive an unqualified audit report for the year 20X6, they may put the audit out to tender.

4   The ICAEW Code implements the IFAC Code.

     ☐  True

     ☐  False

5   The FRC's Ethical Standards for Auditors apply to UK audits and assurance work.

     ☐  True

     ☐  False

Now, go back to the Learning Objectives in the Introduction. If you are satisfied you have achieved these objectives, please tick them off.

## Answer to Interactive question

(a) True – it is an advantage of the principles-based approach

(b) True – it implements the IFAC Code, which is principles-based

(c) False – a rules based system tends to remove the need to evaluate, as accountants can just check whether certain rules are being met or not, rather than applying the principles to given situations.

1   (a) and (b) are correct; (c) is incorrect, as this would be true of a principles-based system, not a rules-based system.

2   (a) is false; this is a description of objectivity. (b) is false; accountants are not entitled to use confidential information for their own personal good. (c) is true.

3   (a)   Self-review
    (b)   Intimidation

4   True

5   False – they apply to UK audits only.

# CHAPTER 15

# Integrity, objectivity and
# independence

Introduction

Examination context

**Topic List**

ICAEW

## Learning objectives

- Understand the concepts of integrity, objectivity and independence ☐
- Recognise the importance of integrity, objectivity and independence ☐
- Identify threats to integrity, objectivity and independence ☐
- Identify safeguards for integrity, objectivity and independence ☐
- Be able to suggest sensible measures to resolve ethical conflicts ☐
- Be able to suggest how conflicts of interest between employee duty and professional duty may be resolved ☐

Specific syllabus references for this chapter are: 4f, g, h, l, m, n, o.

## Syllabus links

All these ethical matters will be considered further in Audit and Assurance.

## Examination context

As we saw in the previous chapter, ethics is an important area for your exam. The sample paper contained six practical, scenario-based questions about issues relating to independence. In addition, there was a question on a conflict for an employed accountant working in industry between the needs of his employer and his professional duty.

In the assessment, candidates may be required to:

- Determine an appropriate course of action in situations that may impair or threaten integrity and objectivity
- Respond appropriately to the request of an employer to undertake work outside the confines of an individual's expertise or experience
- Identify the principal types of threat to independence which arise in a set of given circumstances
- Identify safeguards to eliminate or reduce threats to independence
- Suggest how a conflict of loyalty between the duty a professional accountant has to their employer and the duty to their profession could be resolved

# 1 Integrity, objectivity and independence

**Section overview**

- Independence and objectivity matter because of the trust clients and the public have in the assurance provider.

- Safeguards should be applied when independence and objectivity are put at risk.

- If the risks are too great for safeguards to be effective, then the assurance provider should not accept or should withdraw from the engagement.

We looked at the importance of independence in the IFAC Code in the previous chapter. The fundamental principles of integrity and objectivity were also introduced. In this chapter we shall look more closely at these three issues, the threats to them that exist and the safeguards that can be applied to reduce the risks to a level determined to be acceptable by partners in the audit firm. Remember, however, that the ethical principles state that some risks cannot be reduced by safeguards and should therefore be avoided.

## Definitions

**Integrity**: This means that an accountant must be straightforward and honest. It implies fair dealing and truthfulness.

**Objectivity**: This is a state of mind that excludes bias, prejudice and compromise and that gives fair and impartial consideration to all matters that are relevant to the task in hand, disregarding those that are not.

**Independence** is related to and underpins objectivity – it is freedom from situations and relationships that make it probable that a reasonable and informed third party would conclude that objectivity either is impaired or could be impaired.

In other words, objectivity relates to the state of the accountant's mind, and independence relates to the circumstances surrounding the situation, such as financial, employment, business and personal relationships that affect the assurance provider in connection with the client or potential client.

## 1.1 Why do independence and objectivity matter so much?

Independence and objectivity matter because of:

- The **expectations** of those directly affected, particularly the members of the company. The audit should be able to provide **objective** assurance that the directors can never provide on the financial statements.

- The **public interest**. Companies are public entities, governed by rules requiring the disclosure of information.

Potential general threats to independence and objectivity were outlined in Chapter 14. We shall look at more specific threats in the next section.

What can the auditor do to preserve objectivity? The simple answer is to **withdraw from any engagement** where there is the **slightest threat** to objectivity. However, there are disadvantages in this strict approach.

- Clients may lose an auditor who knows their business.
- It denies clients the freedom to be advised by the accountant of their choice.

The better approach was set out in Chapter 14 too. It is to identify threats to independence, evaluate how significant they are and then apply safeguards if they are significant. We shall look in more detail at safeguards in the next section also.

# 2 Threats and safeguards

## Section overview

- Examples of threats to independence and potential safeguards are given here, categorised by the main type of threat they represent. You should note that some matters can present several types of threat.

- Hard and fast rules are shown in bold.

This section is based on the ICAEW Code of Ethics (revised 2011) and the FRC Ethical Standards for Auditors. It examines a number of specific threats to independence on assurance engagements. They are outlined here, categorised by type of risk and appropriate safeguards. You should, however, note that certain issues fall into several types of threat, not simply one. Where this is the case, issues have been listed under the dominant threat but other threats are noted. Where relevant, rules relating to each threat are set out. We shall also look at how these risks might apply to particular situations, such as when considering whether to accept a new client.

## 2.1 Self-interest threat

The Code of Ethics highlights a great number of areas in which a self-interest threat might arise.

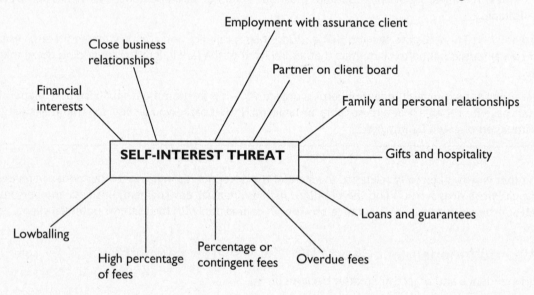

*Figure 15.1: Self-interest threat*

### 2.1.1 Financial interests

### Definitions

Financial interest An interest in equity or other security, debenture, loan or other debt instrument of an entity, including rights and obligations to acquire such an interest and derivatives directly related to such interest.

Direct financial interest A financial interest

- owned directly by and under the control of an individual or entity (including those managed on a discretionary basis by others); or

- beneficially owned through a collective investment vehicle, estate, trust or other intermediary over which the individual or entity has control, or the ability to influence investment decisions.

**Indirect financial interest** A financial interest beneficially owned through a collective investment vehicle, estate, trust or other intermediary over which the individual or entity has no control or ability to influence investment decisions.

**Immediate family** A spouse (or equivalent) or a dependent.

**Assurance team**

(a)    All members of the engagement team for the assurance engagement;

(b)    All others within a firm who can directly influence the outcome of the assurance engagement.

A financial interest in a client constitutes a substantial self-interest threat. **The parties listed below are not allowed to own a direct financial interest or an indirect material financial interest in a client:**

- The **assurance firm**

- Any **partner** in the assurance firm

- Any **person in a position to influence** the conduct and outcome of the engagement (eg, a member of the assurance team)

- An **immediate family member of such a person**

The following safeguards will therefore be relevant:

- Disposing of the interest
- Removing the individual from the team if required
- Keeping the client's audit committee informed of the situation
- Using an engagement quality control reviewer to review work carried out if necessary

Assurance firms should have quality control procedures requiring staff to disclose relevant financial interests for themselves and immediate family members. They should also foster a culture of voluntary disclosure on an ongoing basis so that any potential problems are identified on a timely basis.

### 2.1.2   Close business relationships

A close business relationship will involve a common commercial interest, which in addition to a self-interest threat, could cause advocacy or intimidation threats and a perceived loss of independence.

Examples of when an assurance firm and an assurance client have an inappropriately close business relationship include:

- Operating a joint venture between the firm and the client, or between the firm and a director or other senior manager of the client

- Arrangements to combine one or more services or products of the firm with one or more services or products of the assurance client and to market the package with reference to both parties

- Distribution or marketing arrangements under which the firm acts as distributor or marketer of the assurance client's products or services or *vice versa*

- Other commercial transactions, such as the audit firm leasing its office space from the assurance client

Again, it will be necessary for the partners to judge the materiality of the interest and therefore its significance. However, **unless the financial interest is clearly immaterial and the relationship to the firm and its client clearly insignificant, an assurance provider should not participate in such a venture with an assurance client.** *Appropriate* safeguards are therefore to end the assurance provision or to terminate the (other) business relationship.

If an individual member of an assurance team had such an interest, he should be removed from the assurance team.

Generally speaking, **purchasing goods and services from an assurance client in the ordinary course of business on an arm's length basis does not constitute a threat to independence.** However, if there is a substantial number of such transactions, there may be a threat to independence and safeguards may be necessary.

ES2 states that for **audit clients and firms**, there should be no business relationships except for the purchase of goods and services in the ordinary course of business and on an arm's length basis, and which are not material or clearly inconsequential to either party.

### 2.1.3 Employment with assurance client

**Dual employment** (the same person being employed by both an assurance firm and a client) **is not permitted**.

It is also possible that staff might transfer between an assurance firm and a client, or that negotiations or interviews to facilitate such movement might take place. Both situations are a threat to independence:

- An assurance team member might be motivated by a desire to impress a future possible employer (objectivity is therefore affected)

- A former partner turned Finance Director has too much knowledge of the firm's systems and procedures

These sorts of situations can also present self-review, intimidation and familiarity threats. The extent of the threat to independence depends on various factors, such as the role the individual has taken up at the client, the extent of his influence on the assurance service previously, and the length of time that has passed between the individual's connection with the assurance service and the new role at the client.

Various safeguards may be considered:

- Modifying the assurance strategy

- Ensuring the assurance engagement is assigned to someone of sufficient experience as compared with the individual who has left

- Involving an additional professional accountant not involved with the engagement to review the work done

- Carrying out a quality control review of the engagement

There is a significant threat to objectivity if a partner of an audit firm accepts a key management position at a client of the firm.

ES2 states that when a **partner** leaves the firm and is appointed as a director or to a key management position with an audit client, having acted as audit engagement or independent/key partner in relation to that audit at any time in the previous two years, the firm should resign as auditors. The auditors should not reaccept appointment until two years have elapsed since that partner's involvement in the audit or the former partner leaves the audit client, if earlier.

When any other former member of an engagement team joins an audit client as director/key management within two years of being involved with the audit, the firm should consider whether the composition of the audit team is appropriate.

**An individual who has moved from the firm to a client should not be entitled to any benefits or payments from the firm unless these are made in accordance with pre-determined arrangements.** The individual should not continue to participate (or appear to) in the firm's business or professional activities. If money is owed to the individual, it should not be so much as to compromise the independence of the assurance engagement.

**A firm should have quality control procedures setting out that an individual involved in serious employment negotiations with an audit client should notify the firm and that this person would then be removed from the engagement.** In addition, ES2 states that a review of the employee's work on the current and, where appropriate, most recent audit should take place.

### 2.1.4 Partner on client board

**A partner or employee of an assurance firm should not serve on the board of an assurance client.** This can also cause a self-review and/or a management threat.

It may be acceptable for a partner or an employee of an assurance firm to perform the role of company secretary for an assurance client, if the role is essentially administrative.

## 2.1.5　Family and personal relationships

### Definition

Close family A parent, child or sibling who is not an immediate family member.

Family or close personal relationships between assurance firm and client staff could seriously threaten independence. Each situation has to be evaluated individually. Factors to consider are:

- The individual's responsibilities on the assurance engagement
- The closeness of the relationship
- The role of the other party at the assurance client

**When an immediate family member of a member of the assurance team is a director, an officer or an employee of the assurance client in a position to exert significant influence over the subject matter information of the assurance engagement, the individual should be removed from the assurance team.**

The firm should also consider whether there is any threat to independence if an employee who is not a member of the assurance team has a close family or personal relationship with a director, an officer or an employee of an assurance client.

A firm may wish to establish quality control policies and procedures under which staff should disclose if a close family member employed by the client is promoted within the client.

If a firm inadvertently violates the rules concerning family and personal relationships they should consider applying additional safeguards, such as undertaking a quality control review of the assurance engagement and discussing the matter with the audit committee of the client, if there is one.

## 2.1.6　Gifts and hospitality

**Unless the value of gifts or hospitality are such that a reasonable and informed third party, weighing all the specific facts and circumstances, would consider them trivial and inconsequential, a firm or a member of an assurance team should not accept them.**

### Worked example: Receiving a benefit

Katie, a trainee at West and Co, chartered accountants, is attending the inventory count at Designs Limited, a company that manufactures fashion lines for a number of famous high street stores. During the course of the count, the stores manager tells Katie that after the inventory count, staff are entitled to purchase goods at cost to the value of £30 each. He invites her to take part in this company perk.

In this case, Katie has not been offered a gift, she has been invited to spend £30. However, the benefit that this would confer on her could be substantial. Given the customary mark ups in the fashion industry, cost price could be as low as 25% of ultimate selling price, so in effect, Katie would be receiving a benefit of £90. While this is likely to be immaterial and insignificant to the financial statements of Designs Limited, it could be significant to a trainee in an audit firm. Katie should certainly not accept any such offer without confirming with her engagement partner that it is appropriate to do so. She may be able to determine herself that the best course of action is not to accept the benefit.

In this case, a benefit of £90 is **not clearly insignificant**, and therefore Katie should decline the offer.

In addition, you should note that this practice could represent an audit risk, as it means that there will be inventory movements after the inventory count but before the end of the year, and unless there are strong controls over recording these sales, both inventory and sales could be misstated. Such a benefit to employees is unlikely to cause a material misstatement, but Katie should probably observe the controls over the sales and make a note of the practice for the audit file.

ES4 extends this prohibition to immediate family members or persons able to influence the audit and states that hospitality should not be accepted from an audit client unless it is reasonable in terms of its frequency, nature and cost.

### 2.1.7 Loans and guarantees

The advice on loans and guarantees falls into two categories:

- The client is a bank or other similar institution
- Other situations

If a **loan** or a guarantee of a loan is **made by an audit client which is a bank** (or other similar institution), then this is **not acceptable if the loan is not made under normal lending procedures** (i.e. in the normal course of business).

If the **loan is made under normal lending procedures**, then this **is acceptable provided that appropriate safeguards are applied**. An example of a safeguard would be having the work reviewed by a professional accountant from a network firm that is neither involved with the audit nor received the loan.

If a **loan is made by a bank client to a member of the audit team under normal lending procedures**, then this **is acceptable and no safeguards are necessary**. An example of this would be if a member of the team had a home mortgage, bank overdraft, car loan or credit card with a bank client.

If a loan is made or guaranteed **by a client that is not a bank or other similar institution to either the firm or to a member of the audit team**, then **the self-interest threat created would be so significant that no safeguards could reduce the threat to an acceptable level**, unless the loan or guarantee is immaterial to both (a) the firm or the member of the audit team and the immediate family member, and (b) the client.

Finally, **if the firm, a member of the audit team or an immediate family member, makes or guarantees a loan to a client**, then **the self-interest threat created would be so significant that no safeguards could reduce the threat to an acceptable level**, unless the loan or guarantee is immaterial to both (a) the firm or the member of the audit team or the immediate family member, and (b) the client.

### 2.1.8 Overdue fees

In a situation where there are overdue fees, the assurance provider runs the risk of, in effect, making a loan to a client, whereupon the guidance above becomes relevant. The ICAEW Code states that, generally, the payment of overdue fees should be required before the assurance report for the following year can be issued.

Firms should guard against fees building up and being significant by discussing the issues with those charged with governance (more specifically, the audit committee), and, if necessary, the possibility of resigning if overdue fees are not paid.

### 2.1.9 Percentage or contingent fees

### Definition

Contingent fee A fee calculated on a predetermined basis relating to the outcome of a transaction or the result of the services performed by the firm. A fee that is established by a court or other public authority is not a contingent fee.

---

A firm shall not enter into any fee arrangement for an assurance engagement under which the amount of the fee is contingent on the result of the assurance work or on items that are the subject matter of the assurance engagement.

**Definition**

Public interest entity

- A listed entity; and

- An entity (a) defined by regulation or legislation as a public interest entity or (b) for which the audit is required by regulation or legislation to be conducted in compliance with the same independence requirements that apply to the audit of listed entities. Such regulation may be promulgated by any relevant regulator, including an audit regulator.

A firm should be alert to the situation arising where the total fees generated by an assurance client represent a large proportion of a firm's total fees. Factors such as the structure of the firm and the length of time it has been trading will be relevant in determining whether there is a threat to independence. It is also necessary to beware of situations where the fees generated by an assurance client present a large proportion of the revenue of an individual partner.

Safeguards in these situations might include:

- Discussing the issues with the audit committee
- Taking steps to reduce the dependency on the client
- Obtaining external/internal quality control reviews
- Consulting a third party such as ICAEW

The Code states that where an audit client is a **public interest entity** and, for **two consecutive years**, the **total fees** from the client and its related entities represent **more than 15% of the total fees received by the firm** expressing the opinion on the financial statements of the client, the firm shall:

- Disclose this fact to those charged with governance of the audit client; and

- Carry out an engagement quality control review of the second year engagement, either before the audit opinion is issued (a "pre-issuance review") or after it is issued (a "post-issuance review").

If total fees significantly exceed 15%, then only a pre-issuance review may be sufficient.

**ES4** states that if total fees (audit and non-audit services) are expected to **regularly exceed 10%** of the annual fee income of the audit firm (**5% in the case of a listed company**) the audit engagement partners should **disclose that fact to the ethics partner and those charged with governance** of the audit client and consider whether appropriate safeguards should be applied to reduce the threat to independence. In the case of non-listed companies, an independent quality control review of the engagement should be undertaken before the report is signed. In the case of a listed client, the safeguards might be stricter, such as seeking to reduce non-audit work provided.

If total fees (audit and non-audit services) are expected to **regularly exceed 15% (10% for a listed entity)** of gross practice income, **the firm should not act as the auditors** of that entity, and should resign or refuse reappointment, as appropriate.

It will be difficult for new firms establishing themselves to keep within these limits and firms in this situation should make use of the safeguards outlined above.

## 2.1.11    Lowballing

When a firm quotes a significantly lower fee level for an assurance service than would have been charged by the predecessor firm, there is a significant self-interest threat. If the firm's tender is successful, the firm must apply safeguards such as:

- Maintaining records such that the firm is able to demonstrate that appropriate staff and time are spent on the engagement

- Complying with all applicable assurance standards, guidelines and quality control procedures

ES4 observes that 'the audit engagement partner shall be satisfied and able to demonstrate that the audit engagement has assigned to it sufficient partners and staff with appropriate time and skill to perform the audit in accordance with all applicable Auditing and Ethical Standards, irrespective of the audit fee to be charged'.

Additionally, ES4 states that the audit engagement partner should ensure audit fees are not influenced or determined by the provision of non-audit service to the audited entity.

## 2.2 Self-review threat

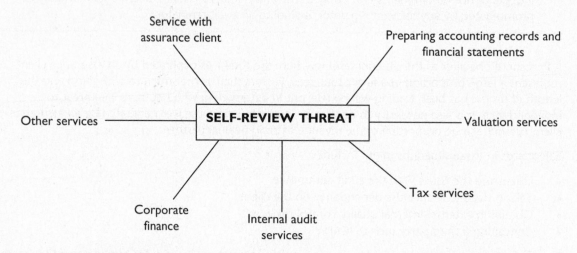

*Figure 15.2: Self-review threat*

The key area in which there is likely to be a self-review threat is where an assurance firm provides services other than assurance services to an assurance client (providing multiple services). There is a great deal of guidance in the rules about various other services accountancy firms might provide to their clients, and these are dealt with below.

### 2.2.1 Service with an assurance client

Individuals who have been a director or officer of the client, or an employee in a position to exert direct and significant influence over the subject matter information of the assurance engagement in the period under review or the previous two years, should not be assigned to the assurance team. ES2 states that **the person should not be assigned to a position in which he or she is able to influence the conduct and outcome of the audit for two years following the date of leaving the audit client.**

Here the key threat is self-review where a member of the engagement team has to report on work they prepared originally, or elements of the financial statement they had responsibility for at the client, but there is also a risk of self-interest and familiarity threats.

ES2 also covers the situation where audit staff are temporarily 'loaned' to a client which is forbidden unless it is not in a management position and the client acknowledges its responsibility for directing and supervising that work. The role should not include making management decisions or exercising discretionary authority to commit the client to a particular position or accounting treatment. The agreement should only be for a short period of time and should not result in the individual performing non-audit services that are disallowed under ES5. When an audit staff member returns to the firm after such a secondment, he should not be given a role in the audit involving any function or activity that he performed/supervised while at the client.

If an individual had been closely involved with the client prior to the time limits set out above, the assurance firm should consider the threat to independence arising and apply appropriate safeguards, such as:

- Obtaining a quality control review of the individual's work on the assignment
- Discussing the issue with the audit committee

### 2.2.2 Preparing accounting records and financial statements

There is clearly a significant risk of a self-review threat if a firm prepares accounting records and financial statements and then audits or reviews them.

On the other hand auditors routinely assist management with the preparation of financial statements and give advice about accounting treatments and journal entries.

Therefore, assurance firms must analyse the risks arising and put safeguards in place to ensure that the risk is at an acceptable level. Safeguards include:

- Using staff members other than assurance team members to carry out work

- Implementing policies and procedures to prohibit the individual providing such services from making any managerial decisions on behalf of the assurance client

- Requiring the source data for the accounting entries to be originated by the assurance client

- Requiring the underlying assumptions to be originated and approved by the assurance client

The rules are more stringent when the client is listed. ES5 states that **firms should not prepare accounts or financial statements for listed clients**, unless an emergency arises.

### 2.2.3 Valuation services

### Definition

Valuation comprises the making of assumptions with regard to future developments, the application of appropriate methodologies and techniques, and the combination of both to compute a certain value, or range of values, for an asset, a liability or for a business as a whole.

---

If an audit firm performs a valuation that will be included in financial statements audited by the firm, a self-review threat arises and also a management threat might arise.

ES5 states that **audit firms shall not carry out valuations which either:**

- **Have a material effect on a listed company's financial statements, either separately or in aggregate with other valuations provided**

- **Involve a significant degree of subjective judgement and have a material effect on the financial statements either separately or in aggregate with other valuations provided to any other audited entity**

If the valuation is for an immaterial matter, the audit firm should apply safeguards to ensure that the risk is reduced to an acceptable level. Matters to consider when applying safeguards are the extent of the audit client's knowledge of the relevant matters in making the valuation and the degree of judgement involved, how much use is made of established methodologies and the degree of uncertainty in the valuation. Safeguards might include:

- Second partner review
- Confirming that the client understands the valuation and the assumptions used
- Ensuring the client acknowledges responsibility for the valuation
- Using separate personnel for the valuation and the audit

### 2.2.4 Taxation services

The Code divides taxation services into four categories:

- Tax return preparation;
- Tax calculations for the purpose of preparing the accounting entries;
- Tax planning and other tax advisory services; and
- Assistance in the resolution of tax disputes.

**Tax return preparation does not generally threaten independence,** as long as management takes responsibility for the returns.

Tax calculations for the purpose of preparing the accounting entities may not be prepared for public interest entities, except in emergency situations. For non-public interest entities, it is acceptable to do so provided that safeguards are applied.

Tax planning may be acceptable in certain circumstances, e.g. where the advice is clearly supported by a tax authority or other precedent. However, if the effectiveness of the tax advice depends on a particular accounting treatment or presentation in the financial statements, the audit team has reasonable doubt about the accounting treatment, and the consequences of the tax advice would be material, then the service should not be provided.

Assistance in the resolution of tax disputes may be provided, depending on whether the firm itself provided the service which is the subject of the dispute, and whether the effect is material on the financial statements. Safeguards include using professionals who are not members of the audit team to perform the service, and obtaining advice on the service from an external tax professional.

The audit firm:

- Provides advice to the audit client in one or more specific matters at the request of the client.

- Undertakes a substantial proportion of the tax planning or compliance work for the audit client.

- Promotes tax structures or products to the audit client, the effectiveness of which is likely to be influenced by the manner in which they are accounted for in the financial statements.

ES5 observes that providing taxation services can cause self-review, self-interest, management and advocacy threats. Safeguards to mitigate these threats include:

- Tax services being provided by partners and staff with no involvement in the audit of financial statements

- Tax services being reviewed by an independent tax partner or senior tax employee

- Obtaining external independent advice on tax work

- Tax computations prepared by audit staff members being reviewed by a partner/staff member of appropriate experience who is not a member of the audit team

- An audit partner not involved in the audit engagement reviews whether the tax work has been properly and effectively addressed in the context of an audit of the financial statements

In addition, there are a number of rules set out in ES5.

The audit firm shall not:

- Promote tax structures or products or undertake an engagement to provide tax advice to an audit client where the audit engagement partner has, or ought to have, reasonable doubt as to whether the relevant accounting treatment involved is based on established interpretations or is appropriate, having regard to the requirement for the financial statements to give a true and fair view in accordance with the relevant financial reporting framework

- Undertake an engagement to provide tax services to an audited entity wholly or partly on a contingent fee basis where the outcome of those tax services is dependent on the application of tax law which is uncertain or not yet established

- Undertake an engagement to provide tax services to an audited entity where the engagement would involve the audit firm undertaking a management role

- Undertake an engagement to prepare current or deferred tax calculations to an audited entity that is a listed entity or significant affiliate for the purpose of preparing accounting entries that are material to the relevant financial statements, with the exception of emergency situations

- Undertake an engagement to provide tax services to an audited entity where this would involve acting as an advocate, before an appeals tribunal or court in the resolution of an issue that is material to the financial statements or where the outcome of the tax issue is dependent on a future or contemporary audit judgement

### 2.2.5 Internal audit services

Providing internal audit services to an audit client creates a **self-review threat** if the internal audit work is relied upon in the external audit. The **key issue is whether the audit firm's personnel assume a management responsibility**. If they do, then **the threat created would be so significant that no safeguards could reduce the threat to an acceptable level.**

Examples of internal audit services that involve assuming management responsibilities include:

- Setting internal audit policies
- Directing and taking responsibility for the actions of the entity's internal audit employees
- Deciding which recommendations resulting from internal audit activities shall be implemented
- Reporting the results of the internal audit activities to those charged with governance
- Performing procedures that form part of the internal control
- Taking responsibility for designing, implementing and maintaining internal control.

Safeguards include ensuring that:

- The client designates an appropriate and competent resource to be responsible at all times for internal audit activities

- The client's management reviews, assesses and approves the scope, risk and frequency of the internal audit services

- The client's management determines which recommendations to implement and manages the implementation process.

ES5 states that the key threats in providing internal audit services are self-review and management. It states that **an audit firm shall not undertake to provide internal audit services to an audited entity where it is reasonably foreseeable that:**

- **For the purposes of the audit of the financial statements, the auditors would place significant reliance on internal audit work performed by the audit firm** (we will look at this situation more deeply in your Audit and Assurance paper); or

- **For the purposes of the internal audit services, the audit firm would undertake the role of management.**

### Worked example: Internal audit

Lee was recently seconded to the internal audit department of his accountancy firm. While on secondment, he carried out a month's internal audit service as part of a four man team at Whitecross plc, an audit client of the firm. He carried out routine controls testing while on this service. He helped to draft the final report to the board of directors at Whitecross, recommending several improvements to the system.

On return to the audit department six months later, Lee has been allocated to the audit team for Whitecross, for the year including the month when he carried out the internal audit service.

Lee should raise this with the training partner or the engagement partner for Whitecross, as it is likely to be a threat to independence if he takes part in this audit. He worked in the internal audit team and made reports to the directors in that capacity. This could form both self-interest (not wanting to discover any work he did was incorrect or inappropriate) and self-review (using work carried out by him to rely on for the audit opinion) threats.

### 2.2.6 Corporate finance services

Certain aspects of corporate finance services will create self-review threats that cannot be reduced to an acceptable level by safeguards. Therefore, **assurance firms are not allowed to promote, deal in or underwrite an assurance client's shares. They are also not allowed to commit an assurance client to the terms of a transaction or consummate a transaction on the client's behalf.**

Other corporate finance services, such as assisting a client in defining corporate strategies, assisting in identifying possible sources of capital and providing structuring advice may be acceptable, provided that safeguards, such as using different teams of staff, and ensuring no management decisions are taken on behalf of the client are in place.

Note that corporate finance services can also constitute an advocacy threat if the audit firm is representing the interests of the client.

### 2.2.7 Information technology services

The key threats in providing IT services, such as designing and implementing a new IT system, are self-review and management. The Code of Ethics states that in the case of **public interest entities**, the audit firm shall **not** design or implement IT services that:

- Form a significant part of the internal control over financial reporting; or

- Generate information that is significant to the financial statements on which the firm will express an opinion.

For **non-public interest entities**, these services may be provided if safeguards are put in place ensuring that:

- The client acknowledges its responsibility for establishing and monitoring a system of internal controls

- The client assigns the responsibility to make all management decisions with respect to the design and implementation of the hardware or software system to a competent employee, preferably within senior management

- The client makes all management decisions with respect to the design and implementation process

- The client evaluates the adequacy and results of the design and implementation of the system The client is responsible for operating the system (hardware or software) and for the data it uses or generates.

Further safeguards would include using only personnel who are not on the audit team to provide the IT services, and having the audit or non-assurance work reviewed by a professional accountant.

### 2.2.8 Litigation support services

An example of a litigation support service is acting as an expert witness. Such services can cause self-review threats if they involve estimating damages or other amounts that affect the financial statements. In addition, management and/or advocacy threats may arise.

Hence ES5 forbids acceptance of litigation support services for listed audited entities that are listed or significant affiliates when the situation above exists. Litigation support services for non-listed entities that do not involve such subjective estimations are not prohibited, provided that appropriate safeguards have been implemented.

## 2.3 Advocacy threat

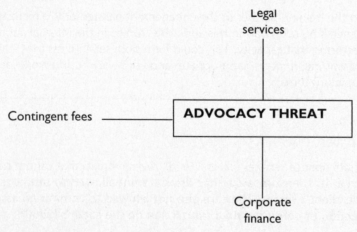

*Figure 15.3: Advocacy threat*

An advocacy threat arises in certain situations where the assurance firm is in a position of taking the client's part in a dispute or somehow acting as their advocate. The most obvious instances of this would be when a firm offered legal services to a client and, say, defended them in a legal case. ES5 forbids the provision of legal services to an audited entity where it would involve acting as the solicitor formally nominated to represent the audited entity in resolution of a dispute or litigation which is material to the financial statements. An advocacy threat might also arise if the firm carried out corporate finance work for the client; for example, if the audit firm were involved in advice on debt restructuring and negotiated with the bank on the client's behalf.

As with the other threats above, the firm has to appraise the risk and apply safeguards as necessary. Relevant safeguards might be using different departments in the firm to carry out the work and making disclosures to the audit committee. Remember, the ultimate option is always to withdraw from an engagement if the risk to independence is too high.

## 2.4 Familiarity threat

A familiarity threat is where independence is jeopardised by the audit firm and its staff becoming over familiar with the client and its staff. There is a substantial risk of loss of professional scepticism in such circumstances.

We have already discussed some examples of when this risk arises, because very often a familiarity threat arises in conjunction with a self-interest threat.

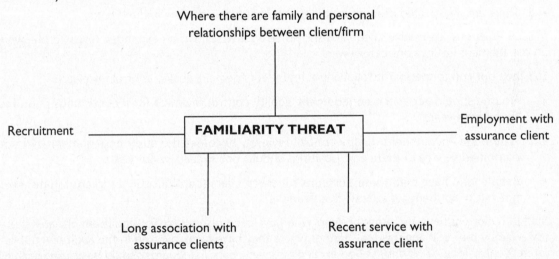

*Figure 15.4: Familiarity threat*

### 2.4.1 Long association of senior personnel with assurance clients

It can be a significant threat to independence if senior members of staff at an audit firm have a long association with a client. All firms should therefore monitor the relationship between staff and established clients and use safeguards to independence such as rotating senior staff off the assurance team and involving engagement quality control reviews. ES3 also contains this requirement. Where appropriate safeguards cannot be applied, the firm should resign.

### Worked example: Long association

Peter has been the audit engagement partner for Santa Ltd for a number of years. During that time, he has formed a friendly relationship with the finance director, to the point that on occasion, usually at client hospitality days organised by the firm, but sometimes not, he might play a round of golf with the FD or attend a dinner function with him and his wife.

There is a risk of a familiarity threat here, particularly if the relationship is growing closer and more personal as time evolves. Peter should monitor this situation and request a review of the audit file by an engagement quality control reviewer to ensure that the risk is not too significant for the audit firm. Alternatively, the audit firm might decide that it would be better to 'rest' Peter from this engagement for a period of time to ensure that independence was not affected, if the firm were confident that this would not affect the professional relationship between the firm and Santa Ltd.

The Code of Ethics sets out general provisions for **all audit engagements**. These state that when an audit engagement partner has held that role for a continuous period of ten years in relation to a non-public interest client, careful consideration must be given as to whether a reasonable and informed third party would consider the firm's objectivity and independence to be impaired. If that individual is still not rotated, alternative safeguards should be put in place, the reason for lack of rotation should be documented, and the facts should be communicated with those charged with governance.

For **public interest entities**, the Code of Ethics has more stringent rules. ES3 states these as follows.

- No one shall act as the audit engagement partner for more than five years.

- Anyone who has acted as the audit engagement partner for a period of five years, shall not subsequently participate in the audit engagement until a further period of five years has elapsed.

However, there may be circumstances in which it is necessary to be flexible about rotation of the audit engagement partner or audit quality control reviewer in relation to the audit of a public interest entity. If the audit committee of the audited entity decides that flexibility is necessary to safeguard the quality of the audit (and the audit firm agrees), then the audit engagement partner may continue in the role for **two more years**. This might happen for example where:

- Substantial change has recently been made or will soon be made to the nature or structure of the audited entity's business; or

- There are unexpected changes in the senior management of the audited entity.

In such situations, alternative safeguards should be applied such as an expanded review of the work by an engagement quality control reviewer.

ES3 then goes on to specify the following rules for engagement quality control reviewers:

- **No one should act as the engagement quality control reviewer for a continuous period longer than seven years**

- **Where the engagement quality control reviewer becomes the audit engagement partner the combined service in these two positions should not exceed seven years**

- **People who have held these positions for seven years (continuously or in aggregate) should not return to them for at least five years**

Staff in senior positions and other partners who have been responsible for significant affiliates should be reviewed by the audit engagement partner where they have been involved in the audit of a public interest entity for a continuous period exceeding seven years. Safeguards should be applied such as the removal of members of staff from, or the rotation of roles within, the engagement team.

**When an audited entity becomes a listed company**, the length of time the audit engagement partner has been involved should be taken into consideration. The engagement partner should only continue in the position for another two years where four or more years have already been served by that individual.

### 2.4.2 Recruitment

Recruiting senior management for an assurance client, particularly those able to affect the subject matter of an assurance engagement creates management, familiarity, self-interest and intimidation threats.

Assurance providers must not make management decisions for the client. Their involvement could be limited to drawing up a shortlist of candidates, providing that the client has drawn up the criteria by which they are to be selected, and makes the final decision in respect of who to hire.

ES5 states that an audit firm should not undertake an engagement to provide recruitment services in relation to a key management position of the audited entity (or significant affiliate of such) for a **listed** entity.

## 2.5 Intimidation threat

An intimidation threat arises when members of the assurance team have reason to be intimidated by client staff.

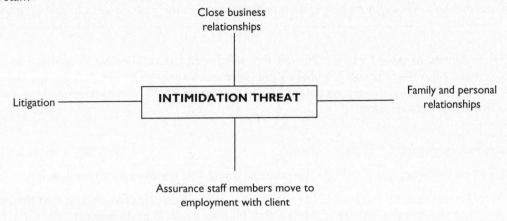

*Figure 15.5: Intimidation threat*

These are also examples of self-interest threats discussed in section 2.1, largely because intimidation may only arise significantly when the assurance firm has something to lose.

### 2.5.1 Actual and threatened litigation

The most obvious example of an intimidation threat is when the client threatens to sue, or indeed sues, the assurance firm for work that has been done previously. The firm is then faced with the risk of losing the client, bad publicity and the possibility that they will be found to have been negligent, which will lead to further problems. This could lead to the firm being under pressure to produce an unqualified audit report when they have been qualified in the past, for example.

Generally, assurance firms should seek to avoid such situations arising. If they do arise, factors to consider are:

- The materiality of the litigation
- The nature of the assurance engagement
- Whether the litigation relates to a prior assurance engagement

The following safeguards could be considered:

- Disclosing to the audit committee the nature and extent of the litigation
- Removing specific affected individuals from the engagement team
- Involving an additional professional accountant on the team to review work

However, if the litigation is at all serious, it may be necessary to resign from the engagement, as the threat to independence is so great. ES4 requires a firm to not continue with/accept an engagement where the threat of litigation is anything other than insignificant, however it is not required to resign immediately in circumstances where a reasonable and informed third party would not regard it in the interests of the shareholders for it to do so.

## 2.6 Management threat

Management threat is identified in the FRC Ethical Standards for Auditors rather than in the IFAC Code or ICAEW Code. A management threat arises when the audit firm undertakes work involving making judgements and taking decisions that are the responsibility of management. There is a significant cross-over with self-review threat here, and, as we have already seen, assurance providers are forbidden to take decisions on behalf of management, therefore this risk should be removed by avoiding situations or not accepting engagements where the client is asking the assurance firm to take management decisions.

An important factor in whether a management threat exists is whether there is 'informed management' at the client.

### Definition

**Informed management** is where the auditors believe that the member of management designated by the audit client to receive the results of a non-audit service provided by the auditor has the capability to make independent management judgements and decisions on the basis of the information provided.

If there is informed management, it is possible that safeguards can be effective to avoid a management threat or reduce it. If there is not, it is unlikely management threat can be avoided. For example, consultancy services are generally acceptable where there is informed management and the auditors do not take management decisions.

### Interactive question 1: Type of threat [Difficulty level: Exam standard]

In each of the following cases, indicate the principal threat that the assurance firm is facing.

(a) Peter Perkins recently resigned as finance director of Assiduous Limited. Peter joined the assurance firm that provides the audit to Assiduous after his notice period of six months.

(b) Artifice Limited has suggested to the engagement partner that a qualified audit report would be unacceptable in the current year because the company is considering a flotation.

(c) Anonymous Limited has requested that the audit team should not be changed from the previous year as they got on well with client staff.

See **Answer** at the end of this chapter.

## 2.7 Accepting new clients

We outlined the issues relating to accepting new clients in Chapter 2. We stated that auditors must consider any ethical issues that might be a bar to acceptance. Any of the ethical issues outlined above could constitute a barrier to acceptance. In addition, the assurance firm must consider whether there appear to be any factors at the client that could be a threat to the firm's integrity or professional behaviour. These are likely to arise from:

- Illegal activities of the client
- Apparent dishonesty of the client
- Questionable accounting practices of the client

It may not be possible to reduce these risks, in which case, the assurance service should be declined. However, some safeguards, such as obtaining a commitment from those charged with governance to improving corporate governance, might be sufficient to make acceptance possible.

### Interactive question 2: Engagement acceptance [Difficulty level: Exam standard]

Notable Co is a small assurance firm that has been asked to take on the statutory audit of the following two companies. For each of the companies, indicate on what basis the audits could be accepted, if at all.

Notorious Limited is a small company that has had a number of HMRC investigations in recent years. The company has had to pay a number of back taxes where incorrect figures had been declared. Recently a director was banned from being a director for five years for wrongful trading. This person has left Notorious and a new managing director has been appointed, who has intimated to the firm that improved corporate governance is at the top of his agenda.

☐ Do not accept

☐ Accept with safeguards

☐ Accept with no safeguards

Pristine plc is a listed company that has good references from all parties whom the firm made enquiries of. It has requested that Notable Co both prepare and audit the financial statements. It does not feel that these services are divisible.

☐ Do not accept

☐ Accept with safeguards

☐ Accept with no safeguards

See **Answer** at the end of this chapter.

# 3 Resolving ethical conflicts

**Section overview**

- The ICAEW Code sets out a framework for professional accountants to follow when faced with an ethical conflict.

- It is generally better to resolve conflicts 'in-house' than to refer to external bodies, although that option is always available and ICAEW has an ethical helpline.

The ICAEW Code sets out a framework that professional accountants can follow when seeking to resolve ethical problems. It states that the professional accountant should consider:

- The relevant facts
- The relevant parties
- The ethical issues involved
- The fundamental principles related to the matter in question
- Established internal procedures
- Alternative courses of action

The accountant should then consider which is the course of action that most aligns with the fundamental principles.

If the accountant cannot determine the best course of action himself, he should refer it to the relevant department within his firm for more advice.

It is generally better for firms to come to conclusions 'in-house', but if needs be, further advice can be sought from ICAEW.

This is a useful structure for you to use when considering ethical problems in the assessment. Think about the facts, parties, issues and fundamental principles involved and try and see the best course of action. Remember that as a trainee, referral to a more senior member of staff may be your most appropriate course of action.

Interactive question 3: Audit trainee issues                    [Difficulty level: Easy]

You are a trainee in the audit department of Harris Brothers & Co. You have recently started your training, have not attended any courses and have attended one audit, where you carried out some simple audit tests under supervision from the audit senior.

An audit manager has asked you to attend the inventory count of Brox Bros, which has a large amount of inventory, which is subject to an annual inventory count. There are very few other controls over the inventory at Brox Bros. Inventory is highly material to Brox Bros' financial statements. No other audit staff will be attending the inventory count.

Which of the following is the most appropriate course of action for you to take:

☐ Perform the work

☐ Refer to training partner

☐ Contact ICAEW

See **Answer** at the end of this chapter.

# 4 Conflicts of interest for the accountant

**Section overview**

- An accountant in industry may face more pressure to behave unethically at times.

- The accountant should evaluate the threats that such pressures bring.

- Safeguards might include:
    - Obtaining advice
    - Using a formal dispute resolution process at work
    - Seeking legal advice

In this section we will consider the problem that an accountant employed by someone other than a practice of other accountants might face if the needs of his professional duty and his employer conflict. This is less likely to be a problem for accountants in practice, as their employers or partners will be bound by the same professional duties as them, but in industry, employers might not understand the importance and nature of an accountant's professional duty.

The Code of Ethics gives advice to accountants in such conflicting situations.

It is important to remember that accountants in a non-practice environment are subject to the same fundamental principles as accountants in practice. However, an accountant in business (as opposed to practice) may find that he is faced with implicit or explicit pressure to:

- Act contrary to law or regulation

- Act contrary to technical or professional standards

- Facilitate unethical or illegal earnings management strategies

- Lie to or mislead auditors or regulators

- Issue or be associated with published reports (for example, financial statements, tax statements) that materially misrepresent the facts

The accountant in question should evaluate the threats that such situations bring (for example, the accountant may face severe intimidation and self-interest threats if he could lose his job by not complying). Available courses of action should be applied as follows:

- First, resolve internally (if possible) using a formal dispute resolution process or audit committee (if the employing organisation has one)

- Second, obtain advice from the ICAEW

- Third seek legal advice

- As a last resort, resign

## Interactive question 4: Conflict of interest [Difficulty level: Exam standard]

Imo is a qualified accountant. She has recently moved out of practice and taken up the position of financial controller of a small, unlisted company, Lavender Lane Limited. The company has a short term cash flow problem.

Imo was recently called into the board meeting and asked if she could defer some income from the previous financial year so as to influence when the tax (both VAT and corporation tax) would be due on those sales. The directors were insistent that such deferral was necessary and that she should consider this request more in the nature of an order.

Which **two** of the following possible courses of action are likely initially to be the most appropriate in this situation?

☐ Report her concerns to the audit committee of the board of directors

☐ Seek advice from ICAEW

☐ Take steps in line with the company's formal dispute resolution process

☐ Take advice from her legal advisors

☐ Resign her job

See **Answer** at the end of this chapter.

## Summary

Assurance providers are required to work with integrity, objectivity and independence

Integrity is being straightforward and honest

Objectivity is the state of mind that has regard to all relevant considerations but no others

Independence is the outward circumstances that surround integrity and objectivity and could affect them, or appear to affect them – for example, the relationships between client and firm

**Objectivity and independence may be threatened by various factors which fall into the following general categories of threat**

Self-interest

Self-review

Familiarity

Management

Intimidation

Advocacy

The ICAEW Code of Ethics recommends a framework for resolving ethical conflicts, and recommends that such conflicts be dealt with 'in house' before reference is made ultimately to ICAEW

The same concept can be applied to resolving conflicts between an employer and an employee's professional duties. The employee should consider:
- Raising concerns with senior staff members/audit committee
- Resolving the problem through company dispute resolution procedures
- If necessary, seeking legal advice or further advice from ICAEW

## Self-test

Answer the following questions.

1 Match the ethical principle with the right description.

Integrity

Objectivity

---

Not allow bias, conflicts of interest or undue influence of others to override professional or business judgements.

Be straightforward and honest in all business and professional relationships.

2 The IFAC Code of Ethics applies only to statutory audits.

☐ True

☐ False

3 Fill in the blanks.

In general, the recurring work paid by the client or group of connected clients should not exceed ........................................ % of the gross practice income.

In the case of........................................ companies, the figure should be 10% of gross practice income.

4 Which of the following services would it be least appropriate for a firm to carry out for an audit client?

A Preparation of tax computation
B Provision of tax advice
C Provision of internal audit services
D Preparation of the financial statements for a public interest entity

5 Audit engagement partners of listed companies should be rotated away from the engagement:

A After 2 years
B After 5 years
C After 7 years
D After 10 years

6 Justine, who is audit senior on the in progress audit of Wedding Planner plc, has recently placed her CV with a recruitment agent. She has had no feedback from the agent, with whom she has a meeting on Friday. The agency is currently carrying an advert for financial controller at Wedding Planner plc, but the advert does not give the company's name.

This represents:

A A self-interest threat
B An intimidation threat
C A management threat
D No threat

7 An ethical conflict should never be referred outside of the assurance firm for advice in relation to resolving that conflict.

☐ True

☐ False

8 When an accountant is faced with a conflict between professional duty and duty to his employer, he should always seek legal advice.

☐ True

☐ False

Now, go back to the Learning Objectives in the Introduction. If you are satisfied you have achieved these objectives, please tick them off.

### Answer to Interactive question 1

(a) Self-review

(b) Intimidation

(c) Familiarity (however, unless any of the members of the team have been on the team for a significant period of time or have close personal relationships with any client staff, this risk is probably insignificant)

### Answer to Interactive question 2

Notorious Limited could be accepted with safeguards. The key safeguard is that the managing director has expressed an intention of improving corporate governance. This safeguard would be strengthened if the audit firm obtained this intention from him in writing.

Pristine plc should not be accepted. This is because the self-review threat associated with preparing the accounts and then auditing them for a listed company is considered too great.

### Answer to Interactive question 3

You should refer this matter to the training partner. You have no experience or training to undertake this work. The risks attaching to the audit tests being carried out are high. The person allocating the work must have allocated you in error.

### Answer to Interactive question 4

It is unlikely to be appropriate to make disclosure to the audit committee in this case, as Lavender Lane Limited, a small, unlisted company, is unlikely to have one. Given the instructions have come from the board of directors, it will be fruitless to take steps in line with the company's formal dispute resolution process. Thus, resolving the situation internally is not possible in this situation.

Imo should seek advice from ICAEW and then take advice from her legal advisors. Resigning her job is not an initial option and should only take place if the other options have been unsuccessful.

1  (a) (ii)

   (b) (i)

2  False. It applies to all assurance services.

3  15, listed/public interest

4  D – Preparation of financial statements for a listed company as this brings a significant self-review threat and is rarely acceptable.

5  B – as laid down by ES3.

6  D – There is currently no threat. If Justine were aware that she was being put forward for a job at an audit client, then she would be faced with a self-interest threat, as she might want to impress client staff to the detriment of doing her job properly.

7  False – however, external referral should be seen as a last option.

8  False – it may not be necessary to seek legal advice unless failure to make a disclosure would constitute a criminal offence. The matter may be resolved internally.

# CHAPTER 16

# Confidentiality

Introduction
Examination context
**Topic List**
    1   Importance of confidentiality
    2   Safeguards to confidentiality
    3   Disclosure of confidential information
Summary and Self-test
Answer to Interactive question
Answer to Self-test

## Learning objectives

- Understand the nature and importance of confidentiality

- Recognise risks to confidentiality

- Identify steps to prevent accidental disclosure of information

- Understand when information may be disclosed

- Understand when information must be disclosed

Specific syllabus references for this chapter are: 4i, j, k.

## Syllabus links

These matters will all be considered again in Audit and Assurance, and in particular, the topical and practically challenging issue of money laundering regulations will be looked at in more detail at the higher level.

## Examination context

Two of the ten ethics questions in the sample paper touched on confidentiality.

In the assessment, candidates may be required to:

- Determine an appropriate course of action in a situation where confidentiality is a potential issue
- Identify situations in which confidential information may be disclosed

# 1 Importance of confidentiality

**Section overview**

- Confidentiality is a fundamental ethical principle.
- Client information must be kept confidential unless there is a genuine exception to this requirement.
- Confidentiality is important as it is a key factor in the trust between client and accountant.

Confidentiality is a fundamental principle of both the IFAC and ICAEW Codes of Ethics, as set out in Chapter 14.

Accountants are required to keep client information confidential. This is an important aspect of the trust between client and accountant, as, to do their job, accountants require access to information about their business that clients would not want made public externally to the business, and, in some cases, such as where it relates to pay or future intentions of the directors, internally to the business either.

In practice this means that an accountant should not discuss client matters with anyone outside the firm of accountants, and, in cases where there is a conflict of interest with another audit client, with anyone outside of the team assigned to that client.

It is appropriate to discuss client matters, where necessary, with other members of staff from the firm; for example, an audit team member may have to *liaise* with a member of the tax department over client affairs, but in general it is better to keep discussions about client affairs to when they are professionally necessary, not merely as gossip.

This is because the greatest risk of breach of confidentiality is likely to be accidental disclosure rather than deliberate disclosure. It is unlikely that an accountant or a firm would make a deliberate disclosure of client information (under the exceptions to the duty of confidentiality noted below) without having taken legal advice and making very sure that it is appropriate to do so. A greater risk of breach of confidentiality is by accidental disclosure (talking about client affairs in the wrong place or leaving client information exposed accidentally).

# 2 Safeguards to confidentiality

**Section overview**

- There is probably a greater risk of accidental disclosure of information than of inappropriate deliberate disclosure.
- Accountants should follow a number of security procedures to prevent accidental disclosure.
- Accountants should always confer with senior staff members when they have a concern that a disclosure is required.

There is probably a greater risk of accidental disclosure of information that is confidential within the business than external to the business. Such risk arises where client staff members are exposed to confidential information by overhearing audit staff conversations or by seeing documents that would normally be kept away from them.

However, there is also a risk of information passing outside the business if assurance providers work on a different client's file at another client's premises, or by losing or leaving files unprotected (for example, in a car, which might be stolen) or through lack of electronic controls (for example, by computer hacking).

The following security procedures are probably wise to prevent accidental disclosure of information:

- Do not discuss client matters with any party outside of the accountancy firm (for example, friends and family, even in a general way)

- Do not discuss client matters with colleagues in a public place

- Do not leave audit files unattended (at a client's premises or anywhere)

- Do not leave audit files in cars or in unsecured private residences

- Do not remove working papers from the office unless strictly necessary

- Do not work on electronic working papers on systems that do not have the requisite protection

In addition, to prevent unauthorised deliberate disclosures of information:

- Raise concerns with more senior staff in the firm (or the MLRO, see section 3.1)
- Seek legal advice before making any disclosures of potentially confidential information

### Worked example: Accidental disclosure of information

Kat is a trainee in the audit department of Fox Brothers & Co. She is working on the audit of Candleworks Limited. Kat is driving to work with two of the audit files in locked cases in the boot of her car. She stops at a petrol station to buy petrol and goes into the petrol station to pay for the petrol. During that time, her car is stolen. When it is found, the cases are missing.

Later that day, Kat arrives at Candleworks Limited and begins work on a different part of the audit file. She leaves the office unattended and unlocked and goes to the toilet. During that time, the purchase ledger clerk goes into the audit office and reviews the payroll. She later raises a complaint with the pay department that the sales ledger clerk earns more than she does.

Kat has breached two simple security measures in this scenario, which has resulted in confidentiality being breached twice.

# 3 Disclosure of confidential information

### Section overview

- Accountants may be compelled by law or consider it desirable in the **public interest** to disclose details of clients' affairs to third parties.

Information acquired in the course of professional work should **only be disclosed** where

- **Consent has been obtained** from the client, employer or other proper source, or
- There is a **public duty** to disclose, or
- There is a **legal** or **professional right or duty** to disclose.

The Code of Ethics identifies three circumstances where the professional accountant is or may be required to disclose confidential information:

- Where disclosure is permitted by law and is authorised by the client or the employer, for example where the auditor has uncovered a fraud and the client is in agreement that the matter should be referred to the police.

- Where disclosure is required by the law.

    Examples include:

    – Reporting clients involved in terrorist activities to the police.

    – Reporting directly to regulators such as the Financial Services Authority on regulatory breaches in respect of financial service and investment businesses or the Charity Commission in respect of charities.

- The reporting of suspected money laundering (for example tax evasion) to the Serious Organised Crime Agency (SOCA).

In making such a report, an auditor is not deemed to have broken the confidence of the client. It is normally addressed by setting out the auditor's right to disclose in the engagement letter.

- Where there is a professional duty or right to disclose, when not prohibited by law. An accountant may defend himself in a negligence claim, for example. The Code of Ethics states that a professional accountant may disclose confidential information to third parties if the disclosure can be justified in 'the public interest' and is not contrary to laws and regulations.

Difficult judgements are required by auditors as to whether the 'public interest' overrides the duty of confidentiality. Usually, the assurance providers should take legal advice on the matter.

A professional accountant acquiring or receiving confidential information in the course of his or her professional work should neither use, nor appear to use, that information for his or her personal advantage or for the advantage of a third party.

Examples of particular circumstances are:

- On a change in employment, professional accountants are entitled to use experience gained in their previous position, but not confidential information acquired there.

- A professional accountant should not deal in the shares of a company in which the member has had a professional association at such a time or in such a manner as might make it seem that information obtained in a professional capacity was being turned to personal advantage ('insider dealing').

- Where a professional accountant has confidential information from Client 1 that affects an assurance report on Client 2 he cannot provide an opinion on Client 2 that he already knows, from whatever source, to be untrue. If he is to continue as auditor to Client 2 the conflict must be resolved. In order to do so, normal audit procedures/enquiries should be followed to enable that same information to be obtained from another source. Under no circumstances, however, should there be any disclosure of confidential information outside the firm.

## 3.1 Money laundering

Accountants are subject to laws concerning money laundering, which make it a criminal offence not to disclose a suspicion of money laundering (the process by which criminals attempt to conceal the proceeds of crime). In addition, it is an offence to let a suspected money launderer know that an investigation may be taking place against him.

Therefore, accountants must report suspicions of money laundering to the appropriate authority, and this disclosure will not constitute a breach of confidentiality. In addition, they should not advise the client that they have done so.

Firms must have a Money Laundering Reporting Officer (MLRO), who will be responsible for making such disclosures. Therefore, trainees and staff carrying out assurance work must make a report to that MLRO when a suspicion of money laundering arises.

Each firm must have an MLRO, so an audit team member will never be required to make a report to the authorities personally. It will always be appropriate for him to make the report of the suspicion to the MLRO, and having made a report to the MLRO is a defence against the criminal offence of failing to report a suspicion of money laundering.

Examples of money laundering in this context could include (but are not limited to):

- Keeping customer overpayments (theft?)

- Offences under the Companies Act that are criminal (such as making a loan to a director – so that the director is in possession of the proceeds of the company's crime)

- Offences that involve a saved cost (such as failure to meet environmental regulations about disposal and dumping waste instead)

The following issues therefore may give rise to suspicions of money laundering:

- Credits on the receivables ledger
- Unusual related party transactions
- Lack of expected costs in income statement
- The existence of a complicated group structure with no obvious business reason for the complexity
- High number of cash transactions without genuine business reason

### Worked example: Money laundering

Jim is carrying out some assurance work in connection with sales at Trying Ltd. He discovers that the owner of the business, who is also the MD, regularly collects cash from customers in respect of sales. In such cases, neither the sale nor the receipt is included in the accounting records of Trying Ltd.

This allows him to bypass accounting for VAT or corporation tax on these sales, so it constitutes money laundering. Jim must therefore report this issue to the MLRO of his firm.

## 3.2 Conflicts of interest

Situations are frequently perceived by clients as 'conflicts of interest' where in reality they involve no more than concerns over keeping information confidential. Hence the issues of confidentiality covered in sections 1 and 2 and conflicts of interest are related.

The Code states that firms should have in place procedures to enable them to identify whether any conflicts of interest exist and to take all reasonable steps to determine whether any conflicts are likely to arise in relation to new assignments involving both new and existing clients.

If there is no conflict of interest, firms may accept the assignment. If there is a conflict of interest, the significance of any threat to compliance with the fundamental principles should be evaluated. If any threats are other than clearly insignificant, the safeguards must be applied to eliminate the threat or to reduce it to an acceptable level.

There is nothing improper in a firm having two clients whose interests are in conflict provided that the activities of the firm are managed so as to avoid the work of the firm on behalf of one client adversely affecting that on behalf of another.

Where a firm believes that a conflict can be managed, sufficient disclosure should be made to the clients or potential clients concerned, together with details of any proposed safeguards to preserve confidentiality and manage conflict. If consent is refused by the client then the firm must not continue to act for one of the parties.

Where a conflict cannot be managed even with safeguards, then the firm should not act.

A self-interest threat to the objectivity of a professional accountant or his firm will arise where there is or is likely to be a conflict of interest between them and the client or where confidential information received from the client could be used by them for the firm's or for a third party's benefit.

The test to apply is whether a reasonable and informed observer would perceive that the objectivity of the member or his firm is likely to be impaired. The member or his firm should be able to satisfy themselves and the client that any conflict can be managed with available safeguards.

Safeguards might include:

- Disclosure of the circumstances of the conflict

- Obtaining the informed consent of the client to act

- The use of confidentiality agreements signed by employees

- Establishing information barriers ('Chinese walls', see below)

- Regular review of the application of safeguards by a senior individual not involved with the relevant client engagement

- Ceasing to act

Information barriers, traditionally known as Chinese walls, include:

- Ensuring that there is no overlap between different teams

- Physical separation of teams

- Careful procedures for where information has to be disseminated beyond a barrier and for maintaining proper records where this occurs

Some commentators argue that the term 'Chinese walls' is culturally insensitive and disrespectful of the ability of the Great Wall of China to keep China's enemies at bay. However the term is in common use and likely to remain so for some time in the future.

### Interactive question: Confidentiality [Difficulty level: Exam standard]

During the course of an assurance engagement, Aleem, a member of the assurance team from Goose Brothers & Co discovers that Dave Milton, the owner of D Manufacturing Limited, has told certain customers to write cheque payments out in favour of DM, rather than the full company name. Mr Milton has then been amending the cheques to read D Milton, and paying them into his personal account rather than the company's, reducing the company's overall tax liability.

Which one of the following is the most appropriate action for Aleem to take in respect of this matter?

A    Discuss the matter with the client and advise him of the legal position
B    Report the matter to HM Revenue and Customs
C    Obtain the client's permission to report the matter to the MLRO within the firm
D    Report the matter to the MLRO within the firm

See **Answer** at the end of this chapter.

## Summary

Assurance providers must comply with the fundamental principle to keep client affairs confidential

They should take basic security precautions, such as:
–   Not leaving assurance files unattended
–   Not leaving assurance files in cars
–   Not working on client files on unprotected computers
–   Not talking about assurance clients to parties outside the assurance firm
–   Not talking about assurance work in a public place

There are occasions when it is appropriate to make disclosures of client information:
–   With client permission
–   When required to by law (for example, when money laundering is suspected)
–   In accordance with auditing standards, such as ISA 250
–   To protect a member's interests
–   In the public interest
–   When compelled by process of law
Assurance providers should generally seek legal advice when making disclosures to ensure that they are made appropriately

## Self-test

Answer the following questions.

1   The principle of confidentiality is the duty to keep client affairs secret in all circumstances.

☐   True

☐   False

2   Which **one** of the following actions would not be recommended with regard to securing professional confidence?

A   Keeping assurance files locked up
B   Carrying out audit work at client premises
C   Discussing client affairs on the telephone at a different client
D   Discussing client affairs in the firm's office

3   If an ICAEW trainee is asked for information about a client by the police, which **four** of the following actions would be appropriate?

☐   Asking his training partner for advice

☐   Seeking legal advice

☐   Ringing the ICAEW ethics line for advice

☐   Answering the police without taking further action

☐   Asking the police what authority they have to ask him

☐   Asking the client if he may talk to the police

4   (a)   Which of the following are legitimate reasons for breach of client confidentiality?

(i)     Auditor **suspects** client has committed treason
(ii)    Disclosure **needed** to protect auditor's own interests
(iii)   Information is **required** for the auditor of another client
(iv)    Auditor **knows** client has committed terrorist offence
(v)     There is a **public duty** to disclose
(vi)    Auditor **considers** there to be non-compliance with laws and regulations
(vii)   Auditor **suspects** client has committed fraud

(b)   Of the above reasons, which are voluntary disclosures and which are obligatory disclosures?

5   Explain what is meant by the term 'Money Laundering Reporting Officer'.

Now, go back to the Learning Objectives in the Introduction. If you are satisfied you have achieved the objectives, please tick them off.

## Answer to Interactive question

D The appropriate thing is to make a report to the MLRO. C is inappropriate, because it could constitute a crime to warn Dave Milton that a report has been made about his money laundering. A is therefore also inappropriate. B might be an appropriate act, but it is better practice for assurance team members always to make reports to the MLRO and let them take responsibility for determining whether a report should be made.

1    False. There are recognised exceptions to the principle of confidentiality.

2    C – this is potentially harmful to the client's confidentiality; the others are sensible security measures.

3    Asking his training partner for advice, seeking legal advice, ringing the ICAEW ethics line for advice and seeking more information from the police about the nature of the enquiry would all be sensible approaches. The trainee should not talk to the police until he was certain that it would not breach his duty of confidentiality to do so, and although while in theory getting the client's permission would solve the problem, it is possible this could constitute a criminal offence, depending on the nature of the police enquiries, so it is better not to do this until more information has been obtained.

4    (i)    Obligatory
     (ii)   Voluntary
     (iv)   Obligatory
     (v)    Voluntary
     (vi)   Obligatory in some cases. The auditor must check/take legal advice about what his duties are.

     (Note: In the case of (vii), the auditor should not take action outside the company until he is certain. When he is certain, he should seek legal advice.)

5    The Money Laundering Reporting Officer is the nominated official in the audit firm through whom disclosures of money laundering suspicions should be made. There should not be a need for other individuals in the firm to make reports direct to the appropriate authority, as having made a report to the MLRO is a defence against the criminal offence of failure to report a suspicion of money laundering.

# Index

Dual employment, 244
Due diligence, 6

## U

UK Corporate Governance Code, 80, 141
Understanding the entity, 38
Users, 8

## V

Valuation, 249
Valuation and allocation, 63
Value for money studies, 6

## W

Website security, 6
Working papers, 151
   automated, 156
   filing, 156
Written representation letter, 193
Written representations from management, 191

# REVIEW FORM – ASSURANCE STUDY MANUAL

Your ratings, comments and suggestions would be appreciated on the following areas of this Study Manual.

| | Very useful | Useful | Not useful |
|---|---|---|---|
| *Chapter Introductions* | ☐ | ☐ | ☐ |
| *Examination context* | ☐ | ☐ | ☐ |
| *Worked examples* | ☐ | ☐ | ☐ |
| *Interactive questions* | ☐ | ☐ | ☐ |
| *Quality of explanations* | ☐ | ☐ | ☐ |
| *Technical references (where relevant)* | ☐ | ☐ | ☐ |
| *Self-test questions* | ☐ | ☐ | ☐ |
| *Self-test answers* | ☐ | ☐ | ☐ |
| *Index* | ☐ | ☐ | ☐ |

| | Excellent | Good | Adequate | Poor |
|---|---|---|---|---|
| *Overall opinion of this Study Manual* | ☐ | ☐ | ☐ | ☐ |

**Please add further comments below:**

**Please return to:**
The Learning Team
Learning and Professional Department
**ICAEW**
Metropolitan House
321 Avebury Boulevard
Milton Keynes
MK9 2FZ
ACAFeedback@icaew.com
www.icaew.com